Crisis and Renewal

THE WESTMINSTER HISTORY
OF CHRISTIAN THOUGHT

Other Books Available in This Series:

Christendom at the Crossroads: The Medieval Era,
by J. A. Sheppard

CRISIS AND RENEWAL
The Era of the Reformations

R. Ward Holder

WESTMINSTER
JOHN KNOX PRESS
LOUISVILLE · KENTUCKY

Scripture quotations from the New Revised Standard Version of the Bible are copyright © 1989 by the Division of Christian Education of the National Council of the Churches of Christ in the U.S.A. and are used by permission.

Book design by Sharon Adams
Cover design by Lisa Buckley

First edition
Published by Westminster John Knox Press
Louisville, Kentucky

This book is printed on acid-free paper that meets the American National Standards Institute Z39.48 standard. ♾

PRINTED IN THE UNITED STATES OF AMERICA

09 10 11 12 13 14 15 16 17—10 9 8 7 6 5 4 3 2 1

Library of Congress Cataloging-in-Publication Data

Holder, R. Ward.
   Crisis and renewal : the era of the reformations / R. Ward Holder.
       p. cm. — (Westminster history of Christian thought)
   Includes index.
   ISBN 978-0-664-22990-0 (alk. paper)
   1. Reformation.   I. Title.
   BR305.3.H65 2009
   270.6—dc22   2008018551

For my parents, Ward and Ellagene,
my first teachers in the faith

Joshua 24:15

Contents

SERIES INTRODUCTION

The Westminster History of Christian Thought series provides a set of resources for the study of the history and development of Christian thought from the period of the early church to the present. The books are designed to be accessible introductory studies. They focus on the issues that were important questions and the theological expressions that emerged during the various eras. Strong attention is also paid to the historical and cultural contexts in which the theology developed. The studies are written by superb teachers who present their work in clear and energetic ways. These experts are committed to enhancing the teaching and learning tasks.

We hope this series will be of help to those who want skilled guidance to the development of Christian thought from the days of early Christianity to contemporary times.

The Publisher

Acknowledgments

With any book, the number of debts of gratitude that pile up demonstrate to the author how much any work of scholarship remains a collaborative effort. The number of conversations that contributed to this volume was somewhat more than a lot, and fewer than infinite. So, to all the people whose conversations sparked any useful thought in me, whether they were my teachers, my colleagues, my friends, or my students, I offer my thanks. That said, there are certain individuals to whom the debt of gratitude is particularly great.

Don McKim brought this project to me, continuing the collaboration on projects that have been a special delight to me these past few years. The thought of a historical introduction to the theology of the Reformation period, designed for those without the prior foundational work in theology or history, is inspired. The book moved more quickly to completion because of a summer grant provided by Saint Anselm College. Samantha Calhoun read many of the draft chapters; her critical comments and drive for the stories of the Reformation figures have shaped my writing in both significant and subtle ways. My class in the spring of 2007 in Reformation theology at Saint Anselm College read and commented upon early chapter drafts and made suggestions that have immeasurably improved the clarity and readability of the text. Numerous colleagues have read parts of the book. I owe special thanks to David Whitford, W. Bradford Smith, Greg Miller, Kristen Post Walton, and Sean Perrone. The greatest debt is to my family, who frequently sacrificed the presence of husband or father, or who listened to endless stories about obscure Reformation figures, always with good humor. Finally, the author of any book of this sort must acknowledge that his greatest inspiration for such a task remains the needs of his students and the motivation they provide in their desire to know and understand.

Chronology

1509–1564	John Calvin
c. 1514–1572	John Knox
1515–1582	St. Teresa of Avila
1516	Publication of Erasmus's *Novum Testamentum* (first edition called *Novum Instrumentum*)
1516–1558	Mary I of England
1517	Publication of Luther's Ninety-five Theses
1519	Charles V elected Holy Roman Emperor
	Leipzig Disputation
1520	Bull *Exsurge Domine*
	Luther's "Reformation Treatises"—*To the German Nobility, The Babylonian Captivity of the Church, Christian Freedom*
1521	Diet of Worms
1522	Luther's German New Testament published
	Affair of the Sausages; Zurich reforms begin
1524–1525	Peasants' War
1525	Thomas Müntzer executed
1526	Tyndale's English New Testament published
1527	Felix Manz executed for Anabaptism
	Schleitheim Confession
	Michael Sattler executed for Anabaptism
1527–1598	Philip II of Spain
1528	Patrick Hamilton executed for evangelicalism in Scotland
1529	Second Diet of Speyer, "protestatio" of evangelical princes and imperial cities
	Colloquy of Marburg
1530	Diet of Augsburg, Augsburg Confession
1531	Second Battle of Kappel; death of Zwingli
1533–1603	Elizabeth I of England
1534	Supremacy Act establishes Church of England
	Luther's German Bible published
1534–1535	Kingdom of Münster
1535	Thomas More executed
1536	First edition of John Calvin's *Institutes of the Christian Religion* published
1537	*Consilium de Emendanda Ecclesia*
1537–1553	Edward VI of England
1540	Founding of the Society of Jesus (Jesuits)
1541	Regensburg Colloquy
	Francis Xavier's mission to India
1542–1587	Mary, Queen of Scots

1542–1591	St. John of the Cross
1545–1547	Council of Trent (first session)
1546	George Wishart executed for evangelicalism in Scotland
1548	Ignatius of Loyola's *Spiritual Exercises* published
1549	Book of Common Prayer
1550	Perpetual Edict of Charles V
1551	Edict of Chateaubriant
1551–1552	Council of Trent (second session)
1553	Michael Servetus executed
1553–1610	Henry of Navarre (Henry IV of France)
1555	Peace of Augsburg
1556	Thomas Cranmer executed
1559	Publication of final edition of Calvin's *Institutes of the Christian Religion*
	Foundation of Genevan Academy
	Publication of *Index Librorum Prohibitorum*
1560	Scots Confession
1561–1563	Council of Trent (third session)
1562	Massacre of Vassy; first French War of Religion begins
1563	Publication of Foxe's *Acts and Monuments* in English
	Thirty-nine Articles
1567	Revolt in the Low Countries
1572	St. Bartholomew's Day Massacre
1576	Pacification of Ghent
1577	Teresa of Avila's *Interior Castle* completed
1588	Defeat of Spanish Armada
1593	Henry of Navarre converts to Catholicism
1598	Edict of Nantes
1611	King James Version of English Bible completed
1618	Defenestration of Prague; Thirty Years' War begins
1618–1619	Synod of Dordt; rising power of Protestant scholasticism
1620	English Protestant dissenters sail to North America on the *Mayflower*
1648	Peace of Westphalia; Thirty Years' War ends

Introduction

Why Another History of the Reformation?

The Reformation stands as one of the most studied eras of Christian history. For those who would enter this labyrinth, that fact stands both as an invitation and a caution. Studying the Reformation seems inviting because finding both primary and secondary sources to consider is an easy task. As the whole of the Reformation happened after the advent of Gutenberg's press, the difficulties associated with manuscript transmission are greatly decreased. Further, the Reformation seems immune to falling completely out of academic favor, so there are always new books being published in this field of study. Studying the Reformation, however, can also cause the student some nervousness. The caution comes from the sheer immensity of material. Instead of the scarcity of printed sources that survived, which is sometimes problematic for other periods of the history of Christianity, the amount of material can be astounding. The American edition of Luther's works takes up fifty-four volumes!

In addition, the profusion of source material and secondary volumes is matched by the plethora of scholarly theories about the Reformation. For instance, is the Reformation properly called *the* Reformation, or a series of Reformations? Should it be studied from the "great minds" who left us texts, or from the artifacts that give us some sense of the common people's reception of those texts? Is the Reformation a continuation of the medieval age of Christianity, or a sharp break from it? All of these and many more questions continue to fascinate the scholars who seek to understand the world of the early modern Christian. A student could study for many years just to be able to recognize the pedigree of the arguments that a scholarly book on the Reformation offered.

But beside the problems I have enumerated, another confronts the new student of the Reformation. Frankly, with such a mass of scholarship available, how can the novice enter it? How can one penetrate the mass of conflicting

1

opinions and conflicting methodologies? Further, how can the undergraduate student who approaches this without significant background (who happens to represent the target audience of this volume) penetrate the specialized vocabulary? The same vocabulary that serves the professional scholar so well stands as a barrier to the apprentice. Speaking our jargon serves not only as a shorthand to make difficult concepts "graspable" for briefer speech, but also as proof that we have mastered the necessary initiation so that we may enter the club. That's rather unhelpful to new students.

Perhaps an anecdote will help illustrate the point. As I was once teaching an undergraduate course in Reformation theology, I had chosen texts I considered the most accessible. As the class and I were working through Erasmus's *Defense of the Faith*, a student raised her hand. She began by pointing out correctly that the editor of the volume from which we were reading had noted that in this dialogue Erasmus had avoided one of the critical Reformation issues—that of justification by faith. I nodded, glad that she'd read the introduction. Then she asked the million-dollar question: "But isn't the whole dialogue a justification of Luther's faith?" Of course it is, but just as certainly, that is not what the doctrine of justification by faith actually means to the professional who examines the period.

So the greatest challenge this work seeks to meet is to provide for the beginning student. To bridge the theological vocabulary gap, and at the expense of sometimes being repetitive, this volume adopts the practice of placing doctrinal vocabulary discussions throughout the work. These are freestanding explanations of specific Reformation issues and vocabulary. Though some of the material may be replicated elsewhere in the book, these will offer summary presentations helpful for reference and for definitions. Further, because this volume is intended as the beginning of a student's effort, a list of further suggested readings is included at the end of each chapter. Where appropriate, the list of suggested readings is broken up into primary readings—modern translated editions of what the figures of the sixteenth century actually wrote—and secondary readings, or other scholarly treatments of the material in that chapter.

This volume adopts an old style of intellectual pursuit that is coming into vogue again—intellectual history. Arguments exist for choosing other methodologies. If the Reformation presents truly popular movements that motivated the common people, then social history seems the more appropriate approach. Or if the Reformation was a series of movements that could not have survived without the atmosphere of the new national identities, then political history must be the correct lens. The list could be lengthened, but the point should be clear. So why the adoption of intellectual history?

This book seeks to offer a theological history of the Reformation aimed at the undergraduate or novice reader. The best historical theological efforts are fully cognizant of the fact that humans live in a web of existence in which they are receiving and giving impulses in a variety of spheres. There is no vacuum in which theology lives. But just as certainly, there is no vacuum in which politics, or culture, or economics can be considered. Further, the insights gained from the other areas of historical research are vital to the historian's full understanding of the period. Historians can and do argue whether the issues were political, social, religious, military, or some mix of these. However, the people of the Reformation thought that the issues at hand were religious. Whether they were Genevan members of the city council voting against toleration of Catholicism, or German peasants marching in the Peasants' War toward Frankenhausen, or citizens of Paris rioting on St. Bartholomew's Day against the Protestants, the people of the early modern period generally thought that the questions of the day were about religion. While it may be impossible to determine objectively what the primary cause of the Reformation was, this volume argues that it is also impossible to understand it at all without sufficient understanding of the religious matters of the period. Finally, I assume that this volume will be a part of the student's education, not its entirety.

So while the narrative will include the general account of the events of the Reformation, special attention will be given to the thoughts of the seminal thinkers of the various movements. After those are clarified, the volume will proceed to consider the reception of the doctrines, what people actually understood, and what differences those doctrines made in their lives.

Following this introductory chapter is a chapter deceptively simply titled "What Is the Reformation?" that will briefly consider the arguments over what the Reformation was and how confessional differences have colored scholarship until almost the present day. Then the chapter will consider the church's history of reform movements, from the earliest period of the church to the sixteenth century. Finally, the chapter will set out the reasons for beginning prior to Martin Luther, with the humanists, and ending in 1648, with the conclusion of the Thirty Years' War.

The second chapter, titled "The Late Medieval Context," will set out the religious conditions of the fourteenth and fifteenth centuries. This chapter will help to prepare students to grasp what the conditions were that had so upset the early sixteenth-century Reformers, both humanist and Lutheran. The scandals of the clergy, both high and low, will be surveyed. The laity will not be spared, for this chapter will take into account the kinds of superstitions that were common in the period.

That chapter will set out the necessary groundwork for the third and fourth chapters, "The Humanistic Call for Reform" and "The Lutheran Reform." In part, I will argue that although the humanists did not always support Luther and the positions he took, one cannot possibly understand Luther's reforms without some grounding in the issues they had raised. Though various thinkers will be briefly covered in the chapter on humanism, we will center on the figure of Desiderius Erasmus, "the prince of the humanists." Erasmus's work as critic of the excesses of the church is important. But for the ongoing history of the church, his philological work on the text of the New Testament, studying exactly what the Greek words meant in their first-century context, was more important. Together, Erasmus's philological investigations of the New Testament and his editions of the church fathers dwarf the importance of his critique of the church. Finally, Erasmus himself excellently illustrates the ambivalence some humanists felt toward the early generation of Reformers, and this will be analyzed in his support for and struggles with Martin Luther.

The chapter titled "The Lutheran Reform" sets out the events that turned into an earthshaking upheaval of the Western church by setting Martin Luther securely in his late medieval context. Luther was not different from the great majority of his contemporaries in his outlook, which was far more medieval than some previous historians have recognized. At times, the desire of later generations to see what they want to see in heroes has led scholars to view Luther as a person who would be comfortable in the twenty-first century. He's not that person, but rather a medieval man who was consumed by the hope of heaven and the knowledge of a world filled with devils. Further, though Luther depended upon some of the insights of the humanists, he himself is rarely considered a humanist. But for better or worse, from Martin Luther's genius came the insights that bound together the various religious issues of the day and combined them into a reform movement that eventually divided the Roman Church.

The next chapter, titled "Zwingli and Zurich: Early Swiss Reform," makes the next crucial point for early students of the Reformation. Truthfully speaking, it was not *a* Reformation, but *many* Reformations.[1] Certainly, the early movements of reform in Switzerland were in contact with Lutheran thought. But the cantons of this federation that did choose the way of reform expressly did not choose some of Luther's answers. Huldrych Zwingli denied that he took all of his reforms from Luther. For these reasons, this chapter will end with some comparison of their differences.

A third reform, the Radical Reformation, arose directly from the regions surrounding Zurich and is the subject of the sixth chapter. Called "enthusiasts" or "Anabaptists" by their opponents, these Christians sought to take what to many seemed like the next logical steps from the principles Luther and Zwingli had set forth. The placement after early Swiss reform is natural, as the Magisterial reform (the reform helped by the various governments) preceded it in Switzerland. Further, this reform movement occurred in the context of persecution. Soon, both Lutherans and Zwinglians, as well as the Church of Rome, would agree on the necessity of stamping out what they saw as deadly heresy.

The seventh chapter takes on Calvin and Geneva, the later Swiss Reformation. Some may question the decision to include two chapters on Switzerland, but Switzerland was the site of two different reforms. Zwingli's reform changed after his death in 1531 and was always a Swiss affair. Calvin's reforming movement did not even truly begin until his second stint in Geneva, which began in 1541, and always looked beyond the borders to the possible foundation of an international movement.

The Church of England is the subject of the eighth chapter. Here is not only another regional difference in the patterns of reform but also a wholly different way of approaching the reform, led by secular rulers rather than theologians or preachers, as well as a different way of organizing the church. Though we tend to look back at England with the eyes of the twenty-first century, the fascinating patterns and movements within the English Reformation easily demonstrate the varieties of ways that religious people in the sixteenth century went about their faith.

The ninth chapter is titled "Catholic Reform: Early Modern Catholicism." Students unfamiliar with the history of Christianity in this period may be unaware that Catholicism itself went through enormous change at this time. Some of the most significant movements of the church, from the Council of Trent, to the foundation of the Jesuits and their missionary zeal, to the blossoming of the mystical explorations of Teresa of Avila and St. John of the Cross, make this an extraordinary opportunity for grasping the history and future of the Catholic Church.

If space were no object, the number of chapters could be multiplied (the third edition of George Huntston Williams's *Radical Reformation* spans over one thousand five hundred pages!)[2] But then, this would no longer be an introduction for the novice. So our study will conclude with two further chapters. The tenth chapter will address the question of religion and violence. For the first time in centuries, believers all claiming to be true Western Christians fought over that claim. Examining this violent history even briefly is helpful for understanding our past and raising questions about our future. The eleventh chapter will briefly survey some of the later reform movements of the period—those that, though no less important, were judged to be less central to the aims of this volume. These will include some of the reform movements in Central and Eastern Europe, how the reforming movements effected some of the structures of daily life, the emergence of Protestant scholasticism in the late sixteenth century and early seventeenth century, and the reformation of Protestant ritual.

Finally, it is fair to ask the question of why people should study the Reformation at all. Brilliant scholars have placed this age of ecclesiastical turmoil into a variety of settings. Arguments have been made that the Reformation was the result of the dawn of nationalism, or that it was the choice of the Reformers to redirect society. Scholars have claimed that the Reformation succeeded because of the flattery of the laity, while others have claimed that the Reformation failed. For every effort to grasp at the core, or to memorize the harmony of the Reformation, there has been at least one counterproposal. After five hundred years, if we cannot come to some decisive conclusion, why keep at it?

This study will not attempt to put forward some new idea of the majesty of the rhetoric of the preachers, or the political craftiness of the magistrates, or even how the spirit of the Reformation simply swept over people, leading them to new visions of Christianity. This volume will be content with simply pointing out that this was an age when religion was a matter of enormous significance for everyone. But for the question of why, I am reminded of Barbara Tuchman's *A Distant Mirror: The Calamitous Fourteenth Century*, in which Tuchman argues that by looking at an age that was so different from ours, we might learn from the things that we do recognize. These things we might realize as permanent elements of the human condition.[3] I suggest that a parallel possibility exists when we look at the age of the Reformation, that as we look at an age which was bewilderingly torn by religious conflict, we find the opportunity to grasp our own place in history more fully. For what other age can better help us to understand the array of different religious options coming from both traditional and pioneering sources? What other time can better mirror the insanity of the acts of religious terrorism today than the religious furor of that not-so-distant past?

This is not to make grander claims than are needed. We will not fully seize our own moment in time by memorizing the theological and religious issues of a time five centuries past. But we might come to see the humanness in the search for unbreakable rules of religious certainty. We might approach the possibility of understanding the need to express the varieties of religious impulses that communities and individuals experience. Finally, we might draw near to understanding *how* we came to be the way we are, if not always why. That would be a good place to start.

QUESTIONS FOR DISCUSSION

1. What images or concepts come to your mind when you think about the Reformation?
2. Why does this volume wish to talk about "reformations" rather than "the Reformation"?
3. This book includes a chapter on religion and violence. What do you think the relationship should be between religion and violence?
4. Why might it be worthwhile to study the Reformation?

1

What Is the Reformation?

We begin with a straightforward and almost unanswerable question. Should not a book about the Reformation be able to define what the Reformation is? Yet reams of pages of scholarship have been written on that topic, with the predictable resulting quarrels between proponents of differing answers. But to try again is a necessity. This book defines the Reformation as a period of time marked by religious change in which several movements occurred almost simultaneously. Each of these movements sought somehow to effect positive religious change.

First, the Reformation is most helpfully thought of as a period of time. During that time, roughly equivalent to the entire sixteenth century and the first half of the seventeenth century, the Christian church in Europe experienced extraordinary changes. Some of those changes had been prepared for by preceding developments in the fourteenth and fifteenth centuries. Some have argued that the theological groundwork laid in the reforms of Jan Hus in the fourteenth century are too important to neglect. But the Roman Church did not change in response to Hus. In the eyes of most observers in the sixteenth century, however, an amazing quantity of change occurred.

Throughout this book, we will consider the time period of the Reformation as roughly bounded by the beginning of the sixteenth century and stretching to the middle of the seventeenth. Traditionally, simply fixing the beginning and ending points of the Reformation has been a difficult task! Some argue for the "great event" theory, which demands that one begin with something specifically dated, such as Luther's publication of his Ninety-five Theses considering indulgences on October 31, 1517. While that option is attractive, it misses some of the ways in which the preceding years and even decades had prepared for Luther's own understanding of the church, and the impact his thought had on the people living at that time. The option I have chosen has the advantage of avoiding the question of what event started the Reformation, giving more time to consider what the reforms were, what they meant, and what they continue to mean.

So to begin with, we can start our definition by stating that the period of the Reformation was a period of change. Whether they understood themselves to be in the midst of a continuation of movements that were already active in the earlier centuries, or a rejection of what had gone before, the people in the era of the Reformation were quite conscious of religious change. There were new options to consider. It did not matter that some options were not acceptable. For the first time in centuries, Christians in Western Europe had religious choices to consider.

One of the questions that the issue of the Reformation brings up is the character of the change. The term "reform" has within it the implied idea not only of change but of change for the better, by some sort of return to an earlier ideal. But if we push that question a bit, the answers still do not become simple. Were these changes for the better or for the worse? That seems the easiest question to answer. For the time of the Reformation, the answer depended upon the perspective of the person giving the answer, as well as the specific time of the question. Let us consider, for instance, a peasant outside Frankenhausen in 1520. If we asked him what was going on in his world, he might have answered that the preaching of the pure gospel was ushering in the true age of the Holy Spirit. He might have offered the opinion that only a brief passage of time would bring the clearest evidence of the fruits of the Spirit that had recently been planted, and he may have spoken bravely of the changes in store for his village. He might have seen these changes as all for the good. In 1525, that same peasant, running for his life from imperial troops, might have offered a bitter rejection of the reforms and of the Reformers themselves. He might have looked at his shattered home, the death surrounding him from the effects of the failed Peasants' War, and concluded that the changes were only for the worse.

Let us shift from a story of an imaginary peasant to a particular person, Ami Perrin, a leader of the city of Geneva in the middle of the sixteenth century. Perrin would have been absolutely certain of the power of the gospel to change his city-state for the good in 1541. He would have pointed to the return of Calvin to be preacher of the city as proof of God's providence and of the power of the gospel. Perrin was a member of the party who worked to bring Calvin back to Geneva after his exile. But only fifteen years later, that same Ami Perrin was in a much different situation. Having become a zealous opponent of Calvin's over points of doctrine and religious discipline, Perrin found himself voted out of office by the immigrants who had come to Geneva because of

Calvin. Soon after, he was found guilty of treason against the city and fled for his life. His answer would no doubt differ from the confident opinion he would have expressed earlier!

A third example comes from England. In 1534, King Henry VIII broke away from the Church of Rome by manner of the Supremacy Act, which recognized the king as the head of the English Church. During his reign, Henry rejected the reforms some of his bishops had envisioned for the new faith. Henry seems to have been rather more conservative than some of his bishops! During this time, many people saw the reforms of the bishops as simply innovations that did not carry the religious power of the traditional religious practices. Following Henry's death in 1547, his son Edward VI ascended the throne. Many saw this time as a golden opportunity to cement the reforms and to make the Church of England conform more closely to some of the ideals of the reformers in Europe. This hope was dashed by the early death of Edward in 1553 and his half sister's rise to the throne. Mary Tudor was a stalwart member of the Church of Rome and was convinced of the necessity of bringing England back to the true church. Her five-year reign was marked by the execution of some of the bishops who had pushed for changes under Henry and Edward.

England is such an instructive example because of the constantly changing political and religious environment. At any point along the line of succession from Henry VIII to Edward VI to Mary I, religion was always changing. If we were to ask a resident of that kingdom whether the change was good or bad, the answer would change with the circumstances of the moment.

Finally, the perspective of the Church of Rome represents another option. One would think that for Rome, the evaluation of the changes occurring would all be negative. But the historical record is far more complicated than that. Soon after Luther's publication of the Ninety-five Theses against indulgences, Pope Leo X was heard to say that he believed the issue was not significant but was only a quarrel between two competing religious orders. Certainly, faithful members of the Church of Rome regularly complained about the changes and tended to consider them as either schism or heresy. *Schism* is the division of the church; *heresy* is the teaching of incorrect doctrine after a person has been corrected. But that general negative attitude toward the Protestant changes hides particular reforms that the Roman Church adopted, changes that frequently seemed inspired by the same issues that excited the Protestant thinkers. Thus, while Catholic writers might have bemoaned the heresies of the "Lutherans," the Council of Trent proceeded to address some of the abuses Luther had pointed out.

What these four historical vignettes have demonstrated is that the evaluation of the changes varied according to a variety of factors. Political, economic, and church issues competed with the "simple" idea of the truth of the gospel.

While the Reformation period was full of change, and the agents of change saw those changes as necessary reforms, the final assessment of such a question has not even yet been written.

The third large issue in our definition has to do with the fact that the Reformation was a time period with several movements. This is a crucial understanding, and one of the reasons that this book adopts the terminology of speaking about a "Reformation period." Quite simply, there were several "Reformations." Some of these can be lumped together, such as the "Protestant Reformation"; others cannot. Obviously, the Catholic reforms of this time were not the same as the Calvinist or Lutheran reforms. Further, and most important, it is essential to any good history to create a description in which the actual historical actors might be able to recognize themselves.[1] This approach will sometimes fail to satisfy our curiosity, because at times we will run up against the fact that the concerns of the sixteenth century are not ours. A Genevan in 1545 might have been a follower of Calvin and thus a Calvinist. But to equate that with the twenty-first-century denominations that trace their heritage to Calvin is a colossal mistake. Instead, we must simply try to understand the people and issues of the Reformation period as they might have seen themselves. To do so, we must recognize that instead of one great Reformation, there were several Reformations.

Another reason to speak of Reformations is to honor the differing aims of the reforms that the various movements put in place. The humanists' call to reform the church on the basis of persuasion and the moral reform of the individual simply cannot be confused with the Radical Reformers' call for a church gathered together and set up outside of and even against the society. This volume will specifically look at the humanist, Lutheran, Zwinglian, Radical, Calvinist, English, and Catholic reforms. We will not consider some of the equally important reform movements that social historians have considered, such as the reform of marriage or the reform of the care of the poor. Our set of "Reformations" will not exhaust the topic but will begin to demonstrate the complexity of the religious landscape at this time.

I have been trying to define the term "Reformation." The root of this term is "reform." But when we examine that term, we should be aware that the Christian church was wholly familiar with the concept of reform long before the sixteenth century. From the earliest days of the church, the reform of the individual had been a common theme. Frequently such goals were reached by a concentration upon the change that could be worked in the soul of the individual. Further reform movements were common through the medieval period. Pope Gregory VII (c. 1020–1085) instituted significant reforms during his papacy. With the popularization of the monastic movement and the various reforms such as the Cluniac reform of the tenth century and the Cistercian reform of the twelfth century, Christians of Western Europe were familiar with the idea of reforming Christian practices.

Further, the term "reform" does not simply mean change. Rather, it has the character of change for the better. Additionally, it has the character of change back to a prior state of being, or at least in accordance with that prior condition. This was crucially important in the sixteenth century. Unlike our own times, when newness is seen as the mark of something desirable, newness in religion was seen as suspect in the period of the Reformation. All of the Reformers, whether Lutheran, Reformed, English, or Catholic, went to great lengths to prove that the changes they supported were not "innovations" but rather reforms in agreement with the beliefs and practices of an earlier, purer state of the church. To support this, the sixteenth century became one of the great centuries of doing history, as a wide variety of thinkers enlisted the "help" of long-dead leaders of the church to demonstrate how particular changes were not new.

If we can grant that sense of reform as new-old, what was new, then, in the Reformation period? Why was this period of time called "the Reformation"? The truly new features of reform in the sixteenth century were the scope of some of the reforming movements and the actors in the reforms. Let's begin by looking at the scope of the reforms. Certainly, some reforming minds did not wish to shift outside the patterns of reform that were already familiar. For instance, some of Erasmus's suggestions for the reform of the church did not require any shifts in the central idea of the nature of the church or in the character of salvation. On the other hand, the Schleitheim Brotherly Union, written in 1527, which became a confessional document of some of the Radical reform movements, envisions a Christianity that cannot be reconciled with the church or societal structures of the sixteenth century. The confession denies the possibility of a Christian fully integrated into civil society.

Similarly, no orthodox church body in the West had set a temporal ruler, in this case a king, at the head of the church. Even the coronation of Charlemagne as Holy Roman Emperor never proclaimed the emperor's sole power as the director of the Roman Church. But the Supremacy Act of 1534 did exactly that, naming King Henry VIII as supreme head of the English Church. Examples can be multiplied, but one begins to grasp the point. The period of the Reformation saw greater possible changes than had been common for the millennium that preceded it.

The change that is frequently less well noted and discussed may be even more important in evaluating the alterations that came about in the time of the Reformation, when new classes of people became far more influential in making decisions about religion. In the centuries before the period of the Reformation, religious decisions were made by two classes of people: the clergy and some members of the nobility. Occasional lay movements did occur, but those that challenged the authority and primacy of the religious status quo were usually successfully defined as heretical. In the period of the Reformation, the lower laity were able to be effective in making decisions. This was true in three ways. The first is that laity made decisions for some cities and towns, as members of councils. The second is that people without ordination or theological training were creating theological stances. The third is that laypeople were making their own decisions about the nurture of their souls on their own.

In the first instance, a case in point comes from Zurich. In January 1523, religious tensions were running high in the city and the countryside that surrounded it. Religious strife between the "people's priest" (*Leutpriester*) Huldrych Zwingli and the Catholic clergy of the town had broken out on numerous occasions. During Lent 1522, Zwingli had been present at the printing shop of Christoph Froschauer, at a time when those working were staying late to try to prepare a book that contained the letters written by Paul. Due to the lateness of the hour, and presumably wanting to keep his helpers working well, Froschauer served a meal, which contained sausage. As this was during Lent, the meal was not simply immoral under the legal code of the city but, more seriously, it was illegal. The incident was reported, and Froschauer was arrested by the city council. Zwingli took this as an opportunity to preach against the action and call for evangelical freedom in whether to eat particular foods during times of the church year. The "Affair of the Sausages" is frequently seen as the beginning of the Swiss Reformation.

By 1523, however, it had become clear that the differences between Zwingli and the Catholic clergy of the city could no longer be ignored. Here we come to that difference we are trying to consider. The city council did not refer the matter to a theological faculty at a university. They did not refer it to a council of learned bishops, or to Rome. Rather, they took it upon themselves to hear a debate between Zwingli and representatives of the Roman position. The elected laymen of the city of Zurich would be the decision makers in the religious course of their city.

This was an enormous change. Popes and bishops made the claim that their authority came from God. Kings and princes and emperors had long argued that they were also given their roles by God and thus should have some input in the religious decisions made in their realms. But ordinary laymen had not successfully made such a claim in more than a thousand years. The authority to make religious decisions was heady stuff, and at least some of the thinkers in the sixteenth century wondered whether laymen were ready for it.[2]

This power of the laity was remarkable in the patterns made by mainstream Reformation movements, movements that normally attempted to reform the practice of religion in a whole region. This pattern of lay leadership and power was even more common in the Radical movements. This represents the second way in which laypeople were making theological decisions. There was almost a tangible distrust of education in some of these movements, which were frequently led by laypeople with no formal theological training but who called upon the Holy Spirit for attestation of their spiritual gifts. Some of these people were literate and even skillful at arguing for the necessity of their spiritual positions. Others, while no less skillful, were illiterate and left only the memories of their audiences as a testimony of their spirit-led power.

The final way in which laypeople were making theological decisions is the most obvious of all. Simply put, laypeople were choosing what religion was true. Whether maintaining allegiance to the old faith, or being persuaded by some reform movement, the fact of choice between competing Christianities changed the character of the task of the laity. While Cardinal Sadoleto could argue to the Genevans in 1539 that it was the task of laypeople simply to do what the church commanded, the very fact that he was appealing to them to make this choice signified that he knew they were decision makers.

Finally, this volume will attempt to avoid the confessionalism that has marred some of the past efforts to understand the time of reform. It has been rather well documented that one of the most significant keys to reading histories of the Reformation in prior times has been knowing the confessional placement of the author. Catholics wrote of the schismatics and heretics, Protestants wrote about the dawning of new light and the breaking away from corruption. Though this was rather limited, it was helpful in one way. Confessional differences provided an interpretive lens through which various authors made sense of the historical developments of the time. Luther's flight to the Wartburg in 1521, after having escaped from being made a prisoner of the Holy Roman Empire, was a triumph for Lutheran historians. Henry IV's conversion to Catholicism so that he could become king of France in 1594 was a failure for Reformed historians. Literally, it meant that movements had success or failure not only in the historical sense of continuing to exist but also in the moral sense. There were "good guys" and "bad guys" for such an approach to the history of the time. Further, the swings of various regions and peoples from one faith to another could simply be seen as wins and losses—lead changes in a ridiculously large football game. This made thinking about the Reformation somewhat easier.

However, if we have any actual desire of understanding the swirling emotions and thoughts and actions of the Reformation period, we have to jump into the messiness of the actual period. People did not always know what they would do next. Some decisions were made on the basis of long careful thought, while others seem to have been made in the heat of the moment. All were made in a vital, existentially urgent time when there was no luxury of knowing who the winners or losers might be, with the added expectation that what was at stake was the very salvation of an individual, a city, or even a nation.

I have argued in this chapter that the answer to the question "What is the Reformation?" is that the Reformation was a period of time marked by religious change in which several movements occurred almost simultaneously, and that each of these movements sought somehow to effect positive religious change. Now, with a working definition, it is time to get to the actual stories and thoughts that make this period so worthwhile.

QUESTIONS FOR DISCUSSION

1. How does the author define the Reformation? After reading this chapter, do you think that is a useful or adequate description?
2. What does it mean to "reform" a religion? Does the pattern of the early form of that religion matter?
3. What things were truly new in the Reformation? How would that have changed religion?
4. How has confessionalism affected the writing of history?

SUGGESTED FURTHER READING

Cameron, Euan. *The European Reformation*. Oxford: Oxford University Press, 1991.
Dickens, A. G., and John M. Tonkin. *The Reformation in Historical Thought*. Cambridge, MA: Harvard University Press, 1985.
Ladner, Gerhart. *The Idea of Reform: Its Impact on Christian Thought and Action in the Age of the Fathers*. Cambridge, MA: Harvard University Press, 1959.
O'Malley, John. *Trent and All That*. Cambridge, MA: Harvard University Press, 2000.

DOCTRINAL-VOCABULARY DISCUSSION

Justification by Faith

Justification by faith is frequently called the most significant issue of the Reformation. More than perhaps any other issue, it divided Catholics from Protestants. Justification is a doctrine about how a person becomes acceptable, or justified, before God. Theologians of all types believed that the basic human problem was sin and the stain of sin, which made humans revolting to their Creator. Justification was how humans regained a good relationship with God. The traditional answer to how this happened depended upon a combination of human and divine action. Humans were responsible to do what they could

(Latin, *facere quod in se est*), and God would supply the rest. Traditionally, the Church of Rome directed believers to the system of the sacraments to help in their justification.

Though several theologians can claim some right to the title of being the first to argue for justification by faith alone, in the Reformation this claim is most frequently given to Martin Luther. Luther saw the problem with human responsibility. How would anyone know whether he or she had done enough to earn God's help? This burning question drove Luther back into the Scriptures, especially the Letter to the Romans, where he discovered a different model. Since humans are affected by sin, they are unable to make the choice(s) to do righteous actions. Instead, God offers justifying grace as a free gift. This gracious gift is received by faith, so the believer is justified by faith, rather than by faith and works that he or she performs. In this idea, the greatest barrier to this justifying is human desire to be active in justification, that is, to earn justification.

Later theologians modified, quarreled with, or rejected Luther's basic insight. Catholic and Radical theologians tended to argue that if justification must be free, then everyone will sin all the time, that there will be no reason to be morally good. Reformed theologians tended to agree with the Lutheran position but attached it to a strong legalistic morality that was a result of the gift of grace.

The result was a basic question of the way of salvation. Does God save humans because they reach out toward him, or does God save humans because they are unable to reach out toward him? The different answers reflect different ways of reading Scripture and different ways of understanding the effects of sin on the human condition. All Christian theologians believed that faith was a part of justification, but the Protestants frequently argued that only faith was involved in justification.

2

The Late Medieval Context

John Donne wrote that "no man is an island." In much the same way, no historical period can really be understood divorced from the time that preceded it. At the very least, the questions that one age considers were asked by the age that went before. But more than that, frequently we see that those things that seemed startlingly new when viewed from the perspective of 1517 are rather less striking when we know the broad outlines of the prior two centuries. Given that, this chapter will seek to outline the accomplishments and difficulties of the late medieval Roman Church. To begin, we must grasp the ways that the late medieval mind frequently saw the whole of life's events as having religious meaning.

THE LATE MEDIEVAL PERIOD AS A TIME
OF CRISIS IN EUROPE

The late medieval period, roughly 1350–1500, experienced a number of crises in Western Europe. These crises were not all religious, but the minds of the people of that time tended to see things religiously. Whether we of a later time would see these phenomena as religious is unimportant to our understanding of that culture. We must take this as a given, so we can remove the blinders that keep us from some appreciation of that time and those people.

By most measures, the fourteenth and fifteenth centuries were times of great difficulty for people living in Western Europe. The population of Europe, which had been steadily climbing from the low levels reached after the fall of the Roman Empire, stopped climbing. The building of the great cathedrals, which had already slowed prior to the middle of the fourteenth

century, came to a halt. Plagues, quite literally of biblical proportions, struck
the land. Two of the greater kingdoms, France and England, engaged in a war,
the Hundred Years' War, that lasted over a century (1337–1453). If a thinker
could see this as a time of tears, as Eustache Deschamps did, could he be faulted
for seeing it so?[1] The late medieval period was a time of crisis in Europe.

Crises for the Population

What were these crises? To begin with, there were various agricultural crises.
These crises took several forms, but all had the same result—namely, widespread hunger and malnutrition. Basic malnutrition made other conditions
worse: young and old died of diseases they might have survived had they been
better fed, some illnesses that were not fatal took longer to recover from, more
children were stillborn. Further, the general religious feeling of the times
caused people to look for divine causes for agricultural failures, rather than
meteorological or economic causes.

Agricultural crises took several forms. Rain had a great deal to do with many
agricultural problems. Too much rain and rivers would flood, washing away
crops in some of the most fertile river valleys. Further, too much rain could
keep crops from maturing in the fields. Too little rain caused a drought, with
total crop failures. But even too little rain at crucial moments in the crop cycle
could cause a drastic drop in yields.

Another form of agricultural catastrophe involved temperature. The late
medieval period saw several extraordinarily severe winters that kept people from
planting until later in the spring, making their crops more vulnerable to early
fall frosts. Of course, excessive heat could also blight crops, and occasionally did.

Meteorological conditions were worsened by insect infestations. Swarms of
locusts, which seemed to come directly from the pages of the Bible,[2] inter-
mittently swept over the land. Although generally more locally concentrated,
such infestations tended to cause total crop losses, with no scrap of food surviving in the affected areas. To a mind-set that saw God's hand in the particular instances of weather and fate, how could a repetition of God's punishment
not be interpreted as God's wrath?

Finally, all of the various agricultural problems were aggravated by storage
and transportation conditions that were simply too primitive to support large
populations. By modern standards, the network of roads was not well maintained, and only water travel was generally secure, though obviously ice from
a severe winter or flooding from too much rain demonstrated that such security was a relative thing. Further, the technologies to store grain dependably
had not been developed. Thus, frequently it was impossible to transport large
amounts of food from areas of abundance to areas of scarcity. All of this led to

a basic fact that hunger was a familiar companion to the medieval person. Such people could far more easily get excited about the frequent biblical references to feasting than people of our own day, when many parts of the developed world do not know systemic and frequent hunger.

Perhaps the medieval imagination could have dealt better with the agricultural issues that the period saw had they been the only kinds of problems people faced. However, that was not the case! Medical crises abounded. In addition to the chronic food shortages that had a general negative effect on the health of the population, new diseases attacked Europe in the fourteenth century, providing further evidence for people to believe that their society was being punished.

The Black Death arrived in Sicily in 1347.[3] Ironically, while the lack of a technological solution to the problem of the storage of grain had contributed to the weakening of the population, it was a series of technological advances in shipping that brought the plague to Europe. The Italian merchant fleet had become proficient enough to bring back plague-infested rats from the Far East so quickly that they did not die on the voyage but survived the journey to spread their disease in port cities. From initial infestations, the disease quickly spread, infecting all of Europe with a disease that still was deadly in the seventeenth century. In 1634, the small village of Oberammergau in Germany was so devastated by the plague and the effects of the Thirty Years' War that the residents offered up a prayer that if God would spare them, they would perform a "passion play," a recounting of the last week of the life of Jesus of Nazareth.

While the Black Death was the most feared disease that afflicted medieval Europe, it was not the only instance of a new threat. Syphilis entered Europe in the late fifteenth century, arriving in Barcelona in 1493. This strange new disease had no name at first, and the residents of various countries termed it the disease of other countries. So Italians and English called it "the French disease," while the French called it "the Neapolitan [from the kingdom of Naples] disease." Further, syphilis was far more to the late medievals than an embarassment. Norman Davies writes, "For reasons that are unclear, the spirochete microbe . . . assumed a specially virulent form when it reached Europe. . . . Within weeks it covered the body in suppurating pustules, attacked the central nervous system, and destroyed all hair. It killed within months, painfully."[4] New threats abounded in the late medieval world, and only the fool felt no fear.

Beyond the obvious effects of sickness and death, these new diseases caused a profound change in what I have been calling the "medieval imagination." This is simply shorthand for a cluster of images, truths, and knowledge that people generally had but that was rarely examined or questioned. For instance, prior to the early part of the twentieth century, people in America generally felt that it was safest to keep money in a bank. This notion was not examined;

had it been, people might have noticed that few regulations safeguarded their money in a bank. After the stock market crash and the run on many banks that caused many people to lose their money, the American imagination was less trusting of banks. In much the same way, the attacks on the general health of the medieval populace resulted in deep alterations in the set of assumptions people made.

First, life, which had always been fragile, became even more so. The tightly knit fabric of society began to unravel as people realized that being in the presence of a plague-infected victim could cause their own deaths. The bonds between family members, members of guilds, and members of the church were all placed under great strain. Further, people were acutely conscious of the possibility of dying without proper preparation. For the medieval Christian, proper preparation meant, among other things, the chance for a good confession to cleanse one's soul. Deprived of that sometimes by the swiftness of death from plague, troubled believers turned to a recent development, the doctrine of purgatory.[5]

What was purgatory? Technically, it was a place reserved for those Christian believers who had failed to make full satisfaction for their sinning during the span of their lives. It was closely related to the sacrament of penance, which was aimed at the cleansing of the individual's soul from sin and its effects. Properly considered, the penitent sinner made a full confession of his or her sins, and the priest pronounced absolution. However, though this removed the guilt from the sinner, there still remained the matter of the punishment. The demands of justice necessitated that those sinned against, including God, be paid. Thus, after the words of absolution, the priest imposed specific works upon the sinner. These might include fasting, special prayers, a pilgrimage, or even a donation of alms.

But what happened to a person who was unable for some reason to complete such works of satisfaction during this life? Obviously, this became a more important question with the increased incidence of and fear of sudden death. Purgatory was a medieval answer to that question. In purgatory a sinner could finish the work so as to enter the gates of heaven. It was no coincidence that the doctrine of purgatory received much more attention in this age of crisis.

Political Crises in the Church

The late medieval period also saw various crises of faith. This does not mean, however, that the Reformation era was brought on by the lack of faith among the laity or clergy. The late medieval church was full of vibrant communities of faith who were passionate about their service to their Lord. However, to turn a blind eye to the series of shocks to the system that the medieval church absorbed, both occasional and systemic, is to choose to fail to understand the history properly.

Two crises in the church had dominated ecclesiastical politics in this period. The first was the Avignon Papacy. If you ask almost any Catholic, even today, where the pope lives, she or he will answer in Rome. Indeed, one of the pope's titles is bishop of Rome. However, in the fourteenth century, that was not always the case. In 1309, during the papal reign of Clement V, the papal court was moved from Rome to Avignon, France. Clement did this because of the pressure of the French, and indeed seven of the popes who served in Avignon were French. This period was frequently termed the "Babylonian Captivity of the Church," a name that would come back to haunt the Roman Church. The papal court remained in Avignon until 1377, when it was moved back to Rome near the end of the reign of Gregory XI. The building program that the popes had undertaken in Avignon to make it look, well, papal, had taken enormous resources from the Roman Church. Further, how could the bishop of Rome not reside in Rome?

However, the resolution of the Avignon Papacy led directly to the next crisis, the Great Schism. Though Gregory XI did move the papal court back to Rome in 1377, he died in 1378. The people of Rome rioted in the streets while the cardinals met to choose the next pope. The demonstrators demanded that the next pope maintain the papacy in Rome. The cardinals elected Urban VI. However, a few months later, the cardinals slipped out of Rome, claimed that they had been intimidated by the mob, and elected Clement VII.

Was Urban's election simply made under duress and thus illegitimate? To answer this fully seems very difficult now. On the one hand, that is exactly the reason that the cardinals gave for their extraordinary action. On the other hand, scholars have pointed out that Urban VI was not a Roman citizen and did not seem to be a choice motivated by the cardinals' fear. Whatever the reason might have been, however, a truly new situation presented itself to the faithful. Two popes existed. Each claimed to be pope. Each had been elected by the same group of cardinals. Each immediately excommunicated the other. How could a believer know who was the true Father of the faithful?

The prestige of the papacy suffered serious damage during this period, which lasted from 1378 to 1417. The Avignonese popes and Roman popes continued to excommunicate each other and demand that none of the faithful associate with the other. Prominent members of the Roman Church also spoke out in favor of one side or the other and frequently criticized the other side harshly. However, there was not unanimity even among the learned, so this did not help. Too frequently, people saw men who claimed to be the vicar of Christ acting in ways that seemed hardly Christian.

The resolution of the schism also battered the stature of the papacy, at least in the minds of theologians, and possibly among the laity. The solution came from the conciliar movement. Councils were an ancient tool of the church. A council was literally the meeting of bishops to decide particular questions of doctrine and discipline. In 325, the first ecumenical, or universal, council was called by the Emperor Constantine and met in Nicaea, outside of the capital city of Constantinople. The calling of an ecumenical council, by long tradition, could be at the will of the pope or emperor. Exceedingly important questions had been decided by councils, such as the doctrine of the Trinity and the question of the relation of Christ to the Father.

The Council of Pisa was called in 1408 and convened in 1409. Significantly, this council was not called by either pope but by cardinals from both camps. Both popes, Gregory XII of Rome and Benedict XIII of Avignon, were invited to attend, but they refused. In their absence the council decided that the highest power in the church did not reside in the pope but in councils. The Council of Pisa deposed both popes and elected a new pope, Alexander V.

This would have been a solution had the popes accepted either the theory that councils had the greatest power in the church or their having been deposed. Since they did neither, the council had simply muddied the waters of the question of authority in the church and had succeeded in making matters worse by electing a third pope. However, help was on the way from a new quarter.

King Sigismund of Germany, who would become Holy Roman Emperor in 1433, was persuaded of the necessity of acting for the good of the church. He arranged for another council to be held, this one in the German city of Constance, and pressured Pope John XXIII, the pope elected by the Council of Pisa, to convoke the Council in 1414. John XXIII seems to have wanted the council to depose the Roman and Avignonese popes, to strengthen his claim. However, the council leaned toward having all three popes resign. When Pope John would not resign, in 1417, the council deposed all three popes and elected Martin V as the new pope. The Great Schism was over.

The papacy held only a shadow of its former power at the end of the council. The council had made two decrees by which it intended to solve the question of authority in the church for good. First, in 1415, it decreed that the highest authority in the church resided in a general council, and that the authority of a general council was even superior to that of a duly elected pope. Second, in 1417, the council decreed that general councils must be held in the church regularly, setting out a pattern of general councils every ten years. Obviously, with such frequency of meetings, the office of the pope had the potential to become simply the office that executed the policy and doctrines of the councils. Later popes protested strongly, and in 1460 Pius II gave a decree titled *Execrabilis*, which stated that it was not permissible for anyone to appeal the ruling of a pope to a later council. The question of the authority of the church in the fifteenth century was just that—a question.

Crises of Discipline in the Church

Not only the politics of the church but also the actions of its clergy came under increased scrutiny in the period leading up to the Reformation. Both the higher and lower clergy were frequently involved in actions that were in some way scandalous to the members of the faithful. Though the church had argued for almost one thousand years that the power of the sacraments was not dependent on the personal holiness of the priest, the church never argued that members of the clergy should abandon common standards of morality. In fact, the church held the clergy to higher standards than the laity. This made any failure on the part of the clergy all the more scandalous.

With regard to the higher clergy, it is worthwhile to consider the example that the popes were setting at the end of the fifteenth century and the beginning of the sixteenth century. Pope Alexander VI reigned from 1492 to 1503. He was a member of the Borgia family and the nephew of Pope Calistus III. Pope Calistus gave great gifts to him as a young man, and he rose rapidly in the church. Alexander engaged in several sexual liaisons and was not shy about showering gifts on the children who came from these illegitimate unions. One of his favorite mistresses was Vannozza dei Cattani. Alexander and she were the parents of Juan, Cesare, Lucrezia, and Goffredo Borgia. At times, his life became so shameful that he was reprimanded by Pope Pius II in 1460. Apparently he did not change his ways after that censure.

Alexander won the papal election after Innocent VIII's death in August 1492. Being the bishop of Rome did not turn his attention from his favorite children. He appointed his son Cesare to be bishop of several dioceses, even though Cesare was still only eighteen years old. He arranged several advantageous marriages for Lucrezia. He was a capable administrator and might have led the Vatican toward greater respectability and greater success in its ministries. However, he seemed, by his actions, to believe that the papacy was simply another princedom he had won. Nowhere was this more apparent than when he battled with the Dominican reformer Girolamo Savonarola. When Savonarola would not stop preaching against Alexander's wishes, Alexander excommunicated and executed him in 1498.

Alexander VI was followed by Pius III. Pius may have been a reformer, but he died after only ten days in office. This paved the way for the election of Julius II in 1503, and he served until 1513. Julius was not from a wealthy family, but his uncle had become pope in 1471 and had given several wealthy posts to Julius. This gave him the power base from which to gain both influence and wealth. After Pius III's brief reign, Julius managed to bribe enough cardinals to gain the papacy. He was not like Alexander VI in having a desire to enrich his family, though he had three daughters from liaisons during his time as a cardinal. However, Julius did have other unseemly characteristics. Julius was a warrior, a leader of armies, which he commanded in battle. His period in office was so marked by war that the humanist scholar Erasmus mocked him in a book published in 1509 titled *The Praise of Folly*.

Julius II had significant gifts. He was able to expand the papal treasuries across the period of his administration. He was an enormously important patron of the arts and supported Michelangelo and Raphael. But the greatness of his vision was tarnished by his methods. To support the costs of rebuilding St. Peter's cathedral in Rome, he proposed the sale of indulgences. This sale of indulgences was widely known, and Niccolò Machiavelli reported them in *The Prince*, written around 1513. This was severely criticized by Protestant reformers, who saw this as a corruption of the idea of the process of salvation.

Leo X followed Julius II. A member of the powerful Medici family from Florence, he served as pope from 1513 to 1521. Leo was interested in the arts but also in the power of his family, which was very influential in Florence. Time and again, he used his authority to benefit Florence and the Medici interests. He spent the papal treasury lavishly, reducing it to nothing within a few years. Leo was like a college student with his first credit card. This habit of spending money he did not have led Leo to authorize even more sales of indulgences. In fact, it was this sale of indulgences that caused the original friction with Martin Luther.

As we have seen, the popes of the late fifteenth century and early sixteenth century were not always setting admirable examples for the body of believers. However, they were not alone in this situation. The lower clergy, whom the faithful might meet on a daily or weekly basis, had problems of their own. Their problems might seem less scandalous because of their lower status, but in a way they were worse, because in small villages the priest was very well known. Far too frequently, that familiarity gave rise to contempt.

One of the difficulties of the lower clergy was that too often they had not been sufficiently trained for their positions. Especially in the smaller towns and villages, some priests were functionally illiterate in Latin. They might be able to repeat memorized portions of the regular church service, but too frequently they were unable to grasp the subtleties of the language or to interpret difficult points of church doctrine, for themselves or for others. Many were unprepared for the interpretation of Scripture, so the preaching to these smaller parishes suffered. University-trained clergy existed, but frequently they were concentrated in the larger towns and cities, where larger and wealthier parishes could mean more substantial livings.

Another issue that caused problems between the clergy and the laity was the abuse of clerical status. In the fifteenth and sixteenth centuries, clergy were simply unaffected by certain laws. For instance, clergy could not be taxed. Further, many towns had laws protecting local craft guilds. Guilds were the medieval equivalent of unions. To be able to produce a certain product, a person, by law, would have to join the guild. This allowed the guild to maintain a standard of quality but also allowed it to monopolize production and maintain a certain price. Clergy were not subject to such laws. Monastic houses commonly produced liquor, beer, and other products that competed with the products produced by the guilds.

Even in the cases where clergy were subject to the law, they were not always subject to the same justice system. The church maintained that clergy were literally not like other members of the population and so should not be liable to trials in regular criminal courts. Thus, if a member of the clergy was accused of a crime, he would generally not have his trial before the magistrates of the town. Instead, his case would be given to an ecclesiastical court. Many times the laity believed that the decisions and punishments given by the ecclesiastical courts were more indulgent than those the regular magistrates would have given.

Another problem for the relationship between clergy and laity at the end of the Middle Ages was clerical concubinage. This was a term used to cover a multitude of practices, all of which related to breaking the discipline of priestly celibacy. Simply put, many of the members of the clergy were not celibate. During the later Middle Ages, while this may have been common, it was never permitted. Pope Gregory VII, who reigned from 1073 to 1085, had demanded that all clergy be celibate. However, at the time directly before the Reformation period, this discipline was not universally obeyed. Many practices were covered by the term "concubinage." Some priests and higher church officials were promiscuous, abusing their spiritual and financial power to engage in many liaisons. On the other hand, sometimes the practice looked simply like clerical marriage, where a man and woman would live together, sharing the work of the household and raising their children together. Neither practice was permitted. How widespread was this phenomenon? Modern historians are unable to say with certainty. However, we do know that it was frequent enough in some dioceses that the bishop had a set price as the penalty for a child born to a priest. That practice suggests that at least in some locales, this custom was not uncommon.

Clergy also abused their flocks by two mutually supporting exploitations of the church's system: absenteeism and simony. Absenteeism was exactly what it sounds like: the priest or bishop would be absent from his parish or diocese. The sacraments could not be effectively administered without the clergy, and the whole medieval system of salvation could grind to a halt without the

sacraments. But absenteeism was not the result of clergy calling in sick or taking extra days of vacation. Frequently, absenteeism was the consequence of a
clergyman having the responsibility for more than one parish or diocese.
Obviously, if a priest had the responsibility for three parishes, he would be
unable to serve all three simultaneously. The problem was the same for a
bishop, but on a larger scale, since a bishop oversaw a diocese and dioceses
were geographically much larger than parishes.

Why would a member of the clergy take on multiple positions? The church
was not shorthanded, needing to use one clergyman to serve where it would
have wished for more.[6] The problem was that each parish or diocese provided
a "living," a salary, for the man who held it. Taking on multiple positions meant
receiving multiple livings. Further, vacant positions could have their income
distributed by higher church officials to lower. Of course, this was done for a
bribe or kickback. This practice was simony. The Church of Rome had claimed
for centuries that simony, the buying or selling of ecclesiastical offices, was both
illegal and a horrible sin. But it was a common sin, and the body of the faithful
suffered for the ability of well-connected clergy to enrich themselves.

One final clerical abuse must be noted. This was the indulgence traffic.
Indulgences were promises sold by agents of the Church of Rome that in
exchange for money, a given person's soul would be released from purgatory.
The church had discovered that when it needed to raise money, it could
depend upon the widespread belief in purgatory, and the love of believers for
those who had already died, to elicit a significant source of income. Many
reformers had questioned the medieval foundations of the doctrine of purgatory for years; even more were convinced that at times indulgence sellers went
too far in their promises, in order to raise money for the church.

All of these abuses and scandalous practices resulted in a predictable mind-
set known as anticlericalism. Anticlericalism is the bias against the clergy, on
the basis of perceived unfairness. Many of the common people saw the clergy
as people who were less moral, even less Christian, than themselves. When
they saw their village priest with a wife and children, when they saw rich nobles
buy particular clerical offices, they had very few illusions about the quality of
the Christianity the clergy held. Frequently, laypeople believed that clergy
were part of the ruling class, trying to take too great a share of the working
class's hard-earned material goods. Anticlericalism was common across Europe
but varied in its intensity. That is not to say that laypeople automatically had
the same problems with clergy abuse that theological reformers did. On the
contrary, Bruce Gordon has argued that some of the things that most upset
theologians like Erasmus and Luther were rather accepted by the laypeople in
the parishes. The laity was prepared to accept oddities in a minister's life if such
did not rise to the level of scandal, as long as he provided what they believed

was essential to their own care.[7] But anticlericalism was a significant factor in the setting out of reforms in several of the reform movements that succeeded in the sixteenth century.

Moral Crises in the Faithful

However corrupt some members of the clergy could be, the body of believers was not without its own problems. Superstition was a normal part of the Christian religion for many believers. Some scholars have estimated that the state of Christianity in Western Europe was rather weak at the beginning of the sixteenth century, so weak that the reforms of the era would be more helpfully termed the "Christianization" of Europe rather than its re-Christianization.[8] The superstitious character of Christianity in the period included a wide variety of practices. Farmers performed rituals to ensure good harvests, attempting to get enough rain at the right times and protection from various insects. Charms and amulets were eagerly bought so that the buyer could guarantee good health or good looks or even a good marriage. These types of superstition were attacked by the clergy, but the people used them anyway.

A further mark of this lack of basic Christianity was the widespread ignorance of even the most basic items of the faith. Many believers could not recite the Lord's Prayer or the Creed. Of those who could, many could only recite these basics of the faith in Latin. But this Latin knowledge was learned by rote. If asked to explain in their everyday speech what it was they had recited, many were helpless to respond.

There was also a lackadaisical character to the observances of many of the faithful. Too frequently, believers only received Communion once a year. At the Fourth Lateran Council in 1215, the doctrine had been decreed that believers should take Communion at least once a year. By 1500, many believers had turned that decree upside down and saw annual communion as a maximum.

This permissive attitude on the part of believers in the area of worship extended to the general acceptance of moral standards that were much less than Christian. Brothels were widely accepted in towns across the Holy Roman Empire. The Christian prohibitions against adultery, fornication, and prostitution simply did not overcome that phenomenon. Beyond sexual immorality, many of the economic practices of the merchants and guilds were based on the desire to maximize profit rather than to give any credence to the Christian ideals of taking care of the poor and sharing the gifts God had given. The practice of guilds to control production and sale of goods was clearly an effort at monopolization, and where successful, it was not hindered by any Christian conscience.

Having noted all of these deficiencies and abuses in the practice of Christianity, and the various agricultural and medical problems that literally plagued Europe in the fourteenth and fifteenth centuries, it would be easy to state that the Protestant reforms were simply the answer to a series of problems, and that the people flocked to this true religion because of the functional death of the traditional religion. However, the historical picture is far more complicated and interesting than that. Simultaneously with the great abuses and problems, the late medieval period saw a number of movements that demonstrated the extraordinary depth of the piety of the people and the vitality of Christianity in the medieval mind.

THE LATE MEDIEVAL PERIOD AS A TIME OF VITALITY IN EUROPEAN CHRISTIANITY

The medieval life of people in Europe was wholly tied up with religion. It is fair to say that there was hardly a single area of life in which religion's impact could not be felt. Further, both common and highborn people did not see this as an imposition brought down upon them by agents of the church, but rather accepted it as the character of life. People believed that God cared about them on a very specific basis and that the faith offered answers to the issues of both daily life and the afterlife. Common Christian practice may have been mixed with a generous helping of superstition, but it was almost unheard of to find someone to question whether the matters of life were touched by religion. To live in the late medieval world in Europe was to live in a world saturated with Christianity.

Because of this, there was a way in which religion permeated life that is hard for people living in the twenty-first century to grasp. The church and religion provided comfort in difficult times, entertainment for leisure times, and a framework for meaningful existence at all times. A popular term for this was "Christendom." Christendom is a concept that expresses the coequality between the empire and the church. In other words, in a Christendom model, all the people are subjects of the king or emperor, while at the same time all the people are members of the church. This idea was supported by the existence of a universal church—the Church of Rome—and by the Holy Roman Empire. The Holy Roman Empire roughly encompassed modern-day Germany. It had been a creation of the early medieval alliance between the popes and the Carolingian kings, beginning formally in the year 800. In the idea of Christendom, the state and church exist in mutual support of each other. Whether this was always true or not is not always important. (In fact, we know that it is not historically true.) People of all orders of society believed that their society held together in part because they were of the true religion, and that their sovereign was supported in the true religion. We shall examine this by considering the medieval mind-set's acceptance of certain ideas about salvation, by examining some of the new movements and doctrines of the late medieval period,[9] by noting one crucial technological development, and by exploring the religious practices of the time.

The Medieval Economy of Salvation

Religion saturated the medieval world and the way that medieval men and women thought about the world. One of the marks of this was the amount of time they spent thinking about the salvation of their souls. This represents one of the great chasms between the modern age and the late medieval and Refor-mation periods. While considerations of salvation were so common then that one cardinal could write in 1539 that the whole point of religion was the sal-vation of one's soul, today that is not the case.[10] One can attend Christian ser-vices where no mention of salvation is made, or where the concept of salvation has become a metaphor for release from bondage to problems such as alco-holism or drug addiction. In the twenty-first century, sincere consideration of heaven and hell, and how one gets there, is far more rare.

To understand this more fully, we must come to terms with the medieval way of thinking about salvation, which would have formed the way that both princes and paupers thought about heaven. The theological term for this is the *ordo salutis*, which simply means the "order of salvation," or the "economy of salvation." The term "economy" suggests an important factor in the ways that the medievals considered the issue. Salvation represented a transaction. Of course, that is a gross simplification of the matter, but when we speak about matters of deep theology, frequently the great majority of people who are affected never get beyond such simplifications.

The medieval economy of salvation was the solution to a particular prob-lem. The problem was the offense to God that humans gave by sinning. Jesus Christ, the divine-human being, had paid the greatest amount of the debt, that which humans could never have paid on their own. The sins were debts, owed to God. Morally good works were payments on account that lessened the total debt owed to God. Sins could be cleansed by confession and absolution granted by a priest. But the payment of the penalty, the actual debt owed to God, needed to be worked off by penances. The priest would assign penances, which could be performed in this life or in purgatory. The penances could be the performing of prayers or other sacred acts, or they could be the giving of charitable contributions, or a special fast. The point was that the cleansing away of sin and its effects was a two-part process.

The advantage of the economic model of salvation is that it was straightfor-ward, understandable, had biblical support, and by the late fifteenth century had hundreds of years of tradition behind it. The weakness was that there was no way to know objectively whether one's "account" was in such a state that one would be permitted entry into heaven, or consigned to hell. Medieval priests did not seek to lessen consciousness of this problem. Time and again, the confessional manuals for priests would direct them to emphasize that no one could know with certainty his own state in the reckoning of salvation. Because of this fear, the bad conscience was a useful tool to encourage believers to greater works of virtue and Christian charity. Such a system did provide significant strengthening for practical morality. In order to be saved, you had to be good. This system also explained the rather frequent consideration of the state of the soul that was characteristic of the medieval woman and man.

Late Medieval Doctrines and Movements

Late medieval society was extraordinarily rich theologically. The major universities were full of theological faculties who engaged the questions of the day with great vigor. The church's leaders demonstrated a sensitivity to the needs of the faithful, declaring doctrines, commissioning religious art, and clarifying truths that were well attuned to the requirements of the faithful. The historian of the period can see several evidences of a rich, varied, and vibrant spiritual culture. One evidence comes in the form of the cult of St. Anne. St. Anne was believed to have been the mother of Mary, the mother of Jesus. Because none of the writings that mention St. Anne were included in the Christian Bible, her status as a saint was slowed, especially in Western Europe. It was in the late thirteenth century that the feast of St. Anne was first celebrated in the West. The late fourteenth century saw the introduction of the cult to England. After that, devotion to her spread throughout the Western Church. We can see in her cult the desire of Christians of the time to know as much as possible about the human side of Jesus, the hunger to grasp the family that generated the mother of God. Her cult moved so quickly and deeply that both Luther and Calvin had instances of piety that prominently depended upon St. Anne. This was true even though the Church of Rome did not formally declare Anne's sainthood until 1584.

Processional accounts for the feast of Corpus Christi give another verification for the strength of piety in the late medieval period. The feast of Corpus Christi was a celebration of the Eucharist, which was to be held on the Thursday after Trinity Sunday. Although this feast was decreed for the universal church in 1264, various problems kept it from being too widely celebrated until the fourteenth century. In the fourteenth and fifteenth centuries, however, this festival became quite popular. One of the signature events in the celebration of Corpus Christi was the processional. Corpus Christi processionals could become almost paradelike.[11] Of course, part of the reason was that it was

a summer feast, and it was possible to have extended religious celebrations out-
doors. But another part seems to be attributable to the desire of the faithful to
proclaim their own faith in a particularly obvious manner.

A significant movement that demonstrates the importance of learning and
of the simple life of devotion in the late Middle Ages is seen in the origins of
the movement called the Devotio Moderna. The Devotio Moderna was a loose
movement that began near the end of the fourteenth century. It was anti-
monastic and somewhat antischolastic in character. The movement gave fundamental emphases to inner devotion, meditation on the passion of Christ (his
sufferings), and the usefulness of frequent eucharistic observance as central to
the life of Christians. The Devotio Moderna spread throughout the Holy
Roman Empire and beyond, representing a strong desire on the part of its
adherents to move toward an inner, lived experience of religion. This represented a deepening of the experiential side of Christianity.

One of the significant advocates of the Devotio Moderna was the Brethren
of the Common Life. The Brethren was an order founded by Gerard Groote,
who had turned away from a university career so as to be able to preach the
primitive Christianity he believed had existed in the first centuries of the
Christian age. He traveled throughout the Netherlands, preaching the simple
apostolic faith. Instead of religious vows, Groote allowed his followers to
maintain whatever life they had before coming to him, but he insisted on a significant level of demonstrable devotion to holiness.

A recognizable group gathered around Groote and his successor, Floren-
tius Radewijns, and were eventually called the Brethren of the Common Life.
Though they took no vows, they did live in communities and had common
possessions. Not wishing to beg for their livings as the friars did, the members
of the community earned money by copying books and eventually by printing.
Education was a principal ministry of the organization, and it founded schools
throughout the Low Countries and eventually in Germany, where Martin
Luther would even attend a Brethren school. Because of their simple piety and
their attachment to learning, their schools frequently offered the best-quality
education available in a given area.

Thomas à Kempis (c. 1380–1471) received an education from a school of the
Brethren and was in a monastic house that was part of the Windesheim movement, a monastic order inspired by the Devotio Moderna. Thomas's book *The
Imitation of Christ* is one of the top devotional manuals of all time. Written in a
humble style, the book concentrates upon humble service to God. Thomas
acknowledges that learning is good but points out that humble piety is even better. He characterizes the Scriptures as being mainly about simple and devout
truths, and he encourages its readers to see themselves as unworthy of the grace
that Christ gives, but invited to receive Christ because of Christ's great mercy.

The broad spread of the Brethren of the Common Life reveals how well in tune with the spirit of the age these emphases were.

The Printing Press

It is impossible to understand the way that the period of the Reformation changed the medieval world without at least mentioning one of the most important technological innovations of the age—the printing press. Johannes Gutenberg is generally credited with the invention of the printing press. This was a crucial ingredient in at least some of the reforming movements, which were hermeneutic movements. Hermeneutics is the study of textual interpretation. At least some of the reforming movements were deeply tied up with matters concerning the interpretation of the Scriptures. Versions of the Scriptures were printed. Commentaries on the Scriptures were printed. Tracts about particular interpretations of the Scriptures were printed. All were bought, frequently quickly, by a public that at times seemed ravenous for the next religious book.

The development of the printing press had two simple and profound functions. First, it made the mass distribution of a tract or book or version of the Bible far easier and quicker than it had ever been before. Never before had an author, religious or otherwise, been able to reach so many readers so quickly. Further, if a particular work was popular and sold out its press run, another printing could easily be done. Second, the printing press made books easier to possess, and they became more attainable marks of status.[12] This easier possession of books helped with the spread of literacy and served some of the Reformers' goals of having a literate, and biblically literate, laity.

The printing press was an enormously important development. We can say without a shadow of hesitation that this development absolutely had a significant role in the development of the Reformation. However, the Reformation was not caused by the availability of print. Gutenberg produced a printed copy of the Psalms in 1457, a good half century prior to the period we are considering. The reforming movements did not simply jump out of the printing press. However, some of the Reformers embraced this new technology, and its impact was both measurable and undeniable.

CONCLUSION

It should be clear by now that a brief summation of the late medieval period can only fail to grasp the rich concentration of religious hunger and exploration that marked the period leading to the time of the Reformation. Medieval people were intensely aware of their own sinfulness and of the gloriousness of the God they needed to worship. This contrast was so firmly in their minds that a variety of responses arose.

Some of the responses we now categorize as abuses. From a distance, we are able to see the desire for money of some churchmen as simple greed, rather than a desire for the building up of the church. We can see the grasping after power as little different from that of secular lords quarreling over a disputed province. But some of the abuses were simply the mark of pious but flawed human beings attempting to make their way through a world in which the realities were changing while the tradition remained static. The period of time was not godless, nor was it perfect. It was a mixture of tradition and innovation that would send forth responses to itself and supply the large numbers of people who would be repulsed and attracted by those very responses.

The late medieval period was not at all a time of religious decline. Far from it. The people of Western Europe, far from being lackadaisical about their religious practices, were fully engaged by a rich panoply of religious beliefs and practices that structured their lives. The Reformation did not simply come about as the answer to an irreligious culture. On the other hand, the facts on the ground in the late medieval period resemble nothing so much as a recipe for religious upheaval. The factors of intense religious piety coupled with a zealous desire to gain heaven and escape hell mixed very badly with a clerical establishment that did not always live up to its own highest ideals. The Reformation came about not out of a lax attitude toward eternal things, but because of a heightened sense of their importance.

QUESTIONS FOR DISCUSSION

1. Why did the people of the late medieval era see so much of their lives religiously? How does that compare to our own time, and what does that say about our time and theirs?
2. How did the political crises of the church in the fourteenth and fifteenth centuries affect the faith of believers in the sixteenth century?
3. How did moral crises of discipline among the clergy affect the laity? Was anticlericalism a logical outcome?
4. What would the effect be of intense spiritual piety and widespread abuses of accepted Christian standards?

SUGGESTED FURTHER READING

Delumeau, Jean. *Catholicism between Luther and Voltaire: A New View of the Counter-Reformation*. Philadelphia: Westminster Press, 1977.

Kelly, J. N. D. *The Oxford Dictionary of Popes*. New York: Oxford University Press, 2006.

Le Goff, Jacques. *The Birth of Purgatory*. Translated by Arthur Goldhammer. Cambridge, MA: Harvard University Press, 1985.

———. *Medieval Civilization*. Translated by Julia Barrow. Oxford: Basil Blackwell, 1988.

Sheppard, J. A. *Christendom at the Crossroads: The Medieval Era*. Louisville, KY: Westminster John Knox Press, 2005.

DOCTRINAL-VOCABULARY DISCUSSION

Heresy, Schism, and Orthodoxy

"Heresy" and "schism" were terms that were thrown around loosely and frequently in the sixteenth century. But what did they mean, and what was the effect when you called someone a heretic or schismatic? Heresy is a theological term with a complex and specific meaning. Heresy and orthodoxy are a matched pair of opposites. Orthodoxy means right belief. But orthodoxy is more complicated than simple right belief. Orthodoxy inherently also means "defined" right belief. Believing in the doctrine of the Trinity is an orthodox belief because the church had defined this idea as true in specific terms at specific councils. While there were and are a wide number of defined orthodox positions across the theological spectrum, the church had not, and has not, defined all correct beliefs.

Heresy is the intentional teaching or spreading of incorrect belief. It is *deliberately* teaching a doctrine that *knowingly* runs counter to something that the church or all believers have *specifically defined*. Therefore, believing something out of ignorance of true doctrine does not rise to the standard of heresy. Technically, that would be a heterodox belief. Further, teaching something that is controversial but on which there is no defined doctrine cannot be heresy. For instance, the Roman Catholic Church did not define the infallibility of the pope in matters of faith and morals until the nineteenth century. Teaching that the pope was fallible prior to that time might have been shocking and offensive, but it would not have risen to the legal standard of heresy.

Schism is the act of dividing the Christian community of believers. Thus, calling someone a schismatic is pronouncing that his or her actions lead to division. Since the New Testament calls unity in Christ a great virtue, schismatic activity is considered sinful. The upheavals of the sixteenth century were not the first schisms. The Great Schism happened in the eleventh century, when the Catholic Church broke with the Eastern Orthodox Church. Both claimed to be the one holy and apostolic church. Roman theologians accused the various Protestant reformers of being schismatics. The Protestants charged back that by accepting human innovative traditions over Scripture, Rome had left the purity of the true church, and reforming it was the only thing a faithful believer could do.

Why did this matter?

Heresy was a civil, capital offense in Europe in the sixteenth century. If someone was intentionally teaching something against defined right belief, that person was in danger of losing his or her life. Heterodoxy, on the other hand, was not a capital offense. If a local peasant had a strange belief that the Trinity included the Father, Son, and Mary but was willing to be corrected, that correction would be the end of the matter. Heresy, however, carried a penalty that civil authorities in both Catholic and Protestant lands were very willing to execute. When you called someone a heretic during the Reformation, you were verbally assigning that person to the stake.

3

The Humanistic Call for Reform

The first call for reform of the Church of Rome in the sixteenth century did not come from Martin Luther, nor for that matter from any group that can meaningfully be called Protestant. The first challenge to the various issues in the church came clearly from a group of men who thought of themselves as true sons of the Church of Rome. This loose movement has come to be called humanism, or Renaissance humanism. It would fuel the ability of the Church of Rome to consider its own heritage, it would supply some of the rocks that Protestant reformers of various types would throw at the practices of Rome, and its impact remains unclear to this day.[1] One cannot take a course on the period of the Reformation or read a book on the matter without soon reading or hearing about the influence of humanism. But what was humanism?

HUMANISM DEFINED

Humanism was the movement that is linked to the time period called the Renaissance. Renaissance simply means "rebirth." The Renaissance and the Reformation periods largely overlapped, and the influences between the two are still widely discussed. The Renaissance was a time of rediscovery of the heritage of the classical period, with a flowering of scholarship, especially scholarship in the classical and biblical languages of Latin, Greek, and Hebrew. Renaissance humanism was an extremely loose movement that valued the classical works and sought to return to the wisdom of the ancient world through reading and understanding the works of an age that was generally and uncritically deemed to be better than the age in which the humanists lived.

Although defining humanism was and is difficult and still causes vigorous scholarly debate, it is useful to set out some of the central characteristics that many humanists shared. This is not a complete list, nor did all those figures who had the marks of this list call themselves humanists. However, both the detractors and supporters of the movement would have recognized this list as characteristic of humanism. Humanism set itself apart from other models of thought by its concentration on language and history, by its turn to the past for models that would change the present, and by a certain confidence about human intellectual and moral possibility.

Language study was the meat and potatos of humanism; if any one thing could legitimately be said to hold for all humanists, it would have been this. The French king Francis I (1494–1547), in seeking to support the new movement in education even set up a college in Paris called the Royal Readers (*Lecteurs Royaux*). The new movement sought to find the wisdom of the classical period by returning to the sources. In fact, that was a common Renaissance humanist slogan—*ad fontes*, which meant "to the sources." When seeking to gain this wisdom, scholars quickly learned that translating the Greek and Hebrew original versions of the Christian Scriptures, as well as translating Greek philosophy into Latin or other languages, caused shifts in meaning. Thus, in order to read well, the learned man had to know Greek, Hebrew, and Latin. One of the highest tributes among the humanists was to call someone a trilingual man (*vir trilinguis*).

In their study of classical texts, the humanists also noted several points of interest. At first, these discoveries were simply fascinating intellectual fragments, but they came to have great impact on the late medieval Latin culture. First, the humanists realized that traditional readings of texts were frequently incorrect. They began to understand this from their close readings and from their own difficulty in understanding texts. This led to the concentration upon historical context. To read a text with the meaning it had to its original audience, humanist scholars had to know things about the original setting: who wrote, under what circumstances, and to whom. History and context became key humanist tools.

A second point humanists grasped was that the meaning of some texts commonly known through translation had been radically changed in the very act of translating. This would affect all of the church's texts, but most especially the Bible. Though the Bible was commonly available to the learned in Latin, that Latin was already a translation of the original languages of Hebrew for the Old Testament and Greek for the New Testament. Obviously, any claim that the church had been using a mistranslation for a thousand years was going to ruffle more than a few feathers!

The third point that humanists came to realize was that some texts, when examined with the new types of tools for reading that the humanists were developing, simply could not be accepted at face value. Erasmus, perhaps the greatest of the humanists, identified many writings as being falsely credited to the pen of Ambrose, the fourth-century bishop of Milan. He demonstrated that they were instead from another author, whom he named Pseudo-Ambrose. Likewise, it was humanist scholars who discovered that Dionysius the Are-opagite, an author who traditionally was believed to have been mentioned in Acts 17:34, must have written much later—hence the name by which most scholars refer to him now: Pseudo-Dionysius.[2] Lorenzo Valla and Nicholas of Cusa also demonstrated in the fifteenth century that the Donation of Con-stantine was a forgery. The Donation of Constantine was a document, sup-posedly from the Emperor Constantine, granting significant land and rights to the papacy. Valla and Cusa independently discovered that the text included terms that were not in use during Constantine's lifetime. This was upsetting because legal scholars had based part of the Roman Church's claims to power on this document. The discovery that the Donation was a forgery was sup-pressed for a time by the Church of Rome, but by the end of the sixteenth cen-tury, claims for its validity had been abandoned.

Reading texts correctly was not the only important issue in language for humanists. The art of speaking well, called rhetoric, was also crucial. In the modern day, rhetoric is a neutral term; we might say in a certain case that a politician's rhetoric does not match his actions. In that case, we would be using the term "rhetoric" in a negative way, meaning that the words were empty of meaning and used to deceive the listeners. For the humanists of the period of the Reformation, the issue was quite different. Rhetoric had to be used for the good of the listener. Rhetoric was the art of speaking well, of using the correct arguments that fit the audience.

Beyond language and beyond history as a guide for understanding docu-ments, humanists were also motivated by a sense of the classical past as a time worthy of emulation. It was the humanist historians of the Renaissance who termed the Middle Ages the "Dark Ages." These centuries were seen as the interim period between the brightness of the classical times of truth and purity and the present rediscovery of those facts. Humanists frequently set about to publish clear editions of classic texts and to give lucid translations of those texts. Had that been their only goal, they would have created far fewer impulses to reform. However, simply creating the availability of the texts was not enough. The humanist scholars tended to see the classical period—the golden ages of Greek and Rome and the apostles—as setting out a model for people to follow. When considering these carefully, many people were able to see the changes that had occurred in the intervening centuries. But would it be a simple matter to throw away centuries of tradition in order to return to another point in time? Was such a thing possible, even if it were desirable? These were some of the issues that humanism raised.

Finally, humanists had a certain confidence about human potential, both moral and intellectual. Broadly speaking, the humanist ideal of reform was that if you explained to people what was good for them and gave persuasive reasons for them to follow certain courses of action, generally people would do so. This was the antithesis of other schools of thought, both traditional and reforming. Significant efforts had been spent over the centuries to compose a system of punishments that, rather than persuading people, sought to threaten them. Likewise, later reformers such as Calvin and Knox were so convinced of the staining effects of sin that they believed that simply attempting to persuade people of good morals was foolish. Penalties also needed to be given so that the wicked would not be able to riot with impunity, and by doing so, draw even more people into their own condemnation.

It is important now to delineate between two different types of humanism. Scholars speak of "humanism" and "Christian humanism," or "biblical humanism." In one sense, the differentiation is meaningless, since almost to a person, the humanists were Christians. The Reuchlin affair is a case in point. Johannes Reuchlin (1455–1522), a jurist, became interested in Hebrew and studied the language with Jews. (In the late fifteenth century, there was no other option for the study of Hebrew.) In 1506, he published a Hebrew grammar and lexicon, which unlocked the world of the Old Testament to serious scholarly study in a way not previously open to Christian scholars. However, he became embroiled in a bitter dispute when Johann Pfefferkorn, a Jew who had converted to Catholicism, urged that all Jewish books should be destroyed. When Reuchlin was the only scholar who spoke against this approach to Emperor Maximilian I, he was accused of heresy. In Latin Europe, to fail to be Christian was quite serious.

In another sense, the distinction is quite important. Though all humanists were involved in the renaissance of learning and the rebirth of the classical voices, not all humanists aimed at the restoration of the church, or of Christianity. Others aspired to change the ways that the government worked or were more interested in other spheres of human learning. Though these humanist scholars were as important for the history of learning and the development of human thought, their contributions are less relevant to our study. Normally, it was the Christian humanists, or biblical humanists, who captured the insights that allowed their reforming ideas to be heard in the broad Christian world of the late fifteenth and early sixteenth centuries. These were the scholars who patterned their ideas and even their rhetorical styles on the Bible and the Christian fathers of the first five centuries of the Christian era.[3]

HUMANISM'S CHARACTERISTIC EMPHASES

Now that we have a rough definition of humanism and have seen the difficulties of defining a loose movement of scholarship, let us consider some of the characteristic emphases of the humanists and what they meant to the sixteenth-century church. The return to the sources for inspiration and reform was important, as was the concentration upon rhetorical arts and persuasion to personal and institutional reform. Two more themes that need some consideration are the struggles between the humanists and the scholastics, and humanism's contest against authoritarianism. Once we have a handle on these traits, we can more profitably consider some of the main humanists whose scholarship made reforming impressions in the church.

Ad fontes was the cry of the humanists. As we have seen, language study was central to the humanists. Giovanni Pico della Mirandola, an early Italian humanist, traveled widely to gain proficiency in Latin, but also Greek, Hebrew, Syriac, and Arabic. This concentration on languages was especially true for the biblical or Christian humanists, because that language study was for the service of understanding the most significant texts of the early Christian period, namely, the Fathers and the Scriptures. The return to the sources became a touchstone of the orthodoxy of a humanist. One found the greatest "truth" by approaching a text in its most original linguistic context. This only seems like a truism to a culture that has accepted its value. Theological students, historical students, classics students, students of political theory—all are taught in the period in which we live that access to the original context and language of a particular document is crucial for grasping its meaning.

But Christian thinkers had collectively spent a millennium creating a tradition of reading and interpretation that did not directly depend upon such tools. The inertia behind that tradition would not make change easy. Though there were significant Christian thinkers in Latin Europe who could read Latin and Greek in the medieval period, such as Boethius and Nicholas of Lyra, the great majority of the Latin West depended upon Latin translations of Greek texts. Scholars depended on the Latin translation of the Scriptures, the Vulgate, as if it were the original text. Eventually, at the Council of Trent, the Church of Rome would settle this problem by setting forth the Vulgate as an inspired translation. But that did not happen until the middle of the sixteenth century, after the legitimacy of the Vulgate had been called into question.

What were the habits of mind that the return to the sources challenged? First, we must note that this method had the possibility and even the tendency to overturn the way that the Bible had come to be read. Over the course of the thirteen centuries prior to the Renaissance, a particular approach to reading had developed. Frequently (and unhelpfully) termed "allegory," this method depended upon the belief that different levels of meaning lay within the scriptural text. Scholars called this the *quadriga*, the fourfold meaning of Scripture.[4] A second-century biblical interpreter, Origen, proposed that at times, when the literal sense of the Bible made no sense to the faithful, God was telling them to look for hidden meanings. Eventually this method took on much greater sophistication. The four senses were the literal, the typological, the moral or allegorical, and the anagogical.

Several things are important to note. First, not all medieval scriptural interpreters, normally called "exegetes," used all the four senses. Nor were all of the four senses of Scripture available in each passage. Some exegetes used different schemes of interpretation, dividing the senses of Scripture into only two or three portions. What is important to realize, however, is that the broadest consensus of the professionals in the church believed that this approach to Scripture was in itself holy, that the method of obtaining the message of Scripture was different from other books because the Bible itself was different from other books. The intrusion of new historical, linguistic, and contextual tools that denied some cherished interpretations was bound to upset people.

Second, this return to the sources denied the power of tradition, as it had come to be conceived by the end of the fifteenth century. Most theologians implicitly believed that the medieval tradition had delivered to later ages a fundamentally unchanging truth. Certainly, some theologians knew that some less significant practices and points of discipline had changed, but the widespread sense was that the present church was unchanging. Tradition had in some sense become its own source of authority: some theologians believed that the church's tradition simply could not be false, that the Holy Spirit protected the church from error in such a way that the dependence on the tradition was a safeguard against any error. The demonstration, made time and again by humanist historians and biblical interpreters, that a traditional practice was simply not the most ancient or was not supported by the biblical texts or the witness of the earliest fathers of the church, was disturbing and could even be offensive. Considerable effort was spent in the sixteenth century debating exactly what the theological and ecclesiastical value of tradition was, a development that was unlikely without the challenges coming from the research of the humanists.

Rhetoric and persuasion were no less central than textual readings to the ideals of the humanists. In the modern period we have come to separate the concepts of rhetoric and persuasion. Rhetoric refers simply to speaking well, without a specific consideration of content. Similarly, persuasion is the ability to change someone's mind or opinion, without a given sense of the moral content of that change. One might use rhetoric to persuade a friend to do something that is clearly morally wrong, such as stealing or murder. However, for the humanists of all stripes, this was not the meaning of rhetorical persuasion. Following the classical patterns of Lucian, Cicero, Augustine, and Chrysostom, humanists defined rhetoric as the use of good arguments, well chosen, to move a specific audience toward a particular good outcome. Thus, rhetorical theology was not simply "convincing," but it moved the hearts and minds and souls of the audience toward being more closely formed to the divine image.

Of course, such an emphasis on persuasion came with a kind of optimism about the human condition. To oversimplify things, humanistic reformers believed that if one made a good argument to a group of people, they would be moved to improvement. Such was the case for Desiderius Erasmus (1466–1536). His *Enchiridion* (*The Handbook of the Militant Christian*), published in 1503, sought to move people to improve their moral character. He tackled this task by several rhetorical methods. At times he demonstrated the poor state in which sick souls might be found and used this metaphor of physical disease to express the importance of spiritually healthy practices. At other moments he simply suggested remedies, such as the frequent reading of Scripture, with directions to which portions of Scripture might be most helpful.

The relatively gentle approach to the laity in the *Enchiridion* was balanced by Erasmus's and other humanists' choice of a variety of approaches to reform of the institutional church. Erasmus wrote colloquies which simply pointed out that certain doctrines were orthodox, rather than heresy. Such was the case in his *Inquiry concerning Faith*, written in 1524. The colloquy is a thinly veiled examination of Martin Luther, on the basis of the Apostles' Creed. The Apostles' Creed was an early definition of Christian faith that had been used in church services since the early ninth century. As such, it was one way of defining "true Christian belief." At the end of the treatise, Erasmus notes that he has not seen such sincerity of faith in Rome itself. At other times, the critiques of the institutional church directed by the humanists could be harsh. When Erasmus took up the character of Julius II, pope from 1503 to 1513, he used a severe tone, demonstrating that Julius had abandoned the model of Peter, the first pope.

The humanists extended this harsher criticism of some of the institutional fixtures of the church to the traditional pattern of theological education and theological method. This was the humanist struggle with scholasticism. Scholasticism had been developed in the period prior to the rebirth of classical studies and wider diffusion of knowledge of the classical languages. It concentrated upon dialectical thought, borrowed from philosophy, especially the philosophical heritage of Aristotle. Logic, rather than historical context, was the more frequent tool of the scholastics as they sought to make sense of the biblical witness and the traditions of the church. For instance, St. Anselm of Canterbury, writing in the eleventh century, believed that he could use logical proofs to demonstrate the correctness of statements of faith. One of his examples was his belief that he could prove why Jesus Christ had to be both God and human, the "God-man" in his terminology. A later scholastic, St. Thomas Aquinas, writing in the second half of the thirteenth century, believed that he could prove the existence of God by using logical proofs that did not rest upon faith or biblical revelation.

Erika Rummel, a modern scholar who has studied this struggle closely, writes:

> Neither the language nor the issues of the debate in the Renaissance was entirely new. The controversy had roots in both classical antiquity and early Christian thought. It revived elements of the Platonic debate over the respective merits of rhetoric and philosophy, translated Lucian's satirical review of the philosophical schools into terms relevant to the Renaissance, reinterpreted the Pauline disparagement of Pharisaical legalism, and borrowed from patristic sermons and commentaries.[5]

In this new-old clash, humanists made several claims about scholasticism. The most damning to the scholastics were two. First, the humanists charged that scholasticism was more concerned with philosophical correctness than it was with producing Christian change in the hearts of the faithful. Second, they argued that the scholastics did not truly understand the biblical texts and the writings of the Fathers by their methods of logic. The humanists argued that the manner of the scholastics, their methodology, was best left alone. Further, they contended that several of the doctrines that scholastics had hammered out over centuries of dispute were of little value in following in the footsteps of Christ.

Both sides in the struggle needed to protect things at stake, and both had a portion of "truth." The humanists saw the scholastics as men who had followed a flawed tradition, which had led to ever more obscure definitions of esoteric doctrines. In this they had a point: little university theology was passed along to the laity in any form. However, the scholastics had some points to make as well. First, the humanists were not all trained as theologians. Many were trained in languages or law. They did not always understand the values of the ideas and doctrines they were discarding. Second, while the humanists might be right that Paul or Augustine did not fully support a particular doctrine, Paul and Augustine had been dead for centuries. The scholastics were the heirs of a great theological tradition, and they had good reason to be suspicious of the humanists' claims to be able to go behind that tradition to a pure truth from antiquity.

Finally, humanists generally did not theoretically support an authoritarian approach to the Christian life or the institutional life of the church. This put them outside the current of mainstream thought. For centuries, the church had defined the faith as something so important to the society that serious mistakes in faith, or stubborn acceptance of the wrong faith, could be punished rigorously. While the humanists may have been precursors to a new way of thinking about the relationship of force to faith, this did not help in the contemporary situation. From Rome's acceptance of the necessity of execution for certain heresies and its acceptance of the Inquisition, to the Genevan execution of Michael Servetus, to the riots in Paris that came to be known as the St. Bartholomew's Day Massacre, people in the sixteenth century believed that religion was something so central to everyday social life that they were willing to accept authoritarian laws specifying the correct religion. In point of fact, the people frequently *demanded* that kind of religious and moral clarity from their rulers.

EARLY HUMANISTS AND REFORM

Having discussed what the humanistic reformers were, and the challenges they posed, it is important to set out specific individuals, to see what kinds of reform they supported and what their techniques were of calling for the betterment of the church. I shall delineate between the early humanists and the later humanists at the dividing line of the first year of the sixteenth century, concentrating upon a few scholars in each period. While in a sense that is arbitrary, in another it is not. Erasmus himself saw that his work was different after the "Luther affair" began, that certain things he had written earlier did not reflect the choices he would have made later. Simply put, the humanist progam of reform always used the same tools, which could have been understood in the same ways across the centuries. But once accusations of revolutionary schism were made, the consideration of how to word each criticism became a far more delicate task.

Marsilio Ficino

Marsilio Ficino was born in Florence in 1433 and died in Corregio in 1499. He was the son of the personal physician of Cosimo de Medici, head of the most powerful family in Florence. After studies at Florence and Bologna, Ficino settled to work on Plato. Medici had given him the task of translating all of Plato's works into Latin. Medici also appointed Ficino as the head of the Florentine Platonic academy. Throughout his career, Ficino translated great numbers of the works of Plato and also works by later philosophers who were inspired by Plato, who came to be called the Neoplatonists. Among these, he translated works of Porphyry, Plotinus, and Proclus.

This concentration upon Platonic thought had consequences. Ficino considered the nature of theology's relationship to philosophy, eventually coming to argue that to reach its highest and clearest expression, theology must depend upon philosophy. This was hardly extraordinary among university theologians in the mid-fifteenth century. However, Ficino soon was arguing that Plato's thought should be the true example of philosophy, rather than that of Aristotle, who then had the dominant position. Further, he asserted that the relationship between Christianity and Platonic thought was so close that Plato and Socrates should be read in churches. He believed that this was proper because Plato and his teacher Socrates were the true intellectual forebears of Jesus Christ. In stating this, he had left orthodox Christianity far behind.

Lorenzo Valla

Lorenzo Valla was born at Rome in 1405 and died in that same city in 1457. Though he wanted an ecclesiastical position, for most of his adult life he was so controversial a figure that he made it difficult for various officials to give him such an appointment. He was trained in Latin under Leonardo Bruni, and in Greek by Giovanni Aurispa. In 1444, he published *De elegantiae linguae latinae*, a work that attempted to formalize the study of Latin according to classical models. While this would seem to the modern eye to be a harmless work, it provoked a storm of controversy. In it, Valla reproached several of his humanist colleagues for their sloppy Latin, especially in allowing popular modern expressions to survive in their texts. Whether Valla was right or wrong on individual points made little difference; he had aggravated a large number of scholars over the very area they believed was their strength.

At the same time, Valla involved himself in a clash with Antonio da Bitonto on the composition of the Apostles' Creed. Bitonto defended the traditional and popular position that the creed was a joint work, to which each apostle had made a contribution. Valla demonstrated that it was impossible to divide it evenly into twelve portions, and that its theology reflected a later time than that of the apostles.

Two more of Valla's efforts demonstrated the kind of reforming potential of the new humanistic tools, while also revealing that Valla himself was not truly interested first and foremost with the reform of the Church of Rome. For Valla, the issue of learning was crucial; the church's self-knowledge was simply an interesting area of study that provided opportunities to exhibit the power of humanistic learning. The first venture was Valla's consideration of the Donation of Constantine, the forged document that claimed that the Roman emperor Constantine had granted to the Roman Church great gifts in gratitude for his own personal health and to strengthen Christianity. The document claimed that Constantine awarded to Pope Sylvester authority over the heads of the largest and most influential churches of the Western world: those in Antioch, Alexandria, Constantinople, and Jerusalem. Constantine gave this to Sylvester and all future popes because they were the true successors to St. Peter. Further, the pope was granted authority over all the bishops in the world. Finally, the document claimed that Constantine gave significant grants of land and other valuables to the church.

Obviously, the document was a significant boost to the church. It stood as a guarantee of both power and possessions. Unfortunately, it was a fake, probably created in the either the eighth or ninth century. Valla, working in the middle of the fifteenth century, was able to demonstrate conclusively that the document simply could not be what it claimed to be, because of the historical problems within it, especially the knowledge of historical items that happened after it was supposed to have been written.

Lorenzo Valla's other project that generated significant controversy was his consideration of the text of the New Testament. Though Valla did not systematically set out to consider the whole of the New Testament, he did consider several textual points of the Vulgate. Frequently, his discoveries showed that the Vulgate was not the most trustworthy translation. Though he did not follow up on these discoveries himself, Valla's work inspired others, most especially Desiderius Erasmus, to consider the whole of the text of the New Testament.

Without going further into the methods and doctrines of Ficino and Valla, it is possible to see what great possibilities and perils were involved in the exploitation of the humanistic tools. Theological doctrines that were supported by biblical texts were at risk when the underlying texts were questioned. Further, casting doubt on particular documents that granted specific powers and gifts to the church was never an easy thing. Again, the Middle Ages was a time when stability was greatly appreciated. Upsetting the workings of a traditional religious complex was neither easy to do nor easily received.

LATER HUMANISTS AND REFORM

In the first third of the sixteenth century, humanism transformed from a movement of academic thinkers who might have been in some sort of rivalry with more traditional scholastics, into a movement of church reform. While this would not have been a remarkable thing in most other ages of the history of Christianity, the outbreak of reform movements, seen by the Roman Church as schismatic and heretical, made the interpretation of humanism far more complicated. Was Erasmus really a Lutheran in disguise? Did Faber

Stapulensis actually support the heretics? Further, the humanistic scholars were criticized from multiple directions. Traditionalists in the Roman Church chastised the humanists for their critiques of familiar practices. As well, those who did make the break with Rome, who believed that their own paths to Christian truth were the most authentic, wondered why other humanistic scholars did not make the same choice, and they criticized these scholars for their fear. Probably neither portrait is wholly correct; undoubtedly both have glimpses of reality within them. But the actual figures are far more interesting than trying to fit them all into a neat classification.

John Colet

John Colet (c. 1466–1519) was one of the more influential English members of the humanistic movement. He was born in an influential political family; his father had twice been Lord Mayor of London. He studied at Oxford and then went to Italy for two years to learn Greek. Around 1496, he returned to Oxford. He received ordination to the priesthood and began to lecture on the Epistles of Paul. These lectures were some of his most lasting contributions to the reforming movement, for they did not follow the old style of lecturing on the meanings of the individual words of the Epistles but sought to grasp the whole of each epistle along with the personality of its author. These lectures also criticized the contemporary church and advocated a return to the simplicity and discipline of the early church.

During these lectures, which lasted for five years, Colet met Erasmus, with whom he became close friends. In 1504, he was made dean of St. Paul's Cathedral of London. In London, he became close friends with Thomas More. During his leadership of St. Paul's, Colet took on the issue of education. In 1505, Colet's father died and left him a substantial inheritance, which was a significant help to Colet's educational plan. In 1509, Colet founded a school at St. Paul's, which was designed to be an experiment in humanistic education. Both Greek and Latin were taught, with almost equal emphasis. Though William Lily was the first headmaster, Colet exercised considerable oversight until his death in 1519.

Colet's example makes obvious two points, one of which has already been considered at some length and another of which needs more emphasis. The first is the emphasis on education. Colet knew that simply blabbering on about the importance of the new education without making specific provision for it was useless; his school was a testament to his commitment to that goal. The second point is that the humanistic movement was not only a movement of ideas but also of friendships. Colet was intimately friendly with other great humanistic scholars. The connections in the sixteenth-century scholarly world were not simply those of great minds who knew each other from their books; these connections were also strengthened by bonds of camaraderie.

Faber Stapulensis

Jacques Lefèvre d'Étaples (c. 1460–1536) was from Étaples in the region of Picardy in France. He was known both by his given name and the latinized form of Faber Stapulensis. After his training at the College du Cardinal-Lemoine of the University of Paris, he was ordained a priest. In 1492, he took a trip to Italy, where he encountered various Italian scholars. Among these were the Aristotelian scholar Barbaro, the Platonist Marsilio Ficino, and Pico della Mirandola—fulfilling the notion of the importance of friendships among the humanists.[6] Returning to France, Stapulensis set about producing an annotated edition of the works of Aristotle. He supplemented this work on the great Greek philosopher with editions of patristic and medieval authors. This stage of his life's work concluded with a monumental edition of Nicholas of Cusa. After that, he turned his attention wholly to the Bible.[7]

In 1517 and 1519, Stapulensis published two articles in Paris arguing that Mary Magdalene was not Mary the sister of Lazarus, nor the woman who annointed Jesus' feet in the seventh chapter of Luke. This opinion was not well received, especially by Noel Beda, the head of the University of Paris. In 1521, Stapulensis was condemned by the university. Only the continuing interventions of the French king, Francis I; Marguerite, Queen of Navarre; and the bishop of Meaux, Guillaume Briçonnet, kept him from further trouble. In general, the Paris theologians suspected that his works were tainted by the doctrines of the Reformers.

Lefèvre continued his biblical work throughout the rest of his career. He published an edition of the Letters of Paul. This was criticized by various other scholars for including the *Epistle to the Laodiceans*, the authenticity of which most sixteenth-century scholars rejected. In 1530, he published a French translation of the Vulgate, which was printed in Antwerp. This translation pulled together several humanistic themes, including the necessity of access to the sources and the placement of the Scriptures into the hands of the more simple, unlearned believers. Further, Stapulensis was a scholar who inspired others. Several important humanists gathered around him at times in his career, so many that it might at times have been appropriate to speak of his "camp" or "party." Among those who congregated around him were François Vatable, Gérard Roussel, Michel d'Arande, and Guillaume Farel. This circle was even termed a "laboratory of preaching."[8] Later circles also gathered and were stimulated by his example.

At his death in 1536, it was an open question whether Stapulensis was a Catholic. Certainly, he never formally broke with the church. However, throughout his career his writings had caused concern among those theologians who were seen as the guardians of orthodox teaching. Further, as Guy Bedouelle points out, he never made any formal statements of "retraction or conformity to the doctrines of the Church as apparently Rome requested of him."[9] Given both his circles of friends and his biblical work, however, there can be no doubt of his impact in the area of humanistic reform.

Thomas More

Thomas More (c. 1478–1535) combined the scholarly brilliance and ironic wit of some of the greatest humanists and added to it a principled stand that would earn him the wrath of King Henry VIII and the martyr's glorification in the Church of Rome. More was born the son of a prominent jurist and seems to have been destined early for a career in law. He attracted the attention of the archbishop of Canterbury, who supported his further education at Oxford. Though he considered the possibility of ordination, he opted instead for the life of the learned layman and followed the career of a lawyer.

While More was content with the life of the layman, he never lost his appetite for learning and the issues of the church. Some of his closest friends were priests and monks. John Colet was his confessor, and Erasmus was a dear friend. In fact, his home became a haven for scholars. His love for learning and humanism is exhibited in his translation into English of a life of Pico della Mirandola. He was a successful lawyer and rose swiftly through the ranks of the bureaucracy, eventually becoming lord chancellor.

More is not, however, famous simply for his legal work and career as a statesman. In 1516, he published his most famous work, *Utopia*. Though this was written as a description of an ideal society, it is also filled with critical observations about the world of the sixteenth century. It poked fun at the shortcomings of the Roman Church, the rulers, and the people. In its own way, it placed More in a conversation with Erasmus's satirical writings. More was recognized as a learned force to be reckoned with.

When the Lutheran affair became known across Europe and in England, More revealed his own loyalties to the traditional church with a series of polemical works, some in Latin and some in English, so as to appeal to the same audience who was reading the vulgar language tracts of the Reformers. Polemical treatises were texts that took part in arguing for or against certain theological positions. In the world of the early sixteenth century, these were the attack ads of the day. More's polemical treatises struck out at the Lutheran ideas and at Luther himself, sometimes in witty ridicule, other times in vulgar name-calling. More was a favorite of the king's, but he never believed that the king's devotion to him was very deep. In this, he would prove to be sadly prophetic.

Though by 1529 More had reached the pinnacle of a legal career in his post as lord chancellor, the king's great affair was destined to bring him down. Henry VIII desired a male heir. He had married the widow of his brother, Catherine of Aragon, but church law had required the pope, Julius II, to give a special allowance—a dispensation—for such an act. By 1526, Henry had no male heir and was beginning to worry, or at least to say that he was worried, that his lack of an heir was a punishment from God for his "adulterous" union with his brother's wife. In 1527, Henry began to seek an annulment of his marriage from the pope. The pope refused, and Henry eventually solved his problem by proclaiming himself head of the Church of England in 1534. More could not accept such a situation and resigned his post as lord chancellor. However, this was not all, for he did not take the oath of obedience to the Act of Succession. He did not accept that Henry's children with Anne Boleyn would be the legitimate heirs to the English throne. Henry had him arrested and eventually executed for treason.

Desiderius Erasmus

With Desiderius Erasmus (1466–1536), we conclude our discussion of individual humanistic scholars by considering the career of the man who was almost universally considered to be the "prince of the humanists." Erasmus's very name advertises the humanistic love of language, for "Erasmus" was a supposed Greek equivalent of his baptismal name, and he took the first name of "Desiderius" because it was the Latin form of "Erasmus." His abilities with language, his sharp wit, and his grasp of the occasional absurdities of the theological tasks all served to make him widely read and, in some quarters, widely rejected. In Erasmus's career, we see the fullest portrait of the powers of the humanistic reform, and we also see most clearly the reasons that this pattern of reform was rejected in part by some among both Catholic and Protestant reformers.

Erasmus was born in Gouda, the illegitimate son of a priest and a local woman. The circumstances of his birth caused difficulties for Erasmus until he was able to gain a papal dispensation from the penalties that would have otherwise come with being born illegitimate.[10] This product of concubinage was not as extraordinary as might have been hoped, and Erasmus seems to have been open about this. The young man was educated at school at Deventer, which was run by the Brethren of the Common Life.

Deventer was the center of learning in that part of Holland. The school at Deventer was marked by the characteristic ideals of the Brethren of the Common Life, valuing simplicity, piety, and devotion. There was within the Brethren an attitude that acceptance of belief and practical piety were better than esoteric theological speculation. The Brethren especially valued an emphasis on inwardness: being conscious of the condition of one's hidden and internal self. All of these influences would have been part of Erasmus's early formation. Erasmus was not a particular fan of the school, claiming that it was old-fashioned in its teaching methods. Still, it was there that the fire of learning was first kindled in him.

In 1487, Erasmus joined the Augustinian order of canons regular, joining the monastery at Steyn. His motive may have been as simple as a desire to continue his education. As Roland Bainton puts it in commenting that Erasmus and Martin Luther joined the same order, "Luther entered the monastery to save his soul by good works, Erasmus to enlighten his mind by good books."[11] Erasmus spent the next seven years at the monastery, reading in its first-rate library and coming in contact with the classics of both pagan and Christian learning. At that time, he also would have had access to Valla's *Elegantiae*, which may have inspired Erasmus to consider the fruits of humanistic learning. After seven years, Erasmus gained permission to leave the monastery for further study, and he eventually ended up at the University of Paris.

At Paris, Erasmus was a student at the Collége de Montaigu, which he hated. In a later treatise, he called it "Vinegar College"; he was thoroughly repulsed by its rigorous discipline, its harsh living conditions, and its devotion to scholastic theology. He never finished his doctorate at Paris; eventually he would be granted that degree from the University of Turin.[12] From Paris he traveled in 1499 to England, where he met Thomas More and John Colet, the leading English humanists. From that point in his life, Erasmus lived by independent scholarship, though he eventually had to gain a papal dispensation releasing him from his vows to the Augustinian canons.

In 1503, Erasmus published his *Enchiridion militis Christiani* (*The Handbook of the Militant Christian*). Erasmus had already begun his publishing career in 1500 with his *Adagia* (*The Adages*). This was an exploration and explanation of common sayings, which Erasmus would continue to collect and edit throughout his life. The *Adagia* was the product of the scholar interested in language for its own sake. The *Enchiridion*, on the other hand, demonstrated a shift in his attention toward a concentration upon the Christian life, especially on how to live the Christian life through moral reform. Though Erasmus wrote the little book in Latin, it was quickly translated into other languages, appearing in English, Czech, German, Dutch, and Spanish between 1518 and 1526.[13]

Erasmus's concern for moral living rings throughout the pages of the *Enchiridion*. Erasmus explained to his readers that in Latin, an *enchiridion* was a dagger, a short knife for self-protection. Likewise, Erasmus told his readers that the Christian life in this world was a battle, and true believers should not be without protection. Having characterized the mortal life so harshly, Erasmus immediately turned to comfort by explaining that although no one can defeat the devil on his or her own strength, Christ's unbeatable power is available to believers. Erasmus urged Christians to look to the quality of their own souls, stating that many of them would find their souls to be sick, in need of spiritual medicine. For Erasmus, the truest spiritual medicine was knowledge of the Scriptures and an inwardly active Christian life. He summarized this life under twenty-two rules for Christian morality, followed by a consideration of the remedies for five particular vices.

Erasmus concluded his advice with a discussion of the Christian life and the simplicity that was vital to following Christ. In this conclusion, he gently critiqued monasticism, denying that it was always a good thing and stating that instead its goodness depended upon the character of the person taking the vows. He then defended the usefulness of the pagan and Christian classics for the contemporary church. Already in 1503 we can see several hallmarks of Erasmus's ideal of Christianity. His concentration upon moral reform is a strong theme, as well as his certainty that the new learning will benefit the faithful. These premises would come back even more strongly later in his career.

In 1509, Erasmus published his *Moriae encomium* (*The Praise of Folly*), it represented a harsh critique of late medieval life, of the system of education, and of the Church of Rome. The title was a play on words; it could either be read as a formal moment of praise of folly, or of Thomas More, his friend the English humanist. The whole of the work is tinged with humor and wit, but the targets of that satire were rarely happy to be criticized. The main speaker of the work is a person named Folly; through her Erasmus castigated various classes of people. He condemned merchants for showing off, grammarians for believing that finding another part of speech was a high achievement, and monks for being careful about touching money but not so careful around women and wine. In the end, Folly announces that the true folly is the foolishness of the cross, that the true Christian does not accept the wisdom of the world. While this was a Christian truism following the first chapter of 1 Corinthians, Erasmus had attacked many powerful groups.

In 1516, Erasmus published his *Novum Testamentum*, the Greek New Testament. This gift to scholarship was not widely read, and there were not multiple editions in many translations flying off the shelves of printers eager to capitalize on Erasmus's fame and witty writing style. However, to the small group of trained scholars who used this work, the door to understanding the Christian Scriptures in a way far closer to their original authors' intentions had been opened. Other giants of the Reformation era, such as Martin Luther and John Calvin, would use this tool to consider what the New Testament was actually saying. As well, it is impossible to understand the attacks Erasmus suffered from Catholic scholars over his choices without remembering the criticisms he had directed at the institutional church in prior years. His translation choices and his demonstrations that some of the traditional ways to read Scripture were not supported by a knowledge of the original languages were not seen as simple and neutral scholarship, but as continued assaults on the church.

The first edition of Erasmus's *Colloquies* was published in 1518. The *Colloquies* demonstrate that sometimes books have a way of escaping their authors. Originally, Erasmus had begun the project by writing student exercises for his tutoring in Paris, but he did so with his customary wit, both to relieve his own boredom and to keep the students' interest. Without Erasmus's knowledge or permission, eventually some of these exercises were gathered together and published. Faced with this, Erasmus made the best of it and expanded the collection over the years. The collection is important because it frequently gave Erasmus an opportunity to speak about the issues of his day in a humorous, self-deprecating manner. For instance, in the colloquy *Cyclops*, first published in 1529, Erasmus disparaged the character of the times, as if the times were as bad as before Noah's flood, and included himself in the inventory of disasters afflicting humanity: "Kings make war, priests are zealous to increase their wealth, theologians invent syllogisms, monks roam through the world, the commons riot, Erasmus writes colloquies. In short, no calamity is lacking."[14]

Erasmus could also use the colloquy to consider places where the Roman Church perhaps was too caught up in political strife to realize common ground with the voices of reform. In *An Inquiry concerning Faith*, first published in 1524, Erasmus demonstrated that Luther held an orthodox faith. Erasmus did this through the invention of a meeting between Luther and himself in which he tested Luther's faith by questioning him on the articles of the Apostles' Creed. Near the end of the colloquy, Erasmus wrote of Luther, "When I was at Rome, I did not find all believing with equal sincerity."[15]

In 1524, Erasmus entered the Reformation era debates with his attack on Luther's position on the freedom of the will in his *Diatribe de libero arbitrio* (*Diatribe on the Free Choice of the Will*). This was remarkable for at least two reasons. First, this publication was a clear attack on Luther's position on the bondage of the choice of the will, and it answered some of Erasmus's critics who had accused him of being Lutheran. Second, the publication appeared only six months after his colloquy *An Inquiry concerning Faith*. Clearly, Erasmus either had a change of heart, or he wished to demonstrate for the intellectual world just where he differed from Luther. Erasmus ended his writing career preparing critical editions of the fathers of the early church.

In a sense, the whole of Erasmus's theological, spiritual, and intellectual effort can be summed up under the term "the philosophy of Christ" (*philosophia Christi*).[16] The philosophy of Christ is rooted in the Christ that is found in the words of Scripture. This philosophy begins in Christ and returns to Christ.

Further, because Christ looked on the inner person, so too does the philosophy of Christ. In Erasmus's ideal, the inner nature of the believer takes precedence over details of theology, especially the kind of details that scholastic theology had labored so long over. Further, the inner reality takes priority over various outward ceremonies. Finally, the philosophy of Christ does not deny the strengths of the pagan classics but rather sees them as a preparation for receiving the more mature wisdom available in the gospel.

While simply knowing the outline of Erasmus's career in the sixteenth century is an important facet of any attempt to grasp the Reformation, more can be taken from this than simple knowledge about him. The brief catalog of Erasmus's writings that we have considered reveals several noteworthy factors in the effect of humanism on the intellectual culture of the early sixteenth century. First, Erasmus and other humanists were vitally concerned with morality and the improvement of both the individual Christian soul and the institutional church. The *Enchiridion* set about persuading individual Christians to improve themselves by paying attention to their inward condition and by turning to the Scriptures. *The Praise of Folly* set out to raise the issues that needed reforming. Of course it was satirical, but the point was not merely to ridicule but also to identify opportunities for reform. We see this same effort in many of Erasmus's colloquies, in which he uses wit to gain a hearing from his audience. We might, from a later point in time, argue that Erasmus was rather foolish in believing that satire would promote reform rather than counterattack. But that is to argue with his method, not the substance of what he was trying to do.

Given the centrality of Scripture in his reform ideal, and his belief in the powers of the classical world to heal his own world, it is no wonder that Erasmus turned his prodigious talents upon the text of the truest classic, the New Testament. Flawed as it may have been, Erasmus's Greek New Testament opened the doors on amazing new developments in both theology and in textual scholarship. The same may be said of his editions of the Fathers. Erasmus demonstrated his confidence in human nature with his simple belief that putting the wisdom of the classical ages before his readers would, almost inevitably, lead them to the truth. Finally, through his dialogue with Luther on the freedom or bondage of the choice of the will, Erasmus proved that humanistic scholarly tools were not simply a "Lutheran" invention but could be turned to the service of the institutional church.

What Erasmus valued was clear, but his ideas about reform are far less so. While we may speak of Erasmian reform, the aim of that reform remains unclear. People in Erasmus's own day were wary of him. Those who were inspired by Erasmus's textual studies of the New Testament frequently went beyond where Erasmus was willing to go: they broke with the Church of Rome and chastised Erasmus for being too cowardly to follow where his own writing led. Those who remained in the Church of Rome, however, frequently accused Erasmus of providing too much ammunition for the attacks of the schismatic sects.

CONCLUSION

As we can see from both the consideration of the contributions of the humanistic movement and the brief sketches of the individual humanistic scholars, humanism was, in some ways, whatever one wanted it to be. Some who took advantage of the new learning believed that it required a conversion to the reform movements that were causing such turmoil and excitement throughout Europe. Others who took advantage of the same new learning saw it simply as a way to support the traditional church and perhaps gently address its shortcomings. Very few scholars in the sixteenth century ignored all of the fruits of the new learning, and its call to return to the sources (*ad fontes*) is most clearly seen in the Bible and the Fathers' becoming the battleground upon which later disputes would be fought.

QUESTIONS FOR DISCUSSION

1. Why were the tools and insights of the humanists, as well as their return to the sources, significant sources of reform?
2. What was the effect of humanism's critique of tradition? Can a church body exist without tradition? Can there be a struggle between historical truth and inherited stability?
3. Why did the humanists and scholastics struggle over the nature of theology?
4. Humanists implicitly called for educational reform as support for Christian reform. What is the relationship between knowledge and Christian faith?

SUGGESTED FURTHER READING

Primary Readings

Erasmus, Desiderius. *The Erasmus Reader*. Edited by Erika Rummel. Toronto: University of Toronto Press, 1990.
———. *The Essential Erasmus: Intellectual Titan of the Renaissance*. Edited and translated by John P. Dolan. New York: New American Library, 1964.
More, Thomas. *Utopia*. Edited and translated by Paul Turner. New York: Penguin Classics, 2003.
Valla, Lorenzo. *On the Donation of Constantine*. Translated by G. W. Bowersock. Cambridge, MA: Harvard University Press, 2007.

Secondary Readings

Bedouelle, Guy. "Jacques Lefèvre d'Étaples." In *The Reformation Theologians*, edited by
Carter Lindberg, 19–33. Malden, MA: Blackwell Publishers, 2002.

Cameron, Euan. *The European Reformation*. Oxford: Oxford University Press, 1991.

Carrington, J. Laurel. "Desiderius Erasmus." In *The Reformation Theologians*, edited by
Carter Lindberg, 34–48. Malden, MA: Blackwell Publishers, 2002.

Keen, Ralph. "Thomas More." In *The Reformation Theologians*, edited by Carter Lindberg, 284–97. Malden, MA: Blackwell Publishers, 2002.

Rummel, Erika. *The Humanist-Scholastic Debate in the Renaissance and Reformation*. Cambridge, MA: Harvard University Press, 1995.

DOCTRINAL-VOCABULARY DISCUSSION

The Process of Salvation

In university theology in the late medieval period, one of the topics of discussion was the *ordo salutis*, the order of salvation. While those discussions could
and did become extremely technical, the idea of an order of salvation is helpful for modern students to use as they envision the various theological options
that arose in the various reforming movements of the sixteenth century. Three
different questions were involved in a consideration of salvation at that time:
What were the elements of salvation? Could salvation be lost? What could a
person know about his or her salvation status?

The possible elements of salvation depended upon one's church. For
instance, theologians of all stripes agreed on the existence and general character of heaven, earth, and hell. However, for Roman Catholics, purgatory was
also part of the geography of salvation. This was a place where people who
were basically good but still owed God some debts went to be purified after
death, prior to going to heaven. To the late medieval Catholic, purgatory was
a good place, even though the time spent there was not thought of as pleasant.
Purgatory was not a middle place between heaven and hell; if you were in purgatory, you were definitely on the way to heaven. Almost all Protestants denied
that purgatory existed, saying that it was not a scripturally supported idea and
that it was an invention of the Church of Rome made up so that Rome could
sell indulgences to grant release from purgatory.

For almost all theologians in the sixteenth century, baptism was a normal
part of God's preparation of souls for heaven. However, beyond that statement, all agreement breaks down. For instance, Catholic doctrine argued that
the unbaptized could not enter heaven, so a circle of hell was reserved for basically innocent people, such as unbaptized babies. Reformed theologians
rejected this doctrine as monstrous and argued that while God *normally* used

baptism in the process of salvation, God was not *required* to do so. Anabaptists agreed that baptism was part of the road to salvation but denied that an infant could actually and meaningfully be baptized.

Could salvation be lost? For some groups, the very question was incorrect. Roman theology on salvation taught that one could never know whether one was saved or not, so to say that salvation was "lost" suggested that you knew something no one could know. For the Reformed and most Lutherans, the idea of losing salvation was outrageous. God saved people; thus, they stayed saved. To suggest otherwise implied that God was not in charge. For the Radical Reformers, salvation could definitely be lost. Once one accepted baptism, one needed to do the works of a Christian. To fail to do so forfeited membership both in the community and in heaven.

Could a person know whether he or she was saved? Both Luther and Calvin argued that the internally felt confidence in God's love and good disposition toward the individual let a person know that God had reached out and saved him or her. They argued that putting the responsibility for salvation wholly in God's charge gave greater assurance to the believer, in contrast to the ongoing doubt of Catholics. Most Radical Reformers argued that believers did know they were saved but could only maintain that status by ongoing works and growth in the Christian life.

What has this shown us? For the sixteenth century, salvation was a vital question. People were ready to go to great lengths to ensure their own salvation. But as the reforms went on, the questions of salvation became ever more complex. By the late sixteenth century, the simple question "Do you believe that Christ saves sinners?" was insufficient to establish exactly what a religiously trained person believed. All Christians believed that Christ was active in salvation. But the devil, as they say, was in the details.

4

The Lutheran Reform

Martin Luther broods like a troubled giant over the face of Reformation studies. Is he the seven-headed monster that his Catholic opponents made him out to be? Is he the true apostle that his closest followers saw? Might we see him as the founder of individual religious freedom, the leader of those who would cast off their shackles and proclaim the true gospel? Can he be the supporter of repression by the state for the good of the people against their will? Could he be the true Christian who invited Jews to consider the truth of the gospel in a new way, or is he the Christian who supplied the Nazis with a ready-made ideology of hatred? All of these characterizations have been written, published, and accepted; none of them captures the genius and depth of Martin Luther. Robert Kolb notes that the various biographers of Luther have "taken the raw material of his life and thought and cast it into forms which would serve their own purposes—with varying degrees of historical accuracy. Few public figures have enjoyed and suffered the process of publicity as has Martin Luther."[1]

Almost from the very beginning of his public career, Martin Luther has gathered the praise due to an apostle, as well as the condemnation reserved for a demon. His very first biographer was a Catholic, Johannes Cochlaeus, who depicted him as a seven-headed monstrosity. The Swiss reformer Huldrych Zwingli wrote in 1520 that Luther was the new Elijah, the Old Testament prophet whose return would signal the coming of the Messiah. This concentration upon his life did not even end in the moment of his death. Heiko Oberman records the poignancy of a politically charged death:

> "Reverend father, will you die steadfast in Christ and the doctrines you have preached?" "Yes," replied the clear voice for the last time. On February 18, 1546, even as he lay dying in Eisleben, far from home, Martin Luther was not to be spared a final public test, not to be

granted privacy even in this last, most personal hour. His longtime confidant Justus Jonas, now pastor in Halle, having hurriedly summoned witnesses to the bedside, shook the dying man by the arm to rouse his spirit for the final exertion. Luther had always prayed for a "peaceful hour": resisting Satan—the ultimate, bitterest enemy—through that trust in the Lord over life and death which is God's gift of liberation from the tyranny of sin. It transforms agony into no more than a brief blow.

But now there was far more at stake than his own fate, than being able to leave the world in peace, and trust in God. For in the late Middle Ages, ever since the first struggle for survival during the persecutions of ancient Rome, going to one's death with fearless fortitude was the outward sign of a true child of God, of the confessors and martyrs. The deathbed in the Eisleben inn had become a stage; and straining their ears to catch Luther's last words were enemies as well as friends.[2]

Luther, in life and death, drew attention. The movement that he began took on his name, though the Lutherans in the sixteenth century normally preferred the term "evangelicals." There can be no better place than Luther's life for us to begin our examination of the movements that came to be called the Protestant Reformation.

LUTHER'S EARLY LIFE

Martin Luther was born in Eisleben, in the mining region of Germany. His father, Hans Luther, had moved his family there because of the good opportunities to be had in the copper mining industry. Martin was born in 1483, and the next year the family moved to Mansfield. Here the family prospered, and Hans eventually became a mine operator. This paid well enough that Hans was able to send his son to school. After attending the school in Mansfield, Martin was sent in 1501 to the University of Erfurt, to study to become a lawyer. His own parents had risen through the application of their own efforts to the opportunities in the new economy; they wished to see Martin rise even higher. Martin dutifully took his master's degree in 1505 and prepared to study law at the university in Erfurt.

This plan ran aground. Whether Luther had already become disenchanted with the idea of being a lawyer is a matter of some historical speculation; some of the sources for his life suggest that might have been the case. What is not in doubt is that on July 2, 1505, Luther was returning to the university from a visit home to Mansfield. He was caught in a tremendous thunderstorm, and in fear for his life he prayed a vow: "Help me, St. Anne, and I will become a monk." Upon surviving the storm, Luther kept his vow and joined the Augustinian Hermits. That choice brought him into contact with the writings of Augustine, which he might not otherwise have known. This would prove important, as we shall see later.

During his first year in the monastery, Luther threw himself into the study of the Scriptures. This year was called the "novitiate," because it focused on the beginners, the novices. Throughout the year, Luther learned about the monastic life and learned the Bible. However, he apparently did not experience the inner spiritual peace that should have followed his taking the beginning vows.

Luther was afflicted by his conscience. Though exceptionally bright, he was not extraordinary in his religious character for his time, except for his inability to come to a sense of spiritual calm through the religious instruments that medieval piety offered. Luther took advantage of these frequently, going to confession regularly and even excessively. He recorded that he once confessed for six hours![3] His confessor, Johann Greffenstein, had his work cut out for him, for Luther was absolutely convinced of the need for a perfect confession, and equally convinced that such a thing was impossible for him. Luther did not have an overactive conscience, but instead realized the demands of purity before a perfectly pure God. The medieval mind believed that to be saved, the believer must perform the works that God commanded. Luther grasped that if God is appeased by the fulfilling of the works that God has commanded, only truly perfect obedience will be sufficient. But Luther also realized that perfect obedience is impossible. This problem would be the source of his eventual break with the Church of Rome.

In 1507, Luther was ordained to the priesthood. While for some this elevated status in the world of medieval Germany would have been a comfort, it only made Luther's struggles more evident. Luther was awestruck before the overwhelming responsibility of coming to celebrate the sacrament of the Lord's Supper with a clear conscience and in a morally pure state. His recognition of his own unworthiness was never alleviated by the instuments of forgiveness. Though he continued the works of a monk and priest, Luther carried within himself severe doubt.

The same year Luther was ordained, he was chosen by his superior to study theology. Of course, he had already studied theology in the course of his preparation for the priesthood, but this was a preparation for teaching at the university level. Luther went back to study theology at the University of Erfurt. However, his studies were divided between the University of Erfurt and the new University of Wittenberg. Though Luther began the normal course of studies at Erfurt, the vicar general—the leader—of his order in Germany, Johannes von Staupitz, requested that he come to Wittenberg. Apparently, Luther's talents were needed to fill a teaching position, called a chair, in philosophy. He was able to do this on the basis of the master's degree that he earned prior to his beginning to study law. In one of the great ironies in the sixteenth century, Luther was required by the university to teach Aristotle, a figure whose influence he would later severely condemn. Luther simultaneously continued his studies at Wittenberg for a year and then was transferred back to Erfurt. After a brief visit to Rome on monastery business in 1510, Luther was transferred back to Wittenberg in the summer of 1511. This small city, really only a large village, would be permanently linked to Luther, and he would live there the rest of his life.

LUTHER IN WITTENBERG: 1511–1519

Wittenberg would have seemed small to Luther, who had become accustomed to a city the size of Erfurt, having been acquainted with it from living in and around it for ten years. Erfurt at this time had approximately 16,000 inhabitants. In comparison, Wittenberg had probably only 2,000 residents.[4] Far more important than its size for our understanding was its position in politics and in education. Though Wittenberg was only a town rather than a full-fledged city, it had both the duke's seat of the Elector of Saxony and a newly endowed university.

An elector had a vote in the election of the Holy Roman Emperor. At the time of Martin Luther, there were seven electors. These included three archbishops and four princes. The three archbishops with electoral power were those of Mainz, Cologne, and Trier. The secular princes with this power were the king of Bohemia, the Count Palatine, the duke of Saxony, and the margrave of Brandenburg. Frequently, the Count Palatine, duke of Saxony, and margrave of Brandenburg were referred to as "the electors" of their respective realms, suggesting the importance of that power. At moments when an emperor seemed to be dying or otherwise passing from office, the political power of the electors grew extraordinarily.

The electoral castle in Wittenberg had been built by the elector Frederick III, called Frederick the Wise. In 1496, he began to build the castle, demonstrating to even the most casual observer that the seat of power was here. Frederick had visions of greatness for his realm and worked to put those in place. Just as important to Frederick as his castle was his university. Though the University of Leipzig was not far away, it was not in his realm. The University of Wittenberg opened its doors in 1502. Several points are worth noting. First, Frederick entrusted the university to men who were open to the new learning; Wittenberg's character was not hostile to humanism. Second, because Frederick saw the importance of education and the university for his dominion, he continued to appoint and attract scholars, printers, and artists. Though the university was rather young, it was not neglected, and it soon had a significant library under the direction of Georg Spalatin, who obtained a collection that demonstrated his own devotion to biblical humanism.[5]

When Martin Luther arrived in Wittenberg, the university's theological faculty was staffed by various orders. Orders were different groups of religious men or women living under a religious rule. The Franciscans, Dominicans, Benedictines, Augustinians, and Carmelites were all different orders. The Franciscan order provided a professor of theology who taught the theology of Duns Scotus, himself a late thirteenth and early fourteenth-century Franciscan. The Augustinian Hermits provided a professor of Bible. This was the post Luther took up when he came to the university as a doctor of theology. Although he had originally come to teach philosophy, Luther's formal career after finishing his doctorate was in theology.

Luther's first works from this time in his life were series of lectures on books of the Bible. He lectured on the Psalms in 1513 and 1514, on Romans in 1515 and 1516, on Galatians in 1516 and 1517, and on Hebrews in 1517 and 1518. This work of commenting upon the Bible was both familiar and strangely new to Luther. The familiarity came from Luther's devotion to the study of Scripture since entering the monastery. The strange newness had to do with Luther's method of commenting. Though one can find instances of Luther's commenting in very traditional fashions in these early lectures, he was also investigating issues of belief and of theological education. Both of these contributed to his foundational insights, which later shattered the sense of unity Christian Europe enjoyed.

The issue of belief is crucial to understanding Luther's breakthrough. According to his own account, Luther discovered the gospel. Luther's conscience was extraordinarily sensitive. He was not able to come to the conclusion that he was in what the Roman Church termed a "state of grace." Instead, Luther believed that there was always more to be done—always more acts of charity, always more prayers, always more confessing to do. Further, one would never know whether enough had been done!

One of the key biblical texts on this issue for Luther was Romans 1:17: "For in it [the gospel] the righteousness of God is revealed through faith for faith; as it is written, 'The one who is righteous will live by faith.'" The key term here for Luther was the "righteousness of God" (Latin, *iustitia Dei*). Luther, and a great number of other theologians, had always read this term to mean a level of moral purity. The righteousness of God represented the gold standard of ethical goodness. That interpretation, however, would not allow Luther out of his difficulty with his own sense of sinfulness. How can a person attain God's level of moral purity? Beyond that, even if humans can reach some exalted level of moral perfection, how can they know they have done so? The interpretation of this passage immediately took Luther's mind into several theological issues, including salvation.

The medieval theologians whose lives and work preceded Luther's struggles with salvation had generated answers to Luther's questions long before he posed them. They believed that people were commanded to perform good works, and that by doing so they might "merit" salvation. However, the question of merit was neither simple nor straightforward. The medieval theologians had discussed two different kinds of merit: "condign" merit and "congruous" merit. Though they are closely related, the distinction between them is important.

Condign merit results in an earned reward. In other words, the pay a worker receives from his or her employer for a job adequately done is a condign merit. No particular gift is involved; if the employer did not pay, the employee would have a legal case, because the payment in return for work is a right. Most theologians of the medieval period believed that there could be no relationship of condign merit between God and humans. (At least some of the disciples of William of Ockham considered the idea at some length, however.)

Congruous merit, on the other hand, results in a granted reward. Here the relationship between the reward and the service is not strictly arithmetic. A possible case might be an indulgent parent rewarding a child for cleaning his or her room when the room, by a strict standard, is not actually clean. Most theologians of the medieval period were convinced that congruous merit was a vital part of the mechanics of salvation. Though humans might not in the strictest sense "earn" their part of the work of salvation, God graciously gives the reward of salvation because of God's inherent goodness and mercy.

While this distinction proved to be widely satisfactory to the theologians of the late medieval period, it was not without several difficulties. First, it was a highly technical distinction that most people without university training in philosophy and theology were unable to grasp. Since that group of people represented the great majority of the Christian populace, this was not a minor problem. Second, because of the lack of theological sophistication on the part of the majority of the believers and probably some of the clergy, frequently the distinction was abandoned, and the belief that salvation could be merited or earned was common. Third, there was the matter of grace. While no theologian denied the action of grace in salvation, the very term "grace" means "free." If God "freely" does something, how is it appropriate to speak of humans earning merit?

In his biblical work, Luther discovered a different way of attacking the problem. What if the "righteousness of God" is not a level of ethical purity demanded by God, but a gift? What if God's righteousness was not ever something that one could earn, but only something that the believer could be given by God? That was Luther's solution. He realized that the righteous person in Romans 1:17 could then simply be the person who lives by faith, by simple and complete dependence on God. Luther grasped that as the heart of his theology, and it changed everything.

Luther's discovery of the freedom of the gospel was the most important of his theological contributions to the world of the sixteenth century. But there was another new issue in Luther's biblical work at Wittenberg. He began to condemn the scholastic models of thought that were part and parcel of the theological studies of the time. In the third chapter, we noted that the humanists quarreled with the scholastic approach to theology. Luther's attack was even more pointed. He believed that the importation of philosophical categories and procedures denied the primary place of the Bible in theology. Luther saved the greatest venom for Aristotle, but his appraisal took in all of philosophy.

This attack was significant. To follow Luther's path on this point meant a change in the entirety of the theological curriculum of the basic university degree. It was not a single course that would be modified, but the entire nature of the education. Many methods for teaching the Bible opened up when the priority of Aristotelian categories was set aside.

Luther's early teaching at Wittenberg was not seen as revolutionary, however. Without the indulgence controversy to give him an accidental platform, Luther might have lived out his life in obscurity. But such was not the case. In 1514, Luther became the town preacher, the *Prädikant*.[6] As such, it was his duty to preach for the townspeople each Sunday. Apparently, Luther took his responsibilities as the guardian of the souls of the Wittenbergers quite seriously and gave significant thought to their spiritual welfare.

In 1515, Pope Leo X proclaimed a plenary indulgence. This would eventually lead to the greatest division the European church had known in hundreds of years, but Leo could not have known that. To understand fully what was going on in this matter, we must investigate the ecclesiastical, financial, and political issues that were involved. As we saw in chapter 2, indulgences were a way for a sinner to return to the fellowship of the church. In the earliest days of the church, this had only come after years or decades of penitential practices. By the late medieval age, the most normal method of obtaining forgiveness of punishment for sins was to be granted indulgences. These could be granted by the church for great service, such as going on a crusade. But as not everyone could go on a crusade, the practice had arisen of paying a monetary gift. By Luther's time, the most normal method of obtaining an indulgence was to pay for it. Further, with the great medieval expansion of purgatory, the greatest fear was for time spent in purgatory, so the greatest selling was for release from purgatory, either for oneself or for one's loved ones. The indulgence Pope Leo proclaimed was a "plenary" indulgence, so named because it claimed to be able to forgive the punishment for almost all sins. Only a very few issues were reserved to Rome. Consequently, the desire for such an indulgence was strong.

Unfortunately, the late medieval desire for knowledge of spiritual safety was so intense that the temptation for the church to abuse this power was great. In Luther's day, great works of the Church of Rome were frequently paid for by the proclamation and sale of indulgences. The 1515 plenary indulgence was backed by the pope's desire to finish the reconstruction of St. Peter's Basilica in Rome, which his predecessor, Pope Julius, had begun. Moreover, the indulgence served the purposes of Archbishop Albrecht of Mainz and of the major banking establishment, the House of Fugger. When Luther began to protest against this indulgence on theoretical and biblical grounds, he had no idea of the stakes that were involved.

The pope had a clear purpose, even if it was somewhat marginal in its attachment to the spiritual kingdom. But why were Albrecht and the Fuggers involved? Albrecht desperately needed money. He had been elected archbishop of the archdiocese of Mainz in 1514. This was a rich post, the largest archdiocese in Germany. Further, it came with electoral dignity. However, the archdiocese had gone through several leadership changes in the past decade, and each time Rome had charged the newly elected archbishop approximately 10,000 ducats to grant the "pallium," the symbol of the archbishop.[7] Of course, each archbishop in turn taxed the archdiocese to make up that cost. By the time of Albrecht, there was significant debt. On top of that, Albrecht was already archbishop of Magdeburg, so he was not eligible for this post, according to church law, called canon law. But again, the right amount of money could cause the church to grant the proper dispensation from the law. Such was obtained, but it added up to Albrecht's having a sizeable debt. To many observers, the whole procedure seemed to be simony, a terrible sin.

Albrecht did not owe the debt directly to Rome. Instead, the third party, the House of Fugger, had financed his costs of election. Of course, this financing came with interest penalties and other values for the Fuggers, but for our purposes, it is enough to know that they wanted to get paid. The details were that the period of the sale of this particular indulgence would last eight years, that Albrecht was allowing it in the archdiocese of Mainz, and that the proceeds were to be divided between Rome and Albrecht, with Albrecht's share covering his debt to the Fuggers. Of course, as Brecht points out, the faithful who would be buying the indulgences knew nothing about the bargain.[8]

Why did Luther not simply ignore the indulgence? It was not allowed in his town of Wittenberg, because the Elector Frederick was a rival of Albrecht of Mainz. For Luther, the issue was both theological and pastoral. His own theological investigations into the practice of indulgences had already led him to doubt some portions of accepted belief, though he did not deny the effect in general. More important, he was the preacher to the town of Wittenberg. The indulgence could not be preached in Wittenberg, but nothing stopped the residents of Wittenberg from traveling to the nearby towns where it was preached and sold. They then returned to Wittenberg, bewildered that Luther was still speaking to them of their need for repentance and a reformed way of life. Had they not bought their forgiveness? Luther believed, with great justification, that the indulgences were causing people to stop believing in and relying on the life of charity, believing that they had "bought" their way out of purgatory, or even into heaven.

Part of the reason that it was difficult to ignore the indulgence was that the pope had secured the services of one of the most successful salesmen available, a Dominican friar named Johann Tetzel. Tetzel zealously followed every advantage the pope's decree allowed him. The regular sermons in the towns and villages of the archdiocese of Mainz were suspended in order that the indulgence and its great powers could be more effectively communicated. Tetzel was a skillful salesman who, like all successful salesmen, was an insightful amateur psychologist. He knew the fears of the people and played upon them. Further, he magnified the glories of the indulgence, even going so far as to come up with his own sales jingle: "As soon as the coin in the coffer rings, the soul from purgatory springs." Though the forces behind the indulgence were far more powerful and distant, Tetzel's ability and audacity made him hard for Luther to ignore.

The politics of the matter were also a crucial part of the mix. Some scholars have claimed that the Reformation was a function of political pressures. That is an oversimplification in two ways. First, it denies the place of real matters of faith and spirituality, which almost everyone claimed were at issue. Second, such a position suggests that politics was a new thing in the business of the church. Very few claims could be more naive; politics had been the sure and certain partner of the faith since at least the time of Constantine, in the early fourth century. What politics were involved? Quite simply, the election of an emperor. Maximilian I's reign was coming to an end, and he wished his grandson, Charles V, elected emperor. The Vatican did not want such an outcome. Part of the reason Albrecht wanted to buy the archbishopric of Mainz was to be an elector, so he could influence the next election. The Elector Frederick, on the other hand, was of a different political family and faction, and he opposed Albrecht on political grounds.

If you are confused by what was going on both in the open and behind closed doors, please do two things. First, note that this is but the briefest possible sketch of the facts; the ecclesiastical and political issues were truly complex in Saxony in 1517. Second, imagine how confusing it was for people living at the time! Without the benefit of hindsight, frequently without any source of news other than word of mouth, people did not know what or whom to believe about the events of their own time.

Into this electrically charged atmosphere Martin Luther introduced his critique. He wrote a treatise titled *Disputation on the Power and Efficacy of Indulgences*, popularly known as his Ninety-five Theses. In popular imagination, Luther is seen as a giant of a man, striding with a hammer and nails, and pounding his testament onto the door of the Wittenberg chapel on October 31, 1517. This view comes with a soundtrack: his hammer strokes were the death knell of the old ways, their sound rolling over the church and the empire. Such an image is thrilling and picturesque but not overly accurate. First, scholars are not even sure Luther nailed his document up on the door at all. Second, the document is not the harsh repudiation of the Roman Church's power and authority that many have assumed. Far from it.

Instead, Luther was simply trying to organize a debate. This was not a call to arms for the common people of Wittenberg to rise up against the church. First, the theses were written in ecclesiastical Latin, hardly the material of popular consumption. Second, this was a university exercise. Luther had written the kind of articles that were common to his profession, and not something aimed at the broadest possible audience. Finally, Luther did not repudiate all of the claims on which indulgences were based. Instead, he argued that works of love were better for the believers than buying indulgences, and that certain facets of the indulgence trade seemed to be getting out of hand and leading believers astray.

Luther seems not to have expected the kind of response his criticism generated. He himself had sent the theses to Archbishop Albrecht; he seems to have originally believed that much of what was going on was happening without the archbishop's knowledge. However, as Carter Lindberg states, "Luther had unknowingly touched some very sensitive nerves concerning papal authority and far-reaching political and ecclesiastical intrigue."[9] Luther's treatise was quickly translated into German and published widely. The affair was soon referred to Rome, and Luther was called upon to answer for his willingness to criticize in such a manner. As is many times the case, the remedy the Roman court suggested turned out to be far worse than the original disease.

In short time, Luther and his theological positions were attacked by various theologians. Johann Tetzel, the indulgence preacher, was the first to answer Luther. But the dispute did not remain at the level of Tetzel versus Luther. Soon other figures, such as Johann Eck, a doctor of theology from the University of Ingolstadt, were involved. As well, Archbishop Albrecht asked for the impudent theologian to be brought in line. The last months of 1517 and first months of 1518 were filled with treatises and countertreatises. These had the effect of bringing the controversy before far more people, as Luther wrote some of this material in German, and making Luther far more famous. Finally, each attack and counterattack made the issue more difficult to heal.

In the time between late 1517 and mid-1518, Luther's thought did not stand still. In the course of writing so many replies and occasional treatises, Luther went further than he had gone in the theses, which he had prepared for an academic audience. Through this period, Luther made several statements that would distance him from Rome. Luther suggested that the Roman Church's power was a historical accident rather than the clear choice of God. He submitted the opinion that the church could make an error. Finally, he allowed that in his estimation neither the pope nor general councils were infallible in matters of the faith.

In August 1518, Luther received a summons from Rome to come to the Vatican to account for his beliefs. Luther appealed to his prince, Frederick the Wise, in order to avoid having his case heard in a venue so hostile to his cause. Frederick negotiated with the pope's representative, the papal legate, Cardinal Cajetan. Cajetan agreed to meet Luther for a private interview at the imperial meeting, the Imperial Diet at Augsburg. Cajetan had express instructions from the pope that Luther had only two options. The first, and preferable choice, was that Luther would repudiate his statements about indulgences and the power of the pope. The technical term is recant. If Luther chose not to recant, however, he was to be arrested and sent to Rome.

Luther's interview with Cajetan did not go well. The cardinal managed to maneuver Luther into a corner over the interpretation of a papal statement, called *Unigenitus*, from 1343. Luther promised to recant if the bull said what the cardinal asserted, namely, that the merits of Christ were a treasure of the church. When the cardinal presented the passage in question, Luther attempted to escape on a weak grammatical point. Pressed further, the next day he reversed his course and simply denied that the pope was the supreme authority in the church, above even Scripture. Here he went much further than to suggest difficulties with indulgences, and both he and Cajetan knew it.

At this point, the interview was basically over, and Luther should have been taken to Rome as a heretic. However, Luther literally sneaked out of Augsburg by night and returned to Wittenberg. Cajetan went back to Rome, and as preparation for a more thorough reckoning of Luther's heresy, a new papal document, called a "bull," was prepared, clarifying the doctrine of indulgences. With this in hand, the forces of the church should have been able to take Luther into custody and bring the affair to a quick end.

Such was not the case. In January 1519, Emperor Maximilian I died. Frederick the Wise, as an elector, became an even more politically significant figure. For some time in early 1519, the pope even supported Frederick as the desirable candidate for emperor, probably to avoid the election of either Charles of Spain or Francis of France. In such a time, Frederick simply could not be alienated by the rushed conviction of the most famous professor at his university. Again, we see that politics and religion were inseparable in the time of the Reformation.

If the institutional church was not actively moving against Luther, that did not stop various theologians from stepping into the campaign. Johann Eck, the Ingolstadt professor, drew Luther into a debate in the summer of 1519. Eck began the debate by directing himself to one of Luther's colleagues at Wittenberg, Andreas Bodenstein von Karlstadt. Luther came to help, as was probably Eck's hope. Held in Leipzig, this Leipzig Disputation, as it would come to be called, took Luther further down the path he had been following. Though the debate was originally to have been about indulgences, the argument soon moved to the issue of papal power and the power of church councils, that is, conciliar power. In the debate, Luther made the blunt statement that councils not only could theoretically make mistakes, but that an actual council had done so in the past. For his example, Luther cited the Council of Constance, noting that when it condemned Jan Hus and his doctrines, it had condemned true Christian teachings. Luther then pointed out that councils sometimes flatly contradict each other, so logically it would be impossible for all councils to be correct. For his example, he noted that the Fifth Lateran Council had overturned the claims of earlier councils that a universal council had more authority than a pope. The debate ended because the duke brought it to a close so he could use his courtroom to entertain a visiting dignitary. However, by that point the two combatants were no longer trying to persuade each other. In a way, both Eck and Luther gained at the Leipzig debate. Eck clearly pushed Luther to the point where he took positions in direct opposition to Rome. Luther, for his part, gained clarity about his own stance vis-à-vis the history of the Roman Church and about the judgment of heresy, especially that of Jan Hus.

LUTHER IN WITTENBERG: 1520–1524

In many ways, 1520 was theologically the key year of the Lutheran Reformation. First, in June the papal bull titled *Exsurge Domine* pronounced Luther's condemnation and the heretical content of some of his teachings. Luther responded to this by burning a copy in the public square. He would later be formally excommunicated in early 1521. But more important than that, Luther wrote three treatises in 1520 that clearly separated his thought from that of the Church of Rome. Though Luther could argue that he was being a good son of the church in the final treatise, by then the break was too great, and the reform of Christianity according to the biblical pattern was too advanced for any reconciliation.

Luther's first treatise was written in German and appeared in August. It was titled *To the Christian Nobility of the German Nation regarding the Betterment of the Christian Estate*. Composing the treatise in German was noteworthy; it was a clear indication of the importance of its intended audience, and it furthered the movement of writing theology in the common languages. In the treatise, Luther argued that the German nobility had a duty toward the Christian estate of their realms. As Christian princes, the nobility had a responsibility to reform religion in their lands when the church refused to do so. Luther pointed out that the Church of Rome had hidden behind three walls, but that these should be denied any validity. The first wall was the division of Christians into a religious class and a secular class. Luther denied that the Scriptures supported such an idea. Instead, all Christians were the religious class, united by one faith, one gospel, and one baptism. The second wall was the claim that the hierarchy of the church, and most especially the pope, possessed the exclusive right to interpret the Scriptures. Again, Luther rejected this idea on the basis of Scripture, claiming that the power of interpretation had not only been granted to Peter, whom Rome believed to be the first pope, but also to the whole Christian community. The third wall was the belief that only the pope could convene a council. Luther renounced this argument by saying that it contradicted Scripture. Since Scripture directed the believer to bring a sinful brother or sister before the church, the pope cannot alone control the power to bring about the possibility of such a chance for reconciliation. Scripture does not grant such a privilege to the pope, nor would such a system work in the case of the pope's own error.

Obviously, Rome was not happy with Luther's turning to the secular lords to bolster his case. Further, the treatise attacked important claims that the popes and the Vatican had traditionally held. In the appeal to the German nobility, Luther had actually fulfilled some of Eck's claims against him. But that was hardly the end of the matter. In September 1520, Luther published *The Babylonian Captivity of the Church*, in both Latin and German. While the first treatise attacked some of the political claims of Rome, here Luther committed himself to a full frontal assault on the theology of the church. Luther attacked the medieval system of sacraments and the theology upon which it was built.

First, Luther condemned the Roman theology of the sacrament of the Eucharist, or Holy Communion. He claimed that the Church of Rome had shackled this sacrament with three manacles that were unbiblical and must be released. The first shackle was the issue of the two elements. Rome had come through long practice to withold the wine from the laity, and after long practice, theologians had made doctrinal arguments maintaining that this was the proper division, that wine should be received only by clergy. Luther demanded that both elements be given to all, as it was clear in the biblical texts from Matthew and 1 Corinthians that such was the case among the apostles.

The second shackle was the doctrine of transubstantiation. In 1215, at the Fourth Lateran Council, the medieval church had declared that the elements of bread and wine become the body and blood of Christ in the sacrament, and that all the faithful must believe this. Across the thirteenth century, the theology of transubstantiation was worked out, most especially in the thought of Thomas Aquinas. According to Aquinas, the true reality of something is its "substance," a term he took from Aristotle's philosophy. This true reality in anything is accompanied by lesser characteristics, called "accidents," another Aristotelian term. The accidental properties of a thing are those things that can change without the thing itself really changing. So, for instance, if a man named Jack has long hair one day but a crew cut the next, his substance has not changed, only the accidents. Jack's friends might remark about his hair, but they will still recognize Jack. The same would be true about a person's clothing or hair color, or even something so drastic as the loss of a limb. To follow this analogy further, Jack's DNA is not accidental but is part of his substance. If Jack's DNA could be changed, even if he did not look different, he would be different. Basically, Aquinas's argument was that the accidents of the bread and wine, such as texture and taste, remained the same; the substance of the underlying reality changed to the very body and blood of Christ.

Luther never denied that the body and blood of Christ were really present. But he did argue that to bind the consciences of the faithful to a mechanism of transubstantiation as an article of faith was going too far. Since Scripture did not give such clarity, demanding it of the believers as a condition of their participation in the church was simply outrageous. Instead, he proposed that it might be simpler to claim that both the bread and the body, or the wine and blood, were present at the same time. This position came to be called consubstantiation, and Luther would hold it until the end of his life.

Finally, the third shackle that Luther identified in the Roman theology of the Eucharist was Rome's belief that in the performance of the mass, a good work and a sacrifice were offered up to God. This was common medieval belief; in fact, people would frequently commission a church or monastery to offer up masses on behalf of a loved one or oneself, so as to gain the merit from such a work. For Luther, in some ways this was the most monstrous idolatry of all. To claim that the mass is a sacrifice that must be performed denied that Christ's actual sacrifice on the cross was sufficient for all time. To claim merit from a good work demonstrated that the believer was actually not a believer in the power of God to save him or her. Instead, such a person was demanding a role in his or her own salvation, and refusing the gift of God.

Having challenged the doctrine of Holy Communion, Luther bolted forward through all the rest of the medieval sacraments. He denied the biblical basis of the sacraments of confirmation, marriage, ordination, and last rites. Further, he discarded the idea that the church could proclaim a sacrament, insisting that only Christ's institution in the Scriptures could warrant the truth of a sacrament. He maintained that the Eucharist, baptism, and penance were sacraments, but reframed their meaning as well. To accept the theology of the *Babylonian Captivity* was theologically to leave the Church of Rome, as even observers of the time knew.

Luther was not finished, however. In November he produced another German treatise, *On the Freedom of a Christian*. Here he clearly set forth his division of the ethical life from the path of salvation. People should not do good works so that they will get into heaven, Luther pronounced. To do so demonstrated a lack of belief in the gracious gifts of God. It also is arrogant to believe that a human can earn his or her way into heaven. Most people cannot even keep a New Year's resolution! For Luther, there can be no hope of helping in one's own salvation. Any such belief or hope only blocks the one true possibility of salvation: faith in God through Jesus.

Instead of the doing of good works for salvation, Luther proposed a radical division between the works of a Christian and the path of salvation. God saves sinners not through any goodness of theirs, but through a divine and gracious choice. No one can do anything to cause God to save him or her. The law in Scripture exists not to direct believers in how to save themselves, but to demonstrate that they are impotent to fulfill its purity. Here we see Luther's dialectic of law and gospel. For Luther, the law brings the judgment of God, which no one can ever withstand. The law brings only condemnation. However, this has a positive function, for when the sinner throws himself or herself on the mercy of Christ, that person finds the word of promise, the grace of the gospel, the only possibility of salvation. The theme of law and gospel remained a key to Luther's thought throughout his career.

Luther's critics said, "Then why would anyone be good?" Luther's answer was simple but profound: Believers know that their works of love do not change their salvation status. However, believers are also continually being filled with the spirit of Christ and growing more into Christ. As well, believers wish to please God, not to earn salvation but as a grateful response to the gifts God has already given. Because of that, the lives of believers are different from those who have not received faith—but that difference is based upon God's decision and action to save the believers.

These "Reformation" treatises effectively severed Luther's connection with the Church of Rome. Not only did Luther depart from Roman theology, but he also had spread his teaching widely. We know this to be the case, because Luther's writings at this time were literally flying off the shelves. The initial printing of the treatise *To the Christian Nobility*, which numbered 4,000 copies, sold out in a few days.[10] To put that in perspective, there were only approximately 2,000 inhabitants in Wittenberg, and probably more than half could not read! With Luther making such a clear break, Rome acted to bring him to trial. Again, the Elector Frederick intervened, and Luther was ordered to make his defense of his doctrine at the next imperial diet, which was a meeting of parliament, of the nobles and their representatives. Luther came to make his defense at the Diet of Worms, in 1521.

Charles V was the new emperor. Whatever the emperor thought would happen at Worms, he could not have imagined the triumphal march Luther made on his way to the diet. Luther's arrival in town after town was the cause of festive celebrations, with dignitaries turning out to see him and to be seen with him. However, if from the perspective of the emperor this parade was bad, the actual interview at Worms was worse. Luther was supposed to come before the emperor and theologians of Rome to recant. Instead, he denied the power of the pope, denied the power of the emperor against his conscience, and stated that the only authority that did bind him was the Bible. Luther pronounced that unless he was convinced by the clear testimony of the Bible, or clear reasoning based upon the Bible, he could not renounce his teachings. Having made his declaration, he retired. On his journey home, his prince, Frederick, arranged to have him kidnapped for his own security. So it came to pass that on May 4, Luther was secretly taken to one of Frederick's fortresses, the Wartburg Castle. He remained there until the spring of 1522. In his absence, the imperial diet proclaimed the Edict of Worms, which declared Luther a heretic and demanded his arrest.

The cause of the Lutheran reform did not cease while Luther was at the Wartburg. Other significant reformers were pursuing their own agendas, some of which were in step with Luther and some of which were not. Andreas Bodenstein von Karlstadt and Philip Melanchthon were two of the important leaders who took over the reins of reform in the town of Wittenberg and realm of Saxony in Luther's absence.

Philip Melanchthon (1497–1560) was Luther's close colleague on the faculty in the university. Melanchthon differed from Luther in the extent of his humanistic training. Though Luther was a fan of the new humanistic learning and a proponent of it for the university, he himself had been trained in the older, formalized scholastic style. He pointed that out to his detractors in later debates, noting that his own training was in the ways of Aristotle and philosophical the-

ology. Melanchthon, on the other hand, had been steeped in humanistic training, even to the point of his family tree. He was the great-nephew of the
Hebraist Johann Reuchlin, who encouraged his language studies. Trained at
Heidelberg and Tübingen, Melanchthon was a noted scholar of Greek. Because
of Luther's reforms of the theological curriculum at Wittenberg, in 1518 the
university hired Melanchthon, who was just twenty-one, to teach Greek.

Melanchthon's command of Greek soon impressed Luther so much that he
turned over the lectures on Romans to him. This led to two results with profound impact throughout the sixteenth century and throughout the Lutheran
Reformation. First, Melanchthon's lectures on Romans led directly to the publication of his commentaries on Romans. The first was published in 1522, but
without Melanchthon's knowledge! Apparently based on class notes, this commentary was an immediate success. However, it embarassed Melanchthon, and
he wrote two further versions, in 1529 and 1532. While the second version did
well, the definitive final version was so significant as to gain praise and attention throughout the academic and ecclesiastical worlds.[11] In this particular case,
we can see the hunger for aids to the reading of Scripture, and Melanchthon's
approach was widely read. Some of the confidence of the early Lutheran
reformers that the people of God simply needed help to read the Scriptures
must in part be credited to Melanchthon.

Second, Melanchthon's work on Romans led him to divide up the letter to
the Romans into sections according to the key doctrines that each section
addressed. This became the foundation of his book *Loci communes*, first published in 1521. The publication of *Loci communes* must be seen as a watershed
event for Reformation theology. For the first time, a handbook of theology
attempting to gather together the whole of Christian doctrine according to a
topical setting was published. The book was so influential in the Reformation
era that Reformation scholars still simply refer to the "loci method." Those
believers who were persuaded by one of Luther's tracts could read more
broadly on other topics by turning to Melanchthon. Further, this early contribution demonstrated that the Lutheran movement was capable of producing more thorough systematic works of theology.

These advances on the theological front were not the only movements in
the Lutheran sphere of influence that were going on while Luther was at the
Wartburg. Fundamental changes were also being made in the daily worship
and practical piety of Wittenberg at this time, changes that were seen as so
potentially dangerous that Luther returned from the Wartburg specifically so
that he might be a calming influence. Andreas Bodenstein von Karlstadt
planned, instigated, and defended these changes.

Andreas Bodenstein von Karlstadt (c. 1480–1541) was a senior colleague of
Luther's at Wittenberg. He had doctorates in theology and law and was widely

regarded as very intelligent, though he was not always friendly to his colleagues. Luther had converted Karlstadt to the cause of reform by his position
on the Fathers. Carter Lindberg writes:

> When Luther declared in a disputation that September [1516] that the
> scholastics understood neither Scripture nor Augustine, Karlstadt
> angrily opposed him and confidently took up Luther's challenge to
> check the primary sources. After buying a new edition of Augustine's
> works, Karlstadt set about to refute Luther. In the process he discov-
> ered to his amazement that Luther was correct and that he, Karlstadt,
> had been "deceived by a thousand scholastic opinions." With surpris-
> ing rapidity Karlstadt's reading of Augustine brought him to the side
> of Luther against scholastic theology.[12]

Karlstadt had converted to Luther's side of the reforming movement. However, his transfer to Luther's camp demonstrates the old saying, "Be careful
what you pray for; you just might get it." Though Luther was at first quite
happy to be joined in his efforts by his colleague, Karlstadt did not simply copy
all of Luther's theology. The bases of the two men's theologies differed, and
Karlstadt did not accept the law-and-gospel distinctions so common to Luther.
Further, there can be no doubt that the two men differed radically on the necessary pace of reform. Luther's ideal was rather slow; while he recognized the
need for reform, he also appreciated that radical and swift changes might bring
as many problems as they solved. Karlstadt took the opposite opinion, holding the belief that allowing unreformed practices to continue at all was to
accept the kingdom of the devil.

Thus, Karlstadt set out in late 1521 to right the wrongs. Luther had called
for priests to be free to marry in his treatise to the German nobility, so in late
1521 Karlstadt announced his intention to marry. Frederick the Wise forbade
him to do so. Karlstadt reported back to Frederick that the marriage was
already a done deal and had been comsummated! Of course, clerical celibacy
was a significant problem in the early modern period. Karlstadt was addressing a real problem, but he was also attempting to demonstrate clearly the freedom that he had, and to lead others to engage in like-minded activities.

A similar contrast in approach to Communion and clerical attire was
evident. Luther had claimed that the laity should have both elements in
Communion in his treatise *The Babylonian Captivity of the Church*; he had
published theological tracts in German and had claimed in his treatise *Christian Freedom* that certain clothes do nothing for a person's spirit. On Christmas Day 1521, Karlstadt tied these things together, and against the Elector
Frederick's wishes, celebrated mass in layman's clothing, in German, while giving both elements to the laity. The number of offenses to common piety of the
day were numerous! The service of the mass had not changed in centuries, and

now so many changes were heaped together that it may have made some pious Wittenbergers' heads spin.

Finally, Luther had argued for a biblical Christianity, a Christian faith that accepted the words of the Bible as the clear standard for Christian practice. It was Luther who had denied authority to Christian tradition if it did not align with clear biblical teaching. Karlstadt read the commandment against the creation of images from the book of Exodus and preached it clearly. He encouraged the people of Wittenberg, against the wishes of Frederick the Wise, to cleanse the town of religious imagery and not to wait for permission from nobles or the courts. In February 1522, a mob pulled down images in Wittenberg and demolished them. Karlstadt preached the duty of the Christian to do this, regardless of the laws of the state.[13] This involved destroying state property as well as private property—religion and law were becoming tangled again.

While Luther generally accepted Melanchthon's contributions to the reforming impulse, Karlstadt gave Luther heartburn. Karlstadt's mercurial temperament and attitude not only annoyed Luther but also were raising problems with Luther's protector, the Elector Frederick. Faced with a reforming movement that seemed to be getting out of hand, Frederick dispatched Luther back to Wittenberg from the Wartburg. Luther responded to Karlstadt's sense of urgency with a sermon series on the power of the Word of God, instead of the world's violence. In March 1522, Luther preached every day for a whole week, giving a series of sermons that came to be known as the "Invocavit Sermons." From that point on, Luther took the guiding role in the German Reformation, so much so that it took on his name.

Of course, a person of Luther's talent and disposition could not sit still and enjoy the view while staying in the Wartburg. While there, Luther wrote sermons, kept in touch with his friends by a lengthy correspondence, and studied the Bible. But most of all, Luther spent his time in Wartburg Castle translating the New Testament into German. While this was not the first translation of the New Testament into German, Luther's linguistic skill and theological ability made it an instant best seller. First offered for sale in September 1522, it quickly sold out. Luther revised this translation and later expanded it by adding the Old Testament in 1534. In providing this translation, Luther furthered his ideal of having Christians know the Scriptures.

Back in Wittenberg, Luther took the supervision of the reform firmly in his own hands. Soon Karlstadt was banished from Wittenberg, although not from the cause of reform. Luther's reforms of the worship service were more cautious than Karlstadt's and slower. But in their own way, they were no less profound. Luther maintained the necessity of worshiping in the language of the people. To support this, he introduced congregational singing in German.

Luther himself wrote many hymns, and he was a sophisticated theorist about the place of music and congregational singing in worship, working out mutually reinforcing schemes so that the texts of hymns would underscore important themes from the Scriptures and sermon.

Since Luther believed that the faithful should be reading the Scriptures and taking responsibility for their own progress in Christian doctrine, it only made sense for the reforming movement to take up the cause of education in Saxony and wider Germany. This supported both his program for the continued building up of the Christian community and for the education of Christian clergy. In this endeavor he was greatly aided by his close friend Melanchthon, who eventually gained the common title "Preceptor of Germany."

THE END OF INNOCENCE: 1525

The year 1525 clearly ended the early period of Luther's reform, when he seemed almost to move effortlessly from one triumph to another. Though under imperial ban, Luther had never been tried for heresy in person and had never spent time in prison for his teachings. Safe within his own geographic area, Luther had conquered all of the difficulties that had arisen. If Luther harbored any hopes that God's grace would protect the reform movement from pain, the stark harshness of 1525 banished such hopes. In that year Luther experienced the double jolt of the Peasants' War and an open fight with the humanist scholar Erasmus. Both cost him, though in different ways.

"The Peasants' War" (*Bauernkrieg* in German) is a term used by historians to describe a loosely connected group of peasant uprisings.[14] These revolts were not at all new; such occurrences could be traced back to the middle of the fifteenth century. However, what was of a different character was the religious quality of some of the uprisings. Some of the religious leaders of these movements had ties to Wittenberg and the Lutheran movement. Andreas Bodenstein von Karlstadt was the leader of the uprising in Rothenburg in March 1521. Thomas Müntzer, who had wandered through Wittenberg on his way to eventual execution, was one of the leaders of the peasant army that took over Mühlhausen and Frankenhausen. Both Karlstadt and Müntzer argued that the peasant armies not only had the right but the responsibility to rise up and create true kingdoms for God. Müntzer went so far as to argue that godless people had no right to live when they stood in the way of the righteous.[15] Both contended that the cause of the gospel was also the cause of the true believers whom they led.

For Luther, this represented a problem. First, it was an excellent opportunity for his Roman opponents to link Luther to criminals. It was easy to say that just as Luther was an outlaw, under an imperial ban, so he was also inciting his followers to be outlaws in ways that even outdid his evils. Second, Luther did not believe that Christian freedom extended to freedom from well-formed human laws. Rather, he judged that the peasants were being led astray by overenthusiastic preachers, who turned the simple sense of Scripture upon its head. When he first wrote a treatise addressing himself to the problem of the uprisings, Luther was pastoral in tone, attempting to be a mediator. When that failed to receive the hearing Luther felt it deserved, and Luther heard reports that towns were being destroyed and saw some evidence of this for himself, he wrote a second treatise, titled *Against the Robbing and Murdering Hordes of Peasants*. In this treatise, Luther encouraged the nobility to find and kill the insurgent forces. When the forces of the princes took the peasant army in Frankenhausen with wholesale slaughter, Luther looked like the cheerleader for might without conscience.

Luther's second battleground of 1525 came from a wholly different quarter, namely, the pen of Erasmus of Rotterdam, the prince of the humanists. In 1524, Erasmus published a book titled *De libero arbitrio* (*On the Free Choice of the Will*).[16] In it, Erasmus took on Luther over the ability of the human will to make choices that lead toward salvation. Erasmus clearly was taking on Luther; he wrote this piece at the urging of King Henry VIII of England and the pope, among others. But the issues involved, both ecclesiastical-political issues and theological issues, are much deeper.

First, in part, Erasmus wrote this treatise to maintain his own standing within the Church of Rome. Erasmus was a reformer in his own right, and he could be a severe critic of the practices and doctrinal quarreling that in part characterized the church in the early sixteenth century. He was occasionally a defender of Luther and in fact had written a treatise only six months earlier in which he clearly endorsed the ways that Luther's faith corresponded to the historic Christian faith as represented in the Apostles' Creed. But his occasional defense of Luther, and his own criticism of the church's practices, had left him open to charges that he himself was a follower of Luther, that he was a "Lutheran." Erasmus pointedly and repeatedly denied such indictments. Writing against Luther clearly may have been one way for Erasmus to demonstrate his own loyalty to the Church of Rome. Luther clearly believed that this was the case, because he accused Erasmus of writing the book against him in return for a red hat—implying that Erasmus was angling for a seat in the college of cardinals.

Second, Erasmus and Luther both knew that they differed on the doctrine in question. Luther had realized as early as 1516 that Erasmus and he disagreed on the proper interpretation of Paul. As Martin Brecht points out, "Humanism's high regard for a person's moral capabilities was incompatible with Luther's teaching of justification."[17] There had been an open debate between

the two thinkers for years over the proper Christian way to construe the powers of the human will. Erasmus's book of late 1524 may also have simply been
his attempt to clarify finally his own position.

What did Erasmus write? First, it is important to point out that the term
"freedom of choice" or "freedom of the will" is not meant here to describe simple choices of everyday life. Thus, the choice to wear blue jeans or khaki slacks
is not what Erasmus and Luther clashed over. Instead, the freedom at issue is
whether humans, in their current state after the introduction of sin into the
world, can make positive choices on their own to turn toward God. Erasmus
believed that they could. He argued several things, but most particularly that
since the Bible contains a great number of God's commands, logically this
must mean that humans *can* fulfill those commands. Perhaps they fulfill them
imperfectly, but they do choose to act to please God. For Erasmus, any other
reading made impossible the kind of moral reform of the church that he envisioned, and made reading the Bible extremely difficult.

In 1525, Luther wrote a book in response to Erasmus. It was clearly a reply;
the title, *De servo arbitrio (The Bound Choice of the Will)*, mirrored that of Erasmus's work. Further, Luther organized his book so that it answered each section of Erasmus's book. When it was finished, Luther believed that it was one
of his finer works—one of a very few he felt worthy of publication.

But what did Luther write? As we have seen, Luther had worked out his
own way of reading the Bible, according to the hermeneutic of law and gospel.
For Luther, the Bible is full of God's commands. However, the fact that commands are present does not mean that humans can accomplish them! Paradoxically, the commands are present in Scripture so that humans will realize
that they are wholly unable to rely upon themselves, that they must throw
themselves on the mercy of Christ. To Luther, this was a key issue, and he com-
plimented Erasmus for getting to the heart of the matter. Luther believed and
maintained that not only the Bible was on his side but also the clearest testimony of the church fathers, especially Augustine.

St. Augustine (354–430) represented one of the issues at stake between
Erasmus and Luther. In a larger sense, Augustine and other important theologians of the early church centuries, who were called the Fathers, formed a
battleground between Catholics and Protestants. Each side tried to prove that
it was the true heir to the heritage of the Fathers and that the other side was
full of innovation. Luther had been formed by a close connection to Augustine in the Augustinian monastery he joined. Augustine was famous for his
reliance on grace for salvation and for his suspicion that humans were not very
active in the process of salvation. Other theologians in both the early church
and the Middle Ages had disagreed with Augustine on this point. In terms of
the debate between Erasmus and Luther, there is no question that Luther was

more closely following Augustine. But Augustine was not the whole of Christian teaching.

Two issues loom large in this conversation. The first, for Luther, was the sense that any initiative given to humans in the path of salvation was taken away from God. This was not something he was prepared to do. For Luther, one is saved wholly by God, not by God with the help of the believer. The second was the issue of predestination. In this text, Luther is at his most forthright in arguing simply that the testimony of Scripture states clearly that God saves those whom he wills to save. Luther was unwilling to go further; he did not develop a clear doctrine of double predestination, as his younger contemporary John Calvin would. But the message was still starkly clear: believers are saved wholly because of God's choice.

For Luther and for the various reform movements, this represented the end of an era of hope that Renaissance humanism and reforming zeal were indivisibly linked. After Luther's reply, Erasmus wrote further treatises on the topic, but Luther never bothered to answer. The hopeful moment that had glimpsed the renaissance of learning fueling the reform of all things Christian in a movement that would be thorough and might change the form of Christianity forever was lost. Historically speaking, such a moment probably never existed, but Luther and the Lutherans could not have known that. In 1525, the Lutheran reform came through challenges, but not without sobering scars.

THE LUTHERAN REFORM: 1525–1546 AND BEYOND

Of course, what we have termed the "end of innocence" did not slow the reforms in Saxony. In June 1525, Luther participated in another reform when he married a former nun, Katerina von Bora. Luther had taken a role in liberating a group of nuns from a nearby convent. Katerina was the last to enter into a settled state, and when Luther tried his hand at matchmaking with disastrous results, she replied that Luther himself was a better choice. Though at first Luther seems to have treated this as a big joke, his father did not, because he wanted Luther to pass on the family name. After some time, Luther came around to the idea, and in a public ceremony trumpeting his new status to the world, Martin married Katerina. To begin, it was not a love match. The early sixteenth century was not the most romantic of ages. But Luther clearly came to love his wife, and her care for him seems evidence of her own devotion. What the marriage did for the Luthers is a matter of biography; what it did for the reform is one of ecclesiology, that is, the doctrine of the church.

For time immemorial, the Roman Church had been directed by a particular caste—celibate men. That many were not celibate added scandal to the situation but did not change the fact that Christian clergy were supposed to be celibate. There were several reasons for this, but certainly one was that it set the clerical estate apart from that of the lay estate. Luther denied this completely. He asserted that all Christians are called to be ministers of the gospel, a belief that he would come to call the "priesthood of all believers." By marrying, Luther demonstrated in the most unambiguous way that the married way of life was not something lesser, given for the spiritual deficiencies of the laity. Rather, it was the fulfillment of the commandment of God and as useful as the celibate way of life, which Luther found to be a very rare gift. Clerical marriage would become a hallmark of Protestant movements.

The reforming movement was also growing in scope, moving from being "Luther's" toward a movement that would be termed "Lutheran." Part of this was due to the reforming actions taken by the princes. After the death of Frederick the Wise in 1525, he was succeeded by John the Constant, who ruled from 1525 to 1532. He was a much more active participant in the reforming movement, partly because of Luther's urging. In 1525, on Christmas Day, Johann decreed that church services would be in German. Other princes also took leading roles in the reform movements, either for or against the reforms. The power of the princes grew at this time, causing the concentration of power in the hands of secular authorities, a theme that we will return to near the end of this volume. While the significance and details of this development are too complex to describe here, the reader should note that Luther had called for the princes to take a part in the affairs of the sacred realm, and they generally responded vigorously.[18]

An important moment in this evolution happened at the imperial diet called for Speyer in 1529. An imperial diet had met at Speyer in 1526 and had given certain allowances of tolerance to Luther's sympathizers, who were in the minority. This was wholly political. Though the Archduke Ferdinand, a Habsburg ruler and Emperor Charles V's brother, wished to put the Edict of the Diet of Worms from 1521 fully in effect, the delegates declared this impossible. Further, the emperor and the archduke were in no position to insist. Internal wars between Christians and the threat of Turkish invasion meant that alienating any part of the empire was too risky.

At the Diet of Speyer of 1529, as usual, the religious question was on the table. The emperor and the majority of nobles within the Holy Roman Empire wished to put a halt to the religious innovations and return to the status quo that had existed before 1517. The political situation had changed, and it was safer for Emperor Charles V to push his religious agenda. The Catholic nobles passed legislation making Lutheran practices illegal. But the minority was also prepared. Though they were divided on many issues, five Lutheran princes and fourteen cities presented a formal protest to the legislation—*Protestatio* in Latin, which is where the term "Protestant" comes from.

Emperor Charles V was not happy with the outcome of the Diet of Speyer in 1529. Though he had won, a significant minority had protested, and the diet had not provided the kind of religious settlement that he had envisioned. Thus, he offered a new opportunity: that at the Diet of Augsburg, to be held the following year, the religious question could be taken up again. This time the "Lutherans" were more prepared. Luther himself could not attend because of his legal status; it was truly unsafe for him to be outside of Saxony. His colleague and trusted friend, Philip Melanchthon, however, could. With Luther's approval, he drafted a confession of faith, using as sources articles of faith that had been previously drafted to clarify the faith that the evangelicals held. The confession was edited until its presentation to the emperor on June 25, 1530. Known as the Augsburg Confession, it was signed by seven princes and the representatives of two cities, and it immediately took on official status as a summary of belief of the evangelical faith.[19]

Though the Augsburg Confession attempted at least in part to be a mediating document that demonstrated to Charles V that the evangelicals held the ancient Christian faith, it also displayed clearly the differences between the evangelical belief and the theology of Rome, which the Lutheran position called "innovations." The emperor did not take the confession lightly but instead referred it to a group of theologians deemed sufficiently loyal to Rome, including Johann Eck, who had attacked Luther in print, and Johannes Cochlaeus, who would be Luther's first biographer, setting his life forward as a warning of the powers of Satan. The group refuted the confession in writing. In response, Melanchthon wrote a defense, titled the Apology of the Augsburg Confession. However, having made up his mind, the emperor refused to receive this document. Charles concluded the Diet of Augsburg by rescinding the religious freedoms that had been granted earlier.

The religious affairs did not simply remain matters of debate. The sixteenth century is far from the twenty-first in its sensibilities. Religion was too important to leave completely in the hands of ecclesiastical officials. Further, it was clear that Charles V and Archduke Ferdinand were growing so weary of the religious dissent that they were considering options beyond the debating of religious positions at councils of the empire. They might resort to armed force, and the minority party of the evangelical faith knew it. Though Luther himself advised that it was sinful to resist the emperor, the Lutheran princes took what they believed was prudent action. In 1531, the princes formed the Schmalkaldic League, named for the town in which the meetings were held. By 1537, this mutual defense organization represented some thirty-five states and embodied a powerful political force within the empire, representing the concerns of the Lutheran areas, cities, and people. The league lasted until 1547, when imperial forces smashed the armies of the League in the Schmalkaldic War.

Beyond Wittenberg, reforms continued. Other religious leaders were continuing the work that Luther had begun in new areas. Far to the southwest of Wittenberg, in Schwäbisch Hall in the region of Württemberg, Johann Brenz (1499–1570) was hard at work expanding the influence of the evangelical faith. Having been trained by a leading humanist scholar, Brenz accepted the evangelical positions Luther took before 1520. He was a solid supporter of these Lutheran positions, preaching against the Mass and supporting Luther's position on the presence of Christ in the Eucharist. Though he was forced to leave Schwäbisch Hall because of the defeat of Lutheran forces in the Schmalkaldic War, Brenz continued to publish, teach, and to influence the faith of Germans in a number of cities in which he preached and taught.

Justus Jonas (1493–1555), was an educator, pastor, and promoter of the works of Martin Luther. Like Luther, he had studied at Wittenberg and Erfurt. In 1519, he became rector of the University of Erfurt, where he immediately began to change the curriculum on the humanistic model, launching the study of Greek and Hebrew. He later taught at Wittenberg, was a great admirer of Luther's, and contributed to the reforms by writing several church orders—directions for how to run local churches. Jonas's later career was north of Wittenberg, in Halle and Eisfeld. His promotion of Luther consisted primarily in his translation work, for he translated Luther's German works into Latin for the more scholarly audience, and his Latin works into German for the popular audience. His devotion to Luther was demonstrated in his rushing from his pastorate in Halle to Luther's side as he lay dying in Eisleben.

The names of other leaders who left their mark on the expanding Lutheran world can be multiplied beyond all value. Lutheranism, or evangelicalism, continued to be a force within Germany and the surrounding lands, even as it had to contend with military losses in the Schmalkaldic War. Two further figures worth mentioning are Matthias Flacius Illyricus and Martin Chemnitz. Matthias Flacius Illyricus (1520–1575) was a professor of theology at Wittenberg. After the defeat of the Schmalkaldic League in 1547, Flacius, instead of adopting a conciliatory tone, took a hard-line approach. He argued that no issues should be compromised, as this would become a slippery slope leading away from the purity of the evangelical faith. Flacius's stance inspired the formation of a movement within Lutheranism that came to be called "Gnesio-Lutheranism," for "true" Lutherans. This movement was centered in the city of Magdeburg and strengthened north German Lutheranism. Martin Chemnitz (1522–1586) taught briefly at Wittenberg in the 1550s. After that, he became a pastor in Brunswick-Wölfenbüttel, where he remained for the rest of his life. He published a book on the Catholic Council of Trent—*Examen Concilii Tridentini (An Examination of the Council of Trent)*. His analysis of the canons and decrees of Trent were devastatingly critical, and even caused some Catholics to convert to Lutheranism. Further, Chemnitz was one of the leaders of a group of Lutheran scholars who worked to hammer out a document that demonstrated the common theology of the Lutheran churches. This document, the Formula of Concord, defined the mainstream position of Lutheranism at a time when there were serious divisions within the various evangelical churches.

Having seen that the Lutheran reforms went on beyond the life of Luther, what other issues impacted Lutheranism? Paradoxically, one of the impacts upon those of the Lutheran faith came from outside. Beyond the Lutheran impulse, other reforms were taking place. In Switzerland, Huldrych Zwingli was leading the town council of Zurich to move toward the evangelical faith. In England, Henry VIII, once a staunch supporter of the Church of Rome, with the approval of parliament set up a state church with himself as ecclesiastical head. In the Low Countries and in Germany, Radical Reform movements were coalescing into a recognizable type. The leaders of the evangelical movement called "Lutheran" had to consider what its relations to these other bodies would be. By the end of Luther's life, issues of religion, while no more urgent than at the start of his career, would be more complicated by the wider variety of choices available to believers.

LUTHER'S THEOLOGY: A SUMMARY

Now that we have considered several points of Luther's theology, it is worthwhile to summarize, especially since so many of the other reformers were influenced by or reacted to Luther's thought. First, we must note with Markus Wriedt that Luther's theology is not presented systematically because it is not worked out as a system.[20] Second, although Luther's thought is frequently presented as a complex, it was worked out over a long career. Some of his insights were not fully developed at their first appearance in his thought.

The first topic that demands the attention of the reader of Luther is Luther's discovery of God's righteousness as a gift rather than a moral standard. Luther read in Romans 1:16—17, "For I am not ashamed of the gospel; it is the power of God for salvation to everyone who has faith, to the Jew first and also to the Greek. For in it the righteousness of God is revealed through faith for faith; as it is written, 'The one who is righteous will live by faith.'" Always previously, Luther had read that word "righteousness" as an exact standard of morality, of the perfection of the Lord. As such, it was not a comfort

but a torment—who can attain the perfection of God? But now Luther discovered a different way to read this passage. What if righteousness was not an
objective standard to be achieved but a gift God gives to those he loves? What
if righteousness is wholly free? Luther concluded that God's righteousness is
a gift, a merciful reaching out to the sinner.

This changes everything. Now, instead of a struggle of conscience and will
to achieve God's favor, the believer is presented with the reality of God's forgiveness. Here we have Luther's emphasis on salvation, or justification, by
faith. Humans are saved. The passive construction in that sentence is crucial.
Humans do not save themselves; they simply are saved by God's gift of grace,
received by faith.

This led Luther to another discovery. If righteousness was a gift, rather than
a standard, what was the point of all the biblical laws? Starting with the Ten
Commandments, Scripture is full of commands for what humans should do in
order to be pleasing to God. What is the purpose of these? Luther's answer
represents another radical break with the medieval model of piety leading to
salvation. The law of God, through the sin of humanity, has fallen from its created purpose to its present function. Originally, the purpose of the law was to
guide humans to please God. But after the introduction of sin into the human
equation—after the fall—everything done by humans was stained by sin and
corrupted. Thus, the law was bent from its original purpose of guidance to its
present function of condemnation. The law exists, in Luther's estimation, to
damn people. No one living can fulfill the law. Anyone who thinks about the
law will eventually realize this.

That may seem harsh. But for Luther it was a crucial linchpin in his theology. Until someone is faced with his or her total inability to do God's will, that
person will continue to attempt to be saved on account of his or her own
efforts. People want to save themselves—and get in God's way. They want to
demonstrate that they do not need God—and in doing so they take away their
only chance of salvation. Until someone realizes that he or she has nothing to
offer, that everything is a gift, that people must throw themselves on God's
mercy, salvation cannot happen. On the other hand, Luther believed that once
humans accept their inherent unworthiness and simply ask for forgiveness, the
message of the gospel is that Christ has already forgiven them. This good news
became Luther's counterbalance to the horrible but necessary message of the
law. In fact, this became a dialectic in his thought—the adversarial nature of
the law and the gospel.

In the debate with Erasmus and elsewhere, Luther made it clear that human
capacity for doing works that are efficacious in the process of salvation is
strictly an illusion. For Luther, the human will had become enslaved, and the
only question was whether it would be mastered by Satan or by God. Of

course, both implicitly and explicitly in Erasmus's critique, this raised the question of the choice of salvation. For Luther, the answer to this was simply that salvation is wholly in God's hands and humans are not able to save themselves. He did not work through a doctrine of double predestination as some later theologians would, but Luther clearly placed the whole of salvation at God's initiative.

Luther did realize that there are different spheres of a human life. The inability to achieve salvation through one's own efforts does not mean complete and total impotence. Rather, there are two kingdoms in human life, each with its own rules. Of course, God's rule presides in the spiritual life. But citizenship in the kingdom of God does not earn one any freedoms in the earthly kingdom. In the kingdom of this world, believers are just as liable to pay taxes, obey their lords, and participate in the needs of the secular community. Without this, the management of the secular kingdom becomes impossible.

Finally, for Luther, all of his authority for his theological positions was grounded in Scripture. Those traditions that might even be helpful to the running of a human enterprise such as the church cannot claim to be authoritative without express legitimation in Scripture. Luther took it as a rock-solid axiom that he could not be argued against on the basis of any other authority. This was the reason for the sacramental stands he took and for the kinds of positions he took on the authority of the papacy. For good or ill, all of Luther's theological ideas became common currency for the sixteenth-century reforms, to be debated, changed, and even refuted. But in no way could or would they be ignored.

CONCLUSION

At the end of this chapter, we return to our starting point: Martin Luther striding over the landscape of the early sixteenth-century Holy Roman Empire like a giant, causing all, whether friend or enemy, to take notice. Though it is impossible to speak of the patterns of reform that came about without the humanistic reforms, it is only with the Lutheran affair that reform meant the necessary structural reform of the church itself. For some, that went too far; for others, it was only the beginning of the reform. No matter what, the early evangelical movements were colored by the personality and theology of Martin Luther.

Several of Luther's characteristic theological emphases became watchwords in the period of the Reformation. The privileging of the Bible as the one true authority in theology, the denial of works-righteousness, and the battlefield of the Fathers—all of these would be common issues for the next generations.

Further, Luther's "self," his personality, became an issue of right belief in Lutheran lands. Within one generation of Luther's death, struggles broke out between those who followed the theological pattern of Luther's friend and colleague Philip Melanchthon, and those who felt that Melanchthon was too open to compromise. The party of Melanchthon was sometimes called the "Philippists," and the other party, led by Matthias Flacius Illyricus, was known as the "Gnesio-Lutherans." Although the parties quarreled partly over theological issues themselves, at least in part they also fought over what positions were truly those that followed the inspiration of Luther. Luther never would have condoned such a fight in his lifetime.

Whether one calls him a demon or an apostle, there can be no doubt that Martin Luther's ability to grasp a certain type of struggle of the soul, and to find a gracious God in the Scriptures who forgave sinners without price, changed the theological world of Christianity. His theological discovery, in turn, changed the world.

QUESTIONS FOR DISCUSSION

1. Martin Luther was tormented by his conscience. Does his solution of radical trust in God make sense as a response?
2. Luther attacked indulgence traffic and the medieval system of salvation. Is there anything a person can do to help earn his or her salvation?
3. Should Luther have been more gentle in his reforming attitude? Did the pace of his reform force him outside of the Catholic Church?
4. Who has the power to interpret Scripture? Can all individuals interpret with equal authority? If so, how are differences of opinion to be settled?

SUGGESTED FURTHER READING

Primary Readings

Luther, Martin. *Luther's Works*. American Edition. 55 vols. Edited by Jaroslav Pelikan. St. Louis: Concordia Press, 1955–1986.
———. *Martin Luther's Basic Theological Writings*. Edited by Timothy Lull. Minneapolis: Augsburg Fortress Press, 2005.
———. *Martin Luther: Selections from His Writings*. Edited by John Dillenberger. New York: Anchor Books, 1951.

Secondary Readings

Brecht, Martin. *Martin Luther: His Road to Reformation, 1483–1521*. Translated by James L. Schaaf. Philadelphia: Fortress Press, 1985.

———. *Martin Luther: Shaping and Defining the Reformation, 1521–1532*. Translated by James L. Schaaf. Philadelphia: Fortress Press, 1990.

Kolb, Robert. *Martin Luther as Prophet, Teacher, and Hero: Images of the Reformer, 1520–1620*. Grand Rapids: Baker Books, 1999.

Lindberg, Carter. *The European Reformations*. Malden, MA: Blackwell Publishers, 1996.

McKim, Donald K., ed. *The Cambridge Companion to Martin Luther*. Cambridge: Cambridge University Press, 2003.

Oberman, Heiko. *Luther: Man between God and the Devil*. Translated by Eileen Walliser-Schwarzbart. New Haven, CT: Yale University Press, 1989.

5

Zwingli and Zurich

Early Swiss Reform

In the popular imagination about the Protestant reformations in the sixteenth century, Martin Luther rose up in Germany, and soon after, John Calvin led the Genevans toward their own reform. Thus the two most recognized branches of the Reformation, the Lutheran and Calvinist, were born. Things were actually messier than that. Calvin did not directly follow Luther; in fact, there was a long period of time when Luther was clearly outside the communion of Rome when Calvin remained a loyal member. Moreover, the central figure in early Swiss reforming movements, Huldrych Zwingli, both preceded Calvin and denied that he was dependent upon Luther! The relationship of the Zwinglian and Lutheran ideals of the reform demonstrate as clearly as any other comparison that the early sixteenth century was difficult to navigate for the people of the time. It remains so for the student who would understand it in a later age.

THE PROBLEM OF "LUTHERAN" THEOLOGY

One of the difficulties that we face as we attempt to understand the thought and movements of the Reformers of the early sixteenth century was that they did not understand everything perfectly themselves. Of course, individuals understood themselves—I am not suggesting mass schizophrenia as the character of the age. But the people, both the theologians and the laity who were reading their tracts, did not always grasp the theological implications or the political meanings that were in the texts they were reading and experiencing. While this seems strange, it is a historical truism. Consider, for instance, the Kennedy assassination on November 22, 1963. If you could gather up the national newspapers from November 23 through November 25, you would find a confused jumble of theories and explanations for what had happened, and for its significance. Even today, a simple search of the Internet about the Kennedy assassination reveals a number of conspiracy theories that are still believable to at least some people. Those living in the period of time closest to the event did not, and could not, grasp everything that had happened. Only later observers had the good fortune of time to come to calmer conclusions. Historians call this the function of distance.

Historically speaking, the Kennedy assassination is a relatively simple event compared to the era of the Reformation. It was a single event in a single location. Reformation movements were happening all over Western Europe and being implemented by different actors for quite different reasons. But that was not immediately clear to the people living at the time. Thus, reforming theological impulses that supported the primary position of the Bible in theology and questioned the way that the church had been run were frequently simply called "Lutheran"—that is, when they were not being called schismatic or heretical or true defenders of the gospel. Erasmus was called a Lutheran, as were several other significant humanist scholars. We have seen that Erasmus and Luther differed intensely on the issue of human freedom, but popular imagination and popular terminology do not always penetrate beyond the surface of issues.

Such is the case in the instance of Huldrych Zwingli (1484–1531). His detractors immediately labeled him a "Lutheran." Meanwhile, Luther himself rebuked Zwingli for some of his doctrines, especially concerning the sacrament of the Lord's Supper. Zwingli battled back against Luther and denied having taken his inspiration from the German monk. In attempting to get a grasp of him and his influence on the Swiss reforms, we frequently run up against a wall. As Gregory Miller states, "Zwingli's reputation suffered from the triple negative of being castigated by Luther as a tool of the devil, being overshadowed by John Calvin in Upper Germany and Switzerland, and perhaps most damaging of all, dying an untimely and violent death on the battlefield of Kappel."[1] In Zwingli, we find an almost exact contemporary of Luther, who forged his own path of reform. Further, in the Swiss Reformation different theological topics were taken up, different theological answers were given, and a wholly different political situation existed than that of electoral Saxony.

At the beginning of the sixteenth century, Switzerland was a collection of states called "cantons." These cantons had banded together for mutual defense and prosecution of their claim to rights within the Holy Roman Empire. This had come about in the fourteenth century, when the three original cantons of Uri, Schwyz, and Unterwalden broke free from the lordship of the Austrian Habsburgs by winning in battle.[2] Later states joined in, and by the time of

Zwingli, there were thirteen cantons. While they were rather expert at coming together to defend themselves against foreign aggression, the confederation had never become a "country" in our modern sense of the word, believing that all cantons had a common destiny. This loose confederated characteristic would greatly impact Zwingli's career and ministry.

HULDRYCH ZWINGLI: EARLY LIFE, EDUCATION, AND MINISTRY

The facts of Zwingli's life are both straightforward and beautifully illustrative of the religiously and ethically ambiguous time in which he lived. Zwingli was born on the first day of January 1484, only weeks after the birth of Martin Luther. He was born in Wildhaus, a region of Toggenburg in the northern reaches of the Swiss confederation. Though he was baptized "Ulrich," he later took the name "Huldrych" for himself, meaning "rich in grace."[3] Zwingli was born to a farming family, but one with ties to the clergy; his uncle was a priest. When young Ulrich showed promise of an academic future, both in his intelligence and in his musical talent, the family managed to send him to school.

Zwingli's first university education came at the University of Vienna. After his early training there, he went to study at the University of Basel, where he received his bachelor's and master's degrees. Basel had been the first university founded in Switzerland, and it was the leading university in the region. When Zwingli arrived there in 1502, the city already had both the influence of humanism and several printing houses. It also was a place where Zwingli could drink deeply at the well of Swiss patriotism, which would shape his later thought and the course of his career, especially around the issue of the mercenary trade. Throughout his education, Zwingli was always in contact with important humanists.[4] While Luther would come upon the new learning rather late in his educational career, Zwingli's formation was always steeped in humanist ideals.

In another contrast to Luther, Zwingli's studies took no detours. He did not begin to study some other discipline and have a lightning-induced conversion to clerical studies. Instead, Zwingli studied theology from the beginning, preparing for a career in the church. He studied the traditional pattern of scholastic theology, as had Luther. However, Zwingli studied the more traditional theology influenced by Thomas Aquinas, the *via antiqua*. Luther had studied the *via moderna*. For our purposes, it is significant that they both studied scholasticism deeply.

In 1506, at the age of twenty-two, Zwingli was ordained as a parish priest in the village of Glarus. He remained in this small village of approximately two thousand inhabitants for the next ten years.[5] This post was crucial to Zwingli's development for several reasons. First, it does not seem to have been so demanding that it took all of his time. Instead, the young priest continued his studies independently, reading the Bible especially, but also the pagan classics and the church fathers. The humanism of Erasmus had by now captured his attention, and Zwingli seems to have been using the models of reading that the humanists preferred. Zwingli's salary and benefices allowed him to buy books, and he amassed a considerable library.

Second, it was at this time that Zwingli learned Greek and Hebrew. By the time of his next position at Einsiedeln, which he added to his duties at Glarus in 1516, Zwingli was an excellent Greek scholar. His ability with Hebrew was not as strong, but it still was remarkable in the world of the early sixteenth century. Prior to the ministry that would make him famous throughout Europe, Zwingli had equipped himself with language—he had become a *vir trilinguis*, a man of the three languages.

Finally, in Glarus, Zwingli became a Swiss patriot. Actually, "became" might be too strong a word. We do not know whether young Ulrich had harbored strong patriotic sentiments. However, we do know that it was in Glarus that his concern for the Swiss came front and center. The lightning rod for this concern was the Swiss mercenary trade.

The Swiss confederation had come about in the late Middle Ages, beginning as a confederation joined together against an external enemy. By the sixteenth century, Switzerland held a reputation for producing soldiers of uncommon skill and ferocity. Machiavelli, writing early in the sixteenth century, attributed the Swiss freedom to their being so skillful at warcraft. This reputation resulted in a mercenary trade. Princes and popes would send recruiting agents into Switzerland to fill their own armies with solders with an aggressive attitude. The men of Switzerland would make some money, but the greatest share of the profits would go to the treasuries of the local town council or local lord.

For poor cantons, this was one of the few profitable enterprises available for bringing money into the area from the outside. But apart from the money to be made, the costs to be paid could be enormous. The Swiss were literally making blood money. The moral price was high. This price was the position that making war for money was appropriate, even though orthodox Christian theologians had long argued that warring for monetary gain was depraved. Further, the human cost could be high, with comparatively few of the young Swiss men returning to their villages if they were engaged in an unsuccessful war.

Zwingli attacked the mercenary trade. In 1510, he wrote a Latin poem, *The Ox*, that confronted this practice. In the poem, the ox represents Switzerland, which is strong, noble, and unpretentious. However, the ox is drawn into fights that are not even his own concern, until finally he is left alone, worse off than when he began. The allegory was not deep; anyone reading the poem got the point immediately. Zwingli was aligning himself with nationalistic Swiss interests. Zwingli was not a pacifist, as we will see. However, his protests can be seen as the beginning of one of his reforming efforts, and one that had no particular influence from Luther.

Later, Zwingli got a closer look at the Swiss mercenary trade. He accompanied a contingent from Glarus in a war of the pope against the French in 1513. As a priest, he preached on the duty of the Swiss to support the pope. But this particular campaign went very badly for the Swiss. The Swiss forces from the different cantons were divided in their allegiances, and some left before the crucial battle of Marignano on September 13–14, 1513. The Swiss were torn apart. G. R. Potter describes the reaction from Zwingli: "The young army chaplain came away with two convictions reinforced—the first, that mercenary service, the sale of flesh and blood for gold, was immoral; the second, that Swiss unity was an indispensable prerequisite for future achievement."[6]

Zwingli took up the crusade against the mercenary trade. This must be seen as his first reforming impulse, and it cannot be seen as influenced by Luther. Was this a reform of the church and Christian morals and life? In Switzerland it was. The pope was a frequent purchaser of Swiss mercenaries and frequently enlisted the help of his bishops, making the Roman Church a major player in the arms-for-hire trade that characterized the era.

In 1516, Zwingli became the *Leutpriester* at Einsiedeln. Basically, this means that Zwingli was not the parish priest but instead was responsible for the spiritual needs, especially the sacramental needs, of the local people and of the pilgrims that came to Einsiedeln. This arrangement is interesting because it illustrates some issues we examined in the chapter on late medieval Christianity. Though Zwingli was too far removed from Glarus to be of much help, living about fifteen miles away, he remained the parish priest there. To fulfill the duties at Glarus, he hired a "vicar," who was paid a portion of what Zwingli was being paid and who did the lion's share of the work while Zwingli was absent.

Pilgrims. Most people were attracted to Einsiedeln for its statue of Mary, the black virgin of Einsiedeln. This was a significant shrine site in that part of Switzerland, and for two years Zwingli directly witnessed the kinds of devotion that were offered to the statue. People believed that the statue contained healing powers. Zwingli's later attacks on religious images and on the superstitions that so frequently arose around such images came from this period of his ministry.

In his two years at Einsiedeln, Zwingli continued to preach and to study. His abilities in Greek and Hebrew reached such a stage that he felt able to enter the company of humanistic scholars, and his correspondence demonstrates that this confidence was not without a sturdy foundation. He became known as a preacher of particular skill, and it is likely that some of the humanists in the area heard him preach and considered him for a position in Zurich, the large city that dominated the region.

In October 1518, the post of *Leutpriester* for the Grossmünster in Zurich became vacant. The Grossmünster was one of the leading churches in Zurich. As Zurich was the principal city in the area, it was probably extremely attractive to Zwingli. He would have a good salary, and because excellent scholars made their homes in the city, his intellectual life might flourish. However, this was an elected position, and Zwingli was not the only candidate. At this point, Zwingli's participation in clerical concubinage became an issue. Scandalous charges were made that Zwingli had taken advantage of a young woman in Einsiedeln. While people might overlook a mature and ongoing relationship as unsanctioned "clerical marriage," the charges essentially made Zwingli out to be a rapist.

Zwingli's response gives a window into the way he conducted himself in times of struggle. Instead of making denials or evading the issue, he dealt with the matter directly. Zwingli candidly admitted that he had had a relationship with the woman. However, while he did not excuse his actions, Zwingli also clarified that the woman in question was the aggressor, that he had been involved with this woman who had had sexual relations with several men of Einsiedeln. Zwingli's candor and his courage seemed to put the issue aside. When his chief rival for the position, Lawrence Mor, turned out to have six children by his clerical marriage, the issue dissolved. In December 1518, Zwingli was elected preacher of the Grossmünster.

ZWINGLI AND ZURICH: 1519–1525

Zurich became the city most aligned with Zwingli, and the capital city of his reforming movement. When he arrived in 1518, Zurich was already leading the charge against the mercenary trade, and this may have had something to do with his election. In 1518, Zurich was both a city and a canton, a true city-state. The city held about 5,000 inhabitants, and the surrounding lands that were under the city's jurisdiction held approximately 50,000 more. The city was an industrial and trading center, with elected large and small councils. Significant power was in the hands of the twelve guilds. Guilds were the late medieval equivalent of labor unions, except that a guild possessed a strict and legally recognized monopoly. If you wanted to weave cloth in the canton of Zurich, you had to belong to the weaver's guild. Thus, considerable amounts of political power were in the hands of the lower classes, rather than being wholly concentrated in the nobility and clergy.[7]

On January 1, 1519, Zwingli announced that the next Sunday, he would begin preaching on the Gospel of Matthew, preaching directly through the text. This was a preaching revolution. For the medieval preacher, the texts for each day were set by long-standing tradition in a collection called the lectionary. The lectionary did not move directly through any book of the Bible in its entirety, and it left some portions of Scripture out. Zwingli was setting aside that tradition in order to take up a method that was much more concentrated upon understanding the text of Scripture, and in a form that laypeople would understand.

For Zurich, this was the first of Zwingli's reforms. Zwingli preached through whole books of the Bible. His inspiration came from John Chrysostom, the famous preacher of the fourth century, and his method of arriving at the simple meaning of the text was clearly dependent on Erasmus.[8] Zwingli later stated frequently that he had abandoned the human inventions that had dragged preaching down in order to preach the pure gospel of the Scriptures. This was one of the key changes that the Protestant reforms brought. There had been preaching in the medieval era, and some of the orders of friars were especially known for their preaching. But the concentration upon preaching, and biblical preaching at that, was new. For most Protestants, preaching became the central act of worship. Further, preaching was now understood to be some sort of explication of the text of Scripture, rather than simply a lesson on moral virtues or on the wonders of the indulgence that was currently being offered for sale. Zwingli's reform of preaching succeeded. In 1520, the city council ordered all preachers in Zurich to preach from the Bible without human additions and explanations.

Had Zwingli's preaching simply been biblically based, it would have been a reform, but its impact would have been gentle. However, Zwingli also pushed his audience to draw the comparisons that he already had made. Bruce Gordon writes:

> In his sermons he asked men and women to contrast the Christian Church in their own time with the teachings of the Gospel. The comparison was not favourable. He spoke of Christian freedom and his message fell on fertile soil; a clash between the hierarchical church and evangelical principles, which were interpreted by many as the rejection of feudal authority and a call for local autonomy.[9]

The people of Zurich were being moved toward reform by this preaching.

In 1522, the next signal event of the Swiss reform movement forced the people and council of Zurich to see that things had changed. The event occurred during Lent, the period of time leading up to the remembrance of the suffering and crucifixion of Jesus of Nazareth on Good Friday, and the celebration of his resurrection on Easter. By long tradition and canon law, the medieval Roman Church had demanded fasting as a proper preparation for this solemn time, and so believers were to avoid eating meat during Lent. Theologians and humanist scholars had for some time known that this was not the most ancient of traditions. Erasmus had poked fun at it by composing a dialogue titled "On the Eating of Fish." No matter what satirists might have been saying, however, the Lenten fast was widely observed and universally acknowledged.

On March 9, 1522, Zwingli and a small group of men were helping the printer Christoph Froschauer prepare an edition of Paul's Epistles. They were under some time pressure, as the book was being prepared for the Frankfurt book fair, which was not far off. After some time, Froschauer prepared a meal for those present, as the print shop and his home were in the same building. At the meal, Froschauer served sausage, and at least some of those present broke the Lenten fast. Zwingli himself did not eat the meat. It is unlikely that he avoided doing so for reasons of principle, but rather for the political necessity of maintaining church law. However, when the occurence came to light, Zwingli wasted little time in using it as an issue. Two weeks later, he preached a sermon on Christian freedom and how Christianity is not about what one does or does not eat. No matter what Zwingli said about his independence from Luther, his sermon makes some of the same theological moves that Luther's treatise on Christian freedom had made. Zwingli argued that only faith makes a person acceptable before God. A month after that, Froschauer printed the text of Zwingli's sermon. This event came to be known as the Affair of the Sausages, and for some it marks the beginning of the Swiss Reformation. When those who had eaten the meat were given very light punishments, some conservatives felt that things were getting out of hand. Further, the city council wrote the local bishop, the bishop of Constance, to ask whether fasting might not be part of necessary Christian piety.

To make matters even hotter, in July 1522 Zwingli requested the bishop's permission to get married. Actually, at some time that year, Zwingli had married a widow, Anna Reinhart. Zwingli attempted to keep the fact of the marriage a secret. However, as anyone even mildly famous knows, keeping a wedding a secret is next to impossible. Keeping such a secret in a town of only five thousand people would have been a miracle. Rumors flew that Zwingli had not made his request to the bishop as a single man.

This went too far for both the bishop and for the new pope, Adrian VI. The pope demanded that the out-of-hand priest be disciplined. However, the Zurich city council did not give in to the demands, but instead chose a different method for dealing with the issues at hand. The council voted to settle the disputed questions by having a debate, which it set for January 1523. This debate would be called the First Zurich Disputation.

By this time Zwingli was becoming powerful in Zurich. He was gathering around himself like-minded churchmen, so that the influence of his theological outlook was magnified. There were "Zwinglian" forces, rather than just one man. Further, the city council's decision raised several issues of interest. First, the council decided to settle the issue by use of an academic standard—the debate. Propositions for debate would be prepared, and the judges would decide on the basis of the responses they heard. Second, this was to be a decision made by laymen for laymen. The members of the council decided that they, rather than trained theologians or ordained clergy, were the proper arbitrators of what was good for the religious care of the people of their canton. Third, the city council meant the disputation to be as all-encompassing as possible, so it invited representatives from all over Switzerland. Fourth, the council set as ground rules two important points: the debate would be held in German, and only the Bible would be allowed as an authority. Any appeal to the tradition of the church that was unsupported by clear scriptural support would fail.

In a way, the very setup of the First Zurich Disputation demonstrated how far the reforming ideas had penetrated into the minds of the council. The debate would be ruled by the authority of Scripture, the language would be the language of the common people, and the arbitrators would be solid citizens of Zurich. Most of the Catholic figures recognized that as such, it would be impossible to compete in such an arena, and so they declined the invitation to participate. Even Johannes Fabri, the representative of the bishop of Constance, always made clear in his remarks that he was attending and speaking as an observer.

The agenda for the proceedings had been prepared by Zwingli and were set out as a set of articles for debate. Known as the Sixty-seven Articles, many of the items were very easily resolved once the central rule for the debate—that only Scripture would be authoritative—was accepted. Thus, for some observers at least, the disputation did not resemble a true contest but simply the acting out of a foregone conclusion. The Catholic position on the whole affair was that the council had no authority to speak about Christianity, as it was not properly called by duly ordained and consecrated members of the hierarchy of the church. Zwingli's answer was that the six hundred members attending the meeting were truly representative of the true spiritual church not because of ordination, but because of their submission to the authority of the Holy Spirit speaking through the Scriptures.[10]

Zwingli won.[11] As it had in 1520, the council again required preachers to preach only from Scripture. No charges against Zwingli were accepted. However, the council did not make further changes. The allowance for married clergy was not made explicit. The role of images in worship and in church buildings was not rejected. The council may have set out for a certain goal, but that goal was not reached, and in a way this "half decision" led directly to further events.

Three areas that the Zurich disputation had not clarified subsequently came to the foreground. First, and as a result of the demand for biblical preaching, iconoclasm broke out. In technical religious terminology, an icon is a particular representation of Christ, or Mary, or one of the saints, executed in a particular repeated fashion. However, the term *icon* historically meant "image," and it referred to any kind of image of Christ, God, Mary, or the saints. The Christian church, while accepting the authority of the Ten Commandments and its prohibition of "graven images," had clashed over the validity of such representations in worship and in worship spaces in the eighth and ninth centuries. Iconoclasts were those who rejected images as inherently flawed, as superstitious and idolatrous and a violation of the commandments. Iconophiles were those who believed that the veneration given to the images was a healthy part of true Christian piety. Iconoclasm refers to the breaking or taking away of religious images from public spaces and worship spaces.[12]

But why was this a result of biblical preaching? As Potter points out, it is all well and good when one demands that all preach from the Scriptures. But problems arise. First, what about those priests who had this responsibility, but not the competency to do so? Zwingli could read Greek, Hebrew, and Latin, and he was quickly becoming acknowledged as one of the foremost scholars of Switzerland. However, many of the priests could barely read Latin, and some could not read it at all. A full version of the Bible in Swiss German was not available until 1529.

Another problem was that Zwingli, like the young Luther, assumed that anyone who read the Scriptures would reach the same conclusions that he did. This is a remarkable phenomenon, widely seen in the first two generations of the Reformation: Protestant thinkers believed that setting Scripture before believers would result in a dependable set of good results. Some of those who were reading the Scriptures and had accepted Zwingli's scriptural principle were pushing the pace of reform. The commandment states, "You shall not make for yourself an idol, whether in the form of anything that is in heaven above; or that is on the earth beneath, or that is in the water under the earth. You shall not bow down to them or worship them; for I the LORD your God am a jealous God, punishing children for the iniquity of the parents, to the third and fourth generation of those who reject me, but showing steadfast love to the thousandth generation of those who love me and keep my commandments" (Exod. 20:4–6). Clearly, the making of religious imagery was prohibited. Why would anyone wait to cleanse the churches? Iconoclastic events began to break out throughout the canton of Zurich.[13]

Two further issues were in the air. Clerical marriage continued to be the object of debate and of scandalous rumor. As well, the marks of Catholic Christianity remained in Zurich. The various orders of monks and friars were still there. Worship was still basically being conducted in the same way. Though Zwingli had clearly argued that hierarchical authority at most was attached to biblical authority rather than being a source of authority in itself, the Zurich church people were still apparently obedient to the bishop of Constance. There was a basic disconnection between some of what Zwingli and other preachers had taught, and what was still going on as business as usual.

Spurred especially by the iconoclastic outbreaks, the Zurich council called for another debate, which it set for late October 1523. This was the Second Zurich Disputation. Again, Zwingli won. The council decided to remove the images from churches, to suppress the Mass, and to close most of the monasteries. These decisions were not immediately put into effect but were accomplished throughout 1524 and 1525. The Second Zurich Disputation had even more people in attendance, but its makeup was different from that of the first. Very few Catholics chose to come, so Zwingli and his supporters had very little traditional opposition. However, with the 20/20 hindsight that our vantage point allows, we can see that another form of opposition arose that was in its own way more challenging. Instead of being disputed by supporters of the traditional ways, Zwingli was occasionally confronted by elements who wished to move faster in reform, who wished to be more radical in their acceptance of the testimony of Scripture and the rejection of human customs. Just as Karlstadt in Wittenberg proved to be difficult for Luther, these more radical reformers proved to be a tremendous test for Zwingli and the cause of reform in Zurich.

ZWINGLI AND RADICAL REFORM

A long book could be written about the effect of "disciples gone bad" in the Reformation. Time and again, influential thinkers gained dedicated followers who then were so inspired that they went beyond the master. These are not accounts of academic jealousy, but rather of the disciples choosing to do things they sincerely believed were demanded by the principles that they had learned, while the masters believed that the actions in question were wrongheaded. This clearly was the case for Luther with Karlstadt and with the Peasants' War, and it would remain the case for Zwingli and the Radicals.[14]

One of those present at the Second Zurich Disputation was Conrad Grebel (c. 1498–1526). Grebel was well educated, though he had never finished his degrees. He was from a wealthy family and had all the privileges that wealth afforded. He had studied his early Latin in the school attached to the Grossmünster, and had studied at the University of Basel, the University of Vienna, and the University of Paris. He was drawn to the teaching and reforming work of Zwingli when he returned to Zurich around 1521. By this time, Zwingli had organized a group of people to study the Scriptures, called the *Prophezei*. Grebel was an enthusiastic participant.

Around the beginning of 1522, Grebel experienced a religious conversion. Though he had always been Christian, he now devoted himself entirely to the cause of Christ. This was something of a contrast to his wilder student days. As a student with an excellent education, Grebel was able to see for himself what Zwingli was taking from the Scriptures and to consider the possibilities of alternate interpretations. This came to a head at the Second Disputation. Grebel there argued for the immediate suppression of the celebration of the Mass; he wished the council to force the pace of change. Zwingli originally supported the elimination of the Mass but saw that the council was not prepared to go so far so quickly, so he compromised. This was the beginning of the breach.

Grebel continued his more activist course. He and a friend, Felix Manz (c. 1498–1527), continued to meet after the Second Zurich Disputation and persisted in considering ways to proceed on what they believed was the true course of evangelical reform. In 1524, Grebel wrote letters to both Andreas Bodenstein von Karlstadt and Thomas Müntzer, who were famously pushing the pace of reform. Finally, Grebel, Manz, and another sympathetic believer, George Blaurock (1491–1529), found an issue upon which to force things into the open. They openly questioned the validity of the baptism of infants.

Infant baptism is the practice of baptizing children, even newborns as young as a few days old. On both the grounds of ancient tradition and the grounds of Scripture, infant baptism is not explicitly supported. Nowhere in the New Testament does Jesus or John the Baptist or one of the apostles explicitly baptize a child. The best support for infant baptism in the New Testament is the story in Acts 10 of the baptism of Cornelius, who was baptized along with his relatives and friends. If one assumes that among his relatives there were children, then one can conclude that the apostle Peter supported the baptism of children. But that case rests on an assumption.

Further, the most ancient traditions of the church did not support infant baptism. For most Christians in the earliest centuries of the Christian era, baptism followed upon a statement of belief and after a long period of learning the basics of the Christian faith. This period of learning was a believer's period of catechesis, when he or she would learn the faith from a priest, bishop, or elder. Only after that time was the believer baptized, and only after baptism was the believer allowed into the "mysteries" of the Christian faith. This meant that only baptized members of the church were allowed to see a baptism, or the eucharistic celebration.

Despite this lack of explicit support for infant baptism in the early tradition and in the New Testament, infant baptism had become central in the medieval church and in society. Official church doctrine in medieval times stated that unbaptized infants could not go to heaven. The frequency of infant mortality in the medieval period intensified the worry about the souls of such children. This intense concern probably contributed to the doctrine of who could baptize. In point of fact, *anyone* who wished to baptize a person could do so. For instance, if a midwife delivered a baby and, fearing for its survival, quickly baptized it in the name of the Father, Son, and Holy Spirit, that baby was truly baptized in the eyes of the Roman Church.

Moreover, baptism mattered in society. Christendom was a popular piece of mental furniture, part of the common worldview. Nowhere is this more clearly seen than in the oddity, to the modern mind, that birth records did not always exist in the early modern period. Towns kept baptism records, not birth records. People might or might not know their date of birth, but they were much more likely to know their baptismal date. Baptism was not only the entry into the church, but it was also the entry into the well-ordered society. When Grebel, Manz, and Blaurock started suggesting that there was no support for infant baptism in Scripture, and that Zwingli's scriptural principle demanded that such a practice be rejected, they were playing with fire. Moreover, they were explicitly denying the model of the relationship of church and state. Tradition held that one was a member of both the church and the city-state. These radicals began to suggest that the true church was only a small portion of the society and was actually held apart from the rest of the society. This was too much to bear for the leaders of Zurich.

Baptism mattered to Zurich. Another disputation was held on January 17, 1525. Zwingli led those who supported the practice of infant baptism, while Grebel directed the adult baptism side. Again, Zwingli won. The city council supported infant baptism and decreed that any unbaptized infants should be brought for baptism within eight days. For many, this was another instance of a foregone conclusion, as Zwingli was aligning himself closely with the views of the council. However, Zwingli's victory was not the end of the story. On January 21, a group met in the home of Felix Manz. George Blaurock asked Grebel to baptize him, after which he baptized the others who were present. This adult baptism was seen by Grebel's group as the only genuine baptism. It was viewed by the more traditional parties, both Protestant and Catholic, as a rebaptism. As such, the group received a name it would thereafter always deny—the Anabaptists.[15]

The Zurich city council, frequently so cautious to act, moved with vigor against this offense. In March, the council declared that adult baptism was a capital offense. The Zurich leadership reflected only a small part of the horror that would be shared by rulers and church leaders across Europe at the specter of rebaptism. Only four years after adult baptism became a crime in Zurich, both Protestants and Catholics, meeting at the Diet of Speyer in 1529, agreed that the appropriate punishment for adult baptism was death. Scholars estimate that between 850 and 5,000 people were executed for adult baptism in the years between 1525 and 1618.[16]

Though Zwingli strongly denied the validity of the claims of the Radicals or Anabaptists, his critics, both Catholic and Protestant, believed that there was something within his thought that supported the Anabaptist position. In turn, Zwingli wrote four different treatises on infant baptism, upholding the traditional practice and attacking adult baptism. His solution to the biblical problem was to make baptism the New Testament and Christian equivalent of circumcision for the ancient Hebrews in the Old Testament. In that way, just as circumcision was done eight days after birth as a mark of God's covenant with the people, so too baptism was done in infancy as a mark of God's enduring covenant with Christians. The child's passive nature in the sacrament was not a deficiency, but rather a reminder that it was God who reached out to humans in baptism, drawing them to himself.

With the city council firmly behind him in the matter of adult baptism, Zwingli was unwilling to compromise on the question. The radicals who had arisen in Zurich fled. Manz and Grebel were captured and imprisoned in Zurich but managed to escape. Manz was caught again and executed in January 1527. The method chosen was especially selected for the Anabaptists: he was drowned, in a mockery of his adult baptism beliefs.

THE GROWTH OF ZWINGLIANISM IN SWITZERLAND

Zwingli's ideas and impact were being felt across Switzerland. In some cantons, Zwinglianism flourished, in others it floundered. Zwingli himself was frequently the lightning rod that caused as much furor as fervor; he was a polarizing figure whose impact is still being measured.[17] Moreover, the impact of the ever easier access to evangelical books was being felt across Switzerland. In 1518, Luther's works were already being published in Basel. While this collection did not contain his treatises of 1520, the text did put in people's hands the work of the most famous, or infamous, theologian of the moment.

Bruce Gordon has drawn some observations that are especially cogent for our grasp of the spread of evangelicalism in Switzerland, outside of Zurich:

The evangelical party was always a minority movement; in every case its success was dependent on winning over the magistrates, who would then impose the new religion. Apart from a brief flirtation during the Peasants' War, the reform movement was neither broad-based nor popular, and the reformers did not ever wish it to be. The evangelical movement spread in the Swiss lands through small networks of friends, most of humanist disposition, who saw themselves as a fraternity committed to the reform of religion and society. Zwingli stood at the centre of this web of contacts and all the key figures were at some point in contact with him. . . . The most significant point of contact for the future reformers, however, lay within the Confederation, and that was the relatively new university in Basle. Although such distinguished scholars such as Ulrich Surgant and Thomas Wittenbach were to be found in Basle, it was not so much what was taught at the university but rather the presence of the printing industry and, more importantly, of Erasmus and his circle which made Basle so influential.[18]

The contact of friendship between committed men made the difference in Switzerland. It caused them to take on frequently violent adversaries and persevere. Supported by friendship and scholarship, the evangelical movement remade the map of Switzerland.

Yet the story of evangelical reform in Switzerland is not one of triumph after triumph. Catholic opposition rose up in Switzerland. As a confederation of cantons, each with its own sense of its own rights and prerogatives, Switzerland was ripe for a division between Protestant and Catholic cantons. In May 1526, a Catholic conference was held in Baden. This was just as much a rigged disputation as those held in Zurich, for each session was begun with a celebration of the Mass, and evangelical preaching was banned. Only Johannes Oecolampadius (1482–1531), a humanistically oriented supporter of the Zwinglian reforms, chose to believe the offers of safe conduct, and he was overmatched by Johann Eck and Thomas Murner. The majority of cantons represented declared certain theological positions, known to be held by Zwingli, as heretical.

In 1526, the city of Saint-Gall voted to join Zurich in accepting the new order of worship. In 1527, another key moment occurred when the municipal elections in Bern brought officials sympathetic to the cause of reform into power. Though the new members of the town government did not immediately institute the evangelical cause, they did arrange for another theological debate. While the conference in Baden had been disastrous for the evangelical cause, the Bern Disputation of January 1528 was a key victory. Several reform-minded theologians attended, including Zwingli and Oecolampadius. The result was an overwhelming vote of support for the evangelical cause. Philip Benedict describes the meeting and its immediate aftermath:

> The city fathers outlawed the mass and ordered all images removed
> from its churches. . . . Two days of iconoclasm followed during which
> children sang triumphantly, "We have been freed from a baked
> God"—a mocking reference to the host—while Zwingli exhorted the
> iconoclasts from the pulpit of the ransacked Minster, "Let us clear out
> this filth and rubbish!"[19]

Bern was clearly and tumultuously in the evangelical camp. This was a crucial
development because it kept Zurich from being alone in its devotion to
reform.

The changes kept coming. In 1529, iconoclastic riots hit Basel. The city
council resigned, and a new regime, favorable to the new reforms, was elected.
Johannes Oecolampadius led the religious reform and even went further than
Zwingli in advocating that certain rights should be reserved to the church,
apart from the city council. In Schaffhausen, the people spoke up against the
city council, which was attempting to block the religious reforms. This reform
was strengthened by the leadership of Sebastian Hofmeister, a Paris-trained
Franciscan. By 1530, four of the urban cantons had declared for the new evangelical faith. Zurich, Bern, Basel, and Schaffhausen were settled in the reform
party, which also included several of the rural areas and the town of Saint-
Gall.[20] The movement was not confined to Switzerland but also crossed into
southern Germany. There were Zwinglian movements in the towns of Ulm,
Strasbourg, Augsburg, Frankfurt, and Constance.

The anti-Zwingli party also was growing in numbers and strength. Some
of this rejection of the new church reforms had very little to do with religion.
Some of the cantons had been resisting Zurich's power since late in the
fifteenth century and were not about to help it become stronger now. As
well, Zwingli was a polarizing figure. Zwingli seems to have been the kind of
person that other people either love or hate. Some of the other cantons did
not want the radical church leader to have the same effect in their home cantons that he had had in Zurich. In 1523, Zwingli's portrait was burned in the
streets of Lucerne.

If some of the rejection of the reforms were rejections of Zurich's growing
power, at least some of the opposition to the types of reforms that Zwingli had
successfully put in place in Zurich was basic rejection of his doctrines and reaf-
firmation of traditional Catholicism. The Catholic cantons of Lucerne, Zug,
Uri, Schwyz, and Unterwalden came together as early as 1524 to consult
together on how best to ward off the new heresy. The Baden Disputation must
be seen as part of that effort. Laws were enacted against evangelical-style
preaching, and in Fribourg in 1527, a law was passed requiring the citizens to
swear allegiance to the Church of Rome.[21] By the late 1520s, Switzerland was
clearly divided by the religious issue.

ZWINGLI'S LATER MINISTRY: 1525–1531

It is against this increasingly fragmented political and religious situation that the final six years of Zwingli's life and ministry must be considered. This is the period of some of Zwingli's most notable triumphs, but also of some of the most damning political failures for the young Protestant cause. The failure to reach a compromise on the Eucharist at Marburg, and the death of Zwingli on the battlefield at Kappel, demonstrated clearly the fragile nature of the institutional reforms.

Zwingli's position in Zurich following 1525 could not have been much stronger. He continued the work of reforming worship in the city and its rural parishes. His marriage to Anna was now open. His position on the rejection of the baptism of adults was swiftly approved by the council, and he was the accuser in the court cases against some of his radical opponents.

However, Zwingli was frequently linked to the Radical Reformers, including those who had taken part in the Peasants' War of 1524–1525. Zwingli's very success in promoting the evangelical reforms caused his Catholic opponents to take him more seriously. The Baden Disputation in 1526, which Zwingli did not dare to attend, was a personal disappointment. The forces against him were gathering themselves together into a coherent league, formed for the purpose of stopping what Zwingli saw as the cause of God.

Into this situation stepped a German prince, Philip, Landgrave of Hesse (1504–1567). Melanchthon had converted Philip to Lutheranism in 1524, and Philip took very seriously his responsibilities toward the transmission of true religion. He was a "Christian" prince. Marburg was a leading city in his realm, and in 1527 he founded a university there. At least part of the purpose of the new university was the training of Protestant theologians. Philip was brilliant, both tactically and theologically, and was able to see the danger to both Lutheran and Zwinglian reforms if the various factions among Protestantism could not cooperate.

Convinced of the need for military and political cooperation, Philip sought to found such cooperation on doctrinal compromise. Thus, in 1529, Philip called the Colloquy of Marburg. Whereas the Diet of Speyer earlier that year had been decidedly anti-Protestant, Philip was attempting to strengthen the position of the various Protestant bodies by coming together to hammer out doctrinal language on various matters on which the Swiss and Germans differed. Essentially, the parties were attempting to write a common confession of faith. This agreement could then be used to leverage the possibility of greater collaboration in politics and defense.

The Colloquy of Marburg met from October 1 to 4, 1529. The leading voices from both the Swiss and German sides were there. Luther and

Melanchthon represented the Lutheran position, and Zwingli, Oecolampadius, and Martin Bucer spoke for the Swiss position. Luther drew up fifteen
propositions for discussion and debate. The parties were able to come to significant agreement on fourteen, but the final proposition, on the meaning of
the presence of Christ in the Eucharist, proved insurmountable. Luther would
later take these fifteen articles and expand them into the first Lutheran confession of faith, called the Schwabach Articles.

What was the problem? As we saw in the last chapter, Luther believed that
in the sacrament of the Lord's Supper, the body and blood of Christ were really
and actually and locally present. Thus, he argued that the body and blood were
on the plate and in the cup—in, with, and under the bread and wine. Luther
accepted very literally Jesus' words from Matthew's Gospel (26:26) that this
was the body and blood of Jesus. Though he argued against Rome's insistence
on transubstantiation, Luther never questioned the literal character of these
words from Scripture.

Zwingli took a different path. His first difference from Luther was biblical.
Zwingli realized that frequently Jesus spoke forcefully through metaphors.
So he argued that Jesus' words in Matthew should be taken figuratively
rather than literally. Second, Zwingli took very seriously Jesus' command
to the disciples from Luke 22:19 and 1 Corinthians 11:24–25 that the meal
was to be taken in remembrance of Jesus. In Zwingli's theology, the Eucharist became a memorial meal and a celebration of the grace Christ gave believers. This solution resolved any tension between the idea of a real and local
presence and the fact that the bread and wine seemed very simply to remain
bread and wine. Zwingli argued that to take a position such as consubstantiation or transubstantiation was to confuse the symbol of a thing with the
thing itself.

Luther was outraged. He attacked Zwingli repeatedly and finally simply
held his ground by sitting at the table in the colloquy and writing "Hoc est
corpus meum," Latin for "This is my body," on the table. The Zwinglians and
Lutherans could not find suitable language or suitable theology to bridge their
differences, and the effort at a Protestant league that would stand on a united
theological footing to provide a union of political and military might failed.

Zwingli's life would never again be peaceful. The struggles between the
Catholic and Reformed cantons became ever more harsh. Zwingli himself was
challenged by Catholics, Lutherans, and Radicals. Added to this was his place
in creating a new reality, the Reformed Church. For Zwingli's ideal of a church
to be effective, greater literacy and especially greater biblical literacy was necessary. As well, he recognized that he could not carry the whole reforming
movement by himself, so he was constantly in conversation with other Swiss
leaders of the reform.

In 1523, the city council of Zurich put Zwingli in charge of a new theological school. This was a necessity for the Reformed program, as it needed both educated laity and educated preachers to teach the Scriptures. Zwingli believed that a grounding in the languages of the Bible would allow pastors to have the right understanding of Scripture and would keep them from falling into the heresies of factions like the Anabaptists.[22] In 1525, Zwingli opened his school in Zurich, calling it the *Prophezei*. This name was a biblical allusion to 1 Corinthians 14, in which Paul directs the prophets to learn from each other. The *Prophezei* was open to all at no cost and met daily. It consisted of a reading of Scripture in the Latin Vulgate, then in Hebrew or Greek with translation back into Latin so as to facilitate learning and to demonstrate the shortcomings of the Vulgate, as well as a German sermon, which gathered together the lesson, especially for those who had no knowledge of the other languages. Throughout, the participants could engage the material in discussion. It may not have been a fully workable program of biblical education, but it was far more than had previously been available.

Zurich's religious power grew. Various other cantons followed the leadership of Zurich, with their own leaders taking up the cause of reform. Inevitably, this caused even greater backlash among those cantons that remained adherents of the Chuch of Rome. Finally, the conflicting views moved from a war of words to actual battles. In 1529, the evangelical preacher Jacob Kaiser was burned at the stake by the Schwyz authorities for preaching in Catholic country.

The reformed cantons threw together a military expedition, which forced the acceptance of the First Peace of Kappel in 1529. The principle of allowing cantons to hold the religion they chose was affirmed, and Zwingli seemed triumphant. However, in 1531, the Second War of Kappel broke out over an economic blockade of Catholic cantons that Zurich had conceived. This time the forces of Zurich were ill prepared. Zwingli accompanied the force, which was demolished on October 11. Zwingli was killed, drawn and quartered, and burned. His ashes were mixed with dung to prevent his followers from turning them into relics. This last image gives us a picture of how badly and ironically the two sides misunderstood each other. Zwingli desperately wanted to get rid of all relics, and his opponents made sure that he himself would not become one.

ZWINGLI'S THEOLOGY

As with Luther, it is valuable to set forth, briefly, a summary of Huldrych Zwingli's theology. One must begin with his norm for theology—the principle of Scripture. This for Zwingli was the basis for all church and proper societal life. He was unwilling to go beyond such a theory, and this sometimes led him to take inflexible positions. On the other hand, he was not a theologian who believed in the guaranteed sanctity of the Scriptures, but rather put his trust in the Holy Spirit, who was the inspiring agent behind the Scriptures.

Zwingli's first reform was the concentration upon Scripture. From 1516 on, he devoted himself to the study of Scripture in its original languages. His emphasis on Scripture changed the way that he preached, caused him to reevaluate the authority of the hierarchy, and led him to support the iconoclastic theory, if not always the particular practices of the iconoclasts. Zwingli applauded Luther precisely where he thought that Luther was following Scripture and for the bravery that Luther showed in not caring for the consequences of his actions. Yet Zwingli was different from Luther in an important way. For Luther, Scripture alone (*sola scriptura*) and faith alone (*sola fide*) went hand in hand. For Zwingli, Scripture alone took priority, and this prepared the way for a very different-looking reformation.

As noted, Zwingli depended upon the word of Scripture, but more upon the Spirit. In fact, he made a distinction between the "outer Word," which was Scripture heard without the Spirit, and the "inner Word," which was Scripture heard under the leading of the Spirit.[23] Thus, an atheist who read the Old and New Testaments would not truly be reading the Word of God, but simply a dead letter that held no life. That is not to say, however, that Zwingli divorced the Word from the Spirit. That is exactly the charge Luther brought against him, but Zwingli denied it, both as an argument and in practice. Zwingli believed that the interpreter needed to be directly taught by God but that the Spirit would never contradict Holy Scripture. Thus, part of the difficulty of deciding whether an interpretation was true was how closely it held to the whole of Scripture.

Zwingli's concentration upon the Word and Spirit also affected his doctrine of the church, his ecclesiology. By the late 1520s, Zwingli was faced with carving out a middle position between the Church of Rome on one hand and the Anabaptists on the other. While facing Rome, Zwingli denied the institutional character of the church, arguing that the necessity for the true church was being led by the risen Christ. His doctrine of Word and Spirit supported this: the church is not only the possessor of the dead and empty Word but also is that society of people who accept that Word, who live under the Spirit of Christ and so hear and obey the genuine Word.[24]

On the other hand, Zwingli also had to face the challenge from the Anabaptists. Their concentration upon adult baptism had led them to see the true church as a small society, composed of those who made the faithful decision against the majority and were set apart. Against them, Zwingli held on to the theory of the church body as encompassing all of the people. The Spirit moves among all the people, and all must be part of the testing to see whether the spirits are truly of God. Otherwise, Zwingli believed that so many small factions would grow up that it would be impossible for many people to find the true church.

Zwingli continued to emphasize the primary place of Scripture in the church when he turned to the topic of Christian worship. Images were to be removed as a violation of the second commandment. Further, images drew people's attention away from the preaching of the Word of God. The centerpiece of worship for Zurich was preaching. This took the form of explanations of passages from Scripture, so that the Word was always central to worship. Likewise, Zwingli argued that since Scripture did not demonstrate clearly that music and instruments should be part of Christian worship, churches should be cleansed of instruments, especially organs. This was extraordinary, not only for the break with tradition but also because Zwingli himself was a talented musician.

Zwingli's reform of Christian worship continued with the sacraments. Like the later Luther, Zwingli believed that only two sacraments actually had biblical support. His fight against the Anabaptists and his later struggles with Lutherans caused him to elaborate his positions on these two sacraments in such a way that Zwinglianism was frequently linked to certain concepts about the sacraments. Gregory Miller's caution about Zwingli's sacramental doctrines is worth noting:

> In his [Zwingli's] treatment of sacrament, a dichotomy between inward and outward is evident. He rejected the view that what is done outwardly in the sacrament causes inward change. A sacrament does not make present what it signifies, but it shows and attests that what it signifies is there. It is the sign of a grace that has been given, but not the instrument of that grace.[25]

Zwingli did not believe that sacraments actually changed things in the soul or the spirit of the person involved in the sacrament. Rather, they were signposts that reminded the viewer that grace was given. Thus, sacraments for Zwingli, to use a crude illustration, are like the road sign "BUMP." The sign is not the actual bump, nor is the bump in the road because the sign was placed in that location. Rather, the sign points out the reality so that the driver will be prepared for it.

Baptism's meaning evolved in Zwingli's thought in response to the Anabaptist threat. He believed that faith followed an order set down by God, in which faith as a gift from God is an effect of God's election of a person. Anabaptists reversed this order by requiring faith prior to being able to be elected by God. Instead, Zwingli argued that the unity of the Old and New Testaments in one covenantal promise to the people of God signified that the promises given in circumcision to the young in the Old Testament now should be attached to the young who receive the sacrament of baptism. The sacrament did not actually create this reality, but pointed to it.

Zwingli's theology of the Lord's Supper is frequently at the center of arguments about his impact. For many scholars of the Reformation, this is the whole story of Zwingli, that he provided another manner of considering Christ's presence in the Eucharist. Zwingli's contribution to the issue of the presence of Christ in the Supper was simple yet desperately profound. He realized in his study of Scripture that "is" does not always mean the same thing. At times in the Gospel accounts, Jesus clearly says "I am" in such a way that it must be taken figuratively, or metaphorically. If readers can see the metaphors in such places, reasoned Zwingli, why is it not possible to see the statement "This is my body" as a metaphor?

In place of the elemental realism of transubstantiation, the Roman position, and consubstantiation, the Lutheran position, Zwingli substituted the memorial character of the Supper. In doing so, his biblical support was clear. Jesus had said to his disciples that they were to break the bread in remembrance of him (Luke 22:19; 1 Cor. 11:24–26). Both Luke's account and that of Paul to the church at Corinth emphasize that the meal shared has a basic function of memorialization. The advantage Zwingli gained from such a theological position was that he no longer had any reason to be caught up in figuring out the method by which the physical presence of the body of Christ was imparted in the sacrament. The burden of such a position was that his critics, both Protestant and Catholic, said that he had emptied the sacrament of its genuine character, making it into an empty ritual.

Another important element of Zwingli's theology was his insistence on the place of the state in the affairs of the church. The preceding statement is anachronistic; the concept of the state in the sixteenth century is not what modern readers would recognize. But Zwingli supported the power of the state in the affairs of the church both theoretically and practically. In theory, that meant that the city council had powers to order the ministers of the church, so long as they did not deny the commandments of God. In practice, Zwingli always sought to work with the council, persuading it of the rightness of his views and accepting the pace of reform it set out.

For Zwingli, God was actively engaged in the whole of the human project. Both civil society and the church were being reformed. Therefore, both the magistrate as the agent of the society and the minister as the agent of the church had their particular God-given roles in God's plan. Magistrates, in forming good laws and in keeping people within the bounds of human righteousness, serve an important function in God's plan for the society. This close relationship between minister and magistrate cannot hide the fact that in many ways, Zwingli subordinated the authority of the church in human affairs to that of the magistrate.

SWISS REFORM AFTER ZWINGLI

The Reformed movement in Switzerland did not die with Zwingli. He was ably replaced in Zurich by Heinrich Bullinger. If not so charismatic as Zwingli, Bullinger was also not such a lightning rod. Bullinger was able to patch up differences between Zurich and Bern and was later able to bridge the sacramental differences between Zwinglian ideas and those of the reformer of French Switzerland, John Calvin. In 1549, Bullinger brought Calvin together with other church leaders to hammer out a compromise agreement on the meaning of the Lord's Supper, which was called the Consensus Tigurinus. This agreement on the Lord's Supper among the German and French Swiss gave some stability to the faith, while driving a wedge between the Reformed and Lutheran Protestants. Frequently, historians underestimate Bullinger's impact on Swiss Protestantism.[26] It was Bullinger who made firm Zurich's stance on Zwingli's legacy and who would write the history of reform. Bullinger served as the leading pastor in Zurich from 1531 until his death in 1575, creating in his own ministry a Reformed "tradition" that would stand the test of time.

Still, if Bullinger was the nurturer of the Swiss Reformation, and especially the German Swiss Reformation, Zwingli's impact on Swiss reform cannot be overestimated. Bruce Gordon writes:

> The Swiss Reformation occurred because of Huldrych Zwingli. He brought about a theological revolution by creating a distinctive understanding of God, the church, and humanity which contrasted sharply with late medieval Catholicism. . . . Zwingli's intense study of scripture and the Church Fathers were realised in his daily activities as a preacher; almost all of his central ideas evolved out of the endless conflicts in which he became entagled. He was a charismatic figure who could lead, and who attracted followers, but most of his time between 1519 and 1531 was spent fighting the fires kindled by his own words.
>
> If Luther's life gave the Wittenberg reformer a profound understanding of the torments of the spirit, and Calvin the Frenchman in Geneva knew what it meant to be a refugee, Zwingli was driven by a visceral hatred of human corruption and impurity. He was repelled by what he saw in the world: bribes, prostitution, poverty, and injustice. Most offensive, for Zwingli, was the grotesque manner in which the church seemed to connive in this despoiling of God's creation.[27]

In Zwingli, the Swiss found a reformer who would lead where he believed Scripture led. The place of Scripture in the church was set forth as a strong wall against any human innovations. Further, the pattern was set in the Swiss Reformation of the cooperation of the clergy with elected government officials, rather than princes. Finally, the theology of Zwingli and the Swiss, whether or not it can be convicted of starting the Anabaptist movement, certainly was always linked to it. Bullinger was always more willing to attack Anabaptists with greater vigor than other opponents. This link of the Zurich theology with Anabaptist and Radical thought was inescapable. With that, we turn to a more detailed look at the Radical Reformation.

QUESTIONS FOR DISCUSSION

1. How was Huldrych Zwingli different from Martin Luther in training and personality. How might this have been reflected in their different reforms?
2. How did nationalism function in Zwingli's reforms? Should national pride have a place in religious issues?
3. The Swiss Reformation was voted upon by the laity, by members of town councils. Should the laity decide matters of Christian faith and practice? What are the strengths and weaknesses of this position?
4. Zwingli struggled against the Anabaptists. Can church movements control their own direction, or must they accept the ideas that arise?

SUGGESTED FURTHER READING

Primary Readings

Bullinger, Heinrich, and Huldrych Zwingli. *Zwingli and Bullinger*. Edited by Geoffrey Bromiley. Library of Christian Classics. Philadelphia: Westminster Press, 1953.

Zwingli, Huldrych. *Commentary on True and False Religion*. Durham, NC: Labyrinth Press, 1981.

———. *Huldrych Zwingli: Writings*. Vol. 1, *The Defense of the Reformed Faith*. Edited by E. J. Furcha. Pittsburgh: Pickwick Publications, 1984.

———. *Ulrich Zwingli: Early Writings*. Edited by Samuel Macauley Jackson. Eugene, OR: Wipf & Stock, 2000.

Secondary Readings

Gabler, Ulrich. *Huldrych Zwingli: His Life and Work*. Translated by Ruth Gritsch. Edinburgh: T&T Clark, 1999.

Gordon, Bruce. *The Swiss Reformation*. Manchester: Manchester University Press, 2002.

Miller, Gregory J. "Huldrych Zwingli (1484–1531)." In *The Reformation Theologians: An Introduction to the Theology of the Early Modern Period*, edited by Carter Lindberg, 157–69. Malden, MA: Blackwell Publishers, 2002.

Ozment, Steven. *The Age of Reform, 1250–1550: An Intellectual and Religious History of Late Medieval and Reformation Europe*. New Haven, CT: Yale University Press, 1981.

Potter, George R. *Zwingli*. Cambridge: Cambridge University Press, 1976.

Stephens, W. P. *The Theology of Huldrych Zwingli*. Oxford: Oxford University Press, 1988.

Wandel, Lee Palmer. *Voracious Idols and Violent Hands: Iconoclasm in Reformation Zurich, Strasbourg, and Basel*. Cambridge: Cambridge University Press, 1994.

DOCTRINAL-VOCABULARY DISCUSSION

Sola Scriptura, Sola Gratia, Sola Fide

Three *sola* slogans dominated Protestant thought in the sixteenth century. *Sola* means "solely," or "wholly." So the three slogans can be translated as "solely by Scripture," "solely by grace," and "solely by faith." But the translations do not yet explain what the catchphrases meant. Further, not all Protestants agreed on what these encompassed.

Sola scriptura meant solely by scripture. The Reformers were basically arguing that the whole of the Christian message and discipline of the church could only be based on Scripture rather than on both Scripture and the human traditions that had grown up over the history of the church. Therefore, when arguing about the right thing to do or believe, Scripture would be the source and battlefield, rather than the statements of long-dead theologians or bishops. Scripture supplied the sole source of authority. The Roman Church felt so strongly that this belief was incorrect that it defined the two sources of authority for Catholicism as Scripture and tradition at the Council of Trent, held in the middle of the sixteenth century.

Sola gratia meant solely by grace. This motto had to do with salvation. When Lutheran or Reformed or Radical theologians stated that salvation was wholly a gracious event, they meant that God saved people wholly as a gift. *Gratia* has the same Latin root as *gratis*, meaning "free." For these theologians, God's action of moving in mercy toward the salvation of any particular person was motivated wholly by God's goodness and mercy, not by anything that the person was or had done. Catholics argued that God was wholly merciful but that humans should do—and in fact had to do—what they could so as to prepare themselves for this grace. Protestant reformers argued back that if one had to do something for grace, then obviously it was not free.

Sola fide meant solely by faith. This saying also was about salvation, or more precisely, justification. Following the reasoning of the apostle Paul in the fourth chapter of Romans, many Protestant theologians argued that the only requirement for being righteous with God was having faith. Roman theologians argued that this was a new innovation, and that no one in the previous history of Christian thought had believed that justification was so easy. Strangely, this immediately raised the issue of what "faith" was. Some Catholic theologians defined faith in such a way as to include the actions of love, making faith more active than some Protestant theologians would allow. Further, Anabaptist theologians argued that faith without works was dead, so works of the believers were required to demonstrate the character of the faith that they held.

Sola scriptura, sola gratia, sola fide. In each case, a whole theological argument, or even a set of arguments, was tied up in two words. Further, the slogans were mutually interlocking—the sole authority was the Bible, the message of the Bible was solely received by faith, the sole reason one received faith was God's grace. For mainstream Protestantism in the Reformation, these terms were shorthand for reforming the church by the authority of the Bible, accepting God's sovereign mercy in salvation, and recognizing the priority of faith in relating to God. For mainstream Catholicism, these represented an abandonment of the faith and practices of a thousand years, and an incorrect understanding of the church's role in God's plan.

6

Radical Reform

The Radical Reformation. Just the sound of the term arouses the imagination. But in its very provoking of our thoughts, the term causes questions. Why a "radical" reformation? Were not all the reforming movements radical in their own way? Further, "radical" in what way? Were the Radicals somehow further out on the reforming scale than figures like Luther and Erasmus and Zwingli? The answers to these questions do not necessarily get easier with deeper study, as Werner Packull acknowledges: "The uninitiated may well despair as to the variety of crusading, pacifist, evangelical, antitrinitarian, sabbatarian, communistic, apocalyptic, mystic-spiritualistic and biblically literalistic Anabaptists. Any attempt at distilling theological essence from such manifest variety seems at best a hazardous undertaking."[1] But let us not give up on the basic question too soon. What was the Radical Reformation?

To answer the question well, we must begin by setting forth a historiographical issue. Historiography is the study of the methods of historians. Historians and theologians did not always use the term "Radical Reformation." Older terms included "the spiritualist movements" or "the Anabaptist movement." Spiritualism is obviously a slippery term, because all of the figures in a reform of Christian belief and practice are, to one extent or another, spiritual. Anabaptism is not slippery at all, but it was a derogatory term, used by outsiders to insult the people in the movement. In Greek, *ana* is a prefix meaning "again." Thus, an Anabaptist is one who has been baptized more than once. The people who believed in adult baptism never believed that they were baptizing again, but that they were instead baptizing or being baptized for the first time, following the biblical pattern.

In 1962, George Huntston Williams published his justly famous book, *The Radical Reformation*.[2] It was an instance of that rare case in which a book truly

117

changes scholars' opinions. He argued for the terminology of "Radical Reformation," balanced by the term "Magisterial Reformation," which he used to
refer to the reform movements led by figures such as Luther and Zwingli.
Williams's idea about terminology was generally accepted.[3] In the terminology, we can see one crucial difference between the two reforms. The Magisterial Reformers generally acted in cooperation with the ruling authorities, the
magistrates. Thus, Luther worked with Frederick the Wise, the electoral
prince of Saxony. Zwingli worked with the elected council of Zurich, persuading and arguing but always accepting their authority in their sphere. The
Radical Reformers generally denied such a model of cooperation, arguing
instead that it was necessary for a pure community of Christians to separate
from the general populace.

Another factor worth noting in the Radical Reformation is the lack of a central figure. For the Lutheran reforms, the obvious giant is Luther. Zwingli
occupied a similar place in Swiss reform until a later figure, John Calvin,
replaced him in the popular imagination. The Radical Reformation did not
come with a central protagonist. This is not to say that there were not significant and sophisticated thinkers among the Radicals. Rather, it has much to
say about the dangers of being counted as Radical in the sixteenth century.
Many of the noteworthy theologians of the movement were executed or spent
much of their lives hiding.

Now that we have looked at the Radical Reformation in terms of what it
was not—that is, in terms of the Magisterial Reformation—what was it positively? The Radical Reformation was a loosely allied set of movements that
sprang up in the 1520s, characterized most especially by anticlericalism, the
glorification of the common man, apocalypticism, and a biblical notion of suffering. The movement suffered several setbacks, most especially the defeats in
the Peasants' War of 1524–1525 and the scandal of the kingdom of Münster
in 1534–1535. But it also attracted thousands of people and proved its dura-
bility through the persecutions it suffered, to emerge as an important molder
of Christian thought in the era of the Reformation.

What were these identifying factors? What were anticlericalism, the glorification of the common man, apocalypticism, and a biblical notion of suffering?
We considered anticlericalism briefly in the second chapter. In the mind-set of
those who were attracted to the Radical Reformation, anticlericalism took an
especially substantial role. Anticlericalism was the basic mistrust of the clergy
by the laity. All clergy were included in the disgust the laity felt. But a special
loathing was reserved for higher clergy and monks. As Luther and Zwingli
preached and wrote popular works that were pouring out of the printing
presses, the issue of how Christianity had reached such a sorry state was frequently graphically put before anyone who would listen, or anyone who could

read. Protestant pamphlets displayed the higher clergy and monks as drunkards and friends of the devil. Since the Roman Church had regularly put forward the necessity of a moral life among believers, it did not have a leg to stand on when its clergy were found to be demonstrably less moral than the laity.

This anticlerical sentiment was also economic in character. At least some people believed that members of the clergy were using spiritual power to get rich. When one examines the families of the men who gained the papacy and other high posts in the early sixteenth century, it is hard to argue against that. Time and again, influence was simply bought. People knew of this and understood that far from being shepherds of the flock, some of the clergy were wolves.

The glorification of the common man was the reverse side of the coin of anticlericalism. Instead of turning to money-grubbing priests, people turned to good, solid citizens as their spiritual heroes. This was probably not the lowest economic class, not the beggars and truly poor. Rather, the common man was seen in the newly growing merchant class, or the artisans such as weavers, or millers. Luther had trumpeted the priesthood of all believers—why should people not take him at his word? Why should not the working man be the leader of Christ's followers? Christ himself had called fishermen rather than priests as his chosen leaders. Why should not common men, burning with their Lord's words in their heart, lead the simple people of the Lord?

The admiration for peasant agricultural life became so widespread that "Karsthans" developed into a common figure in theological pamphlets. Karsthans, or Hans Karst, was an "everyman" figure for the farming peasants. Steven Ozment notes that "in numerous pre-1525 pamphlets 'Karsthans' appears as a quick-witted, God-fearing, Bible-savvy defender of the Reformation, able to rebut all critics."[4] Luther praised peasant work and believed that it was the work God wanted most for humans. There was a certain romanticism in Luther's view, for he had never actually been a peasant and had no actual experience with the harsher facts of peasant life. The conception was widespread that the common man who held a sincere belief in the truth of the gospel was the true disciple and an excellent defender of God's truth.

Apocalypticism was also important in the Radical Reformation. It was not something new in the sixteenth century; apocalyptic strains are present throughout the Christian era and are even found in Scripture. Apocalyptic beliefs hold that God is about to intervene in human history and will save out a righteous remnant. In the sixteenth century, people believed that the reign of Christ was about to take place, that some form of the end of the world was near. They trusted that the new kingdom of God would look very different from the world in which they lived, and they saw the symbols of the world around them as clear indications of the coming change.

The biblical notion of suffering was another crucial element of the Radical Reformation, both in its self-understanding and in its critique of the Magisterial Reformation. Radical theologians and believers took John 15:20 as a prediction that was coming true in the present time: Jesus said, "The servant is not greater than the master—if they persecuted me, they will also persecute you." Radicals thus saw themselves as the servants who were taking on the roles that their divine master had predicted. Further, Radicals believed that this verse was normative, that it set out Jesus' idea of what must be. If people were persecuting them, believers knew they were truly Jesus' followers. Additionally, they could turn this rule on its head, to demonstrate that some of their critics were not true servants of Jesus. Since many of the Lutherans, Zwinglians, and Catholics were not being persecuted, Radicals reasoned that clearly they were not the followers of Jesus. The ideal of persecution went so far as to support the creation of "martyrologies," books or pamphlet accounts that told the stories of the martyrs and how their witness to the end of their lives demonstrated the truth of the convictions of the Radical Reformers and the people who accepted their message.

People believed that God was about to intervene in the working of the world, that the clergy were both irresponsible and dangerous as spiritual leaders, that to follow Christ one must suffer, and that good, common citizens were probably just as good as university-trained theologians at explaining and discerning God's will. These were the people who were more than likely to follow the various strains of the Radical Reformation. So let us come to know them through the figures they followed, the thoughts that moved them, and the stories they have left behind.

Sigrun Haude has recorded the story of Anna Jansz of Rotterdam, who was executed by drowning in 1539. While on her way to the spot where she was to be executed, she turned to the crowd and asked if someone would raise her fifteen-month-old son. A baker stepped forward; the mental portrait of the moment is full of emotion and evokes Jesus' search for a guardian for his mother during his own execution. Jansz could leave very little to her son; part of what she did leave was a will, directing her son in the true life of piety:

> Listen, my son, to the instruction of your mother. Today I go the path
> of the prophets, apostles and martyrs; I drink the cup that all of them
> drank before me; I go the path of Jesus Christ who had to drink this
> cup as well. I urge you, my son, submit to the yoke of Christ; endure
> it willingly, for it is a great honour and joy. Do not follow the major-
> ity of the people; but when you hear about a poor, simple, repudiated
> handful of men and women cast out of the world, join them. Do not
> be ashamed to confess your faith. Do not fear the majority of the peo-
> ple. It is better to let go of your life than to deviate from the truth.[5]

We see the power of the Anabaptist call in Jansz's words. Death was better than failure to follow Christ. In the will she urges her son to look for the small group known for being cast out by the great majority and to join them. Jansz takes every common argument and turns it on its head. If people hate you— good! If you are persecuted—you are like the apostles and Jesus himself! Here was a strength of religious piety that asked for no quarter from a society it had already determined was godless. Let us trace out the development of this movement, beginning with those who claimed Luther as their opening inspiration.

THE RADICAL RESPONSE TO LUTHER

Luther's reforms took on a life of their own while he was hiding in the Wartburg. In 1521, Andreas von Karlstadt took the reformation of the basic rituals of the Christian church into his own hands, at the greatest speed he could generate. For Karlstadt, the rule was that no one should do the works of Christ slowly. On Christmas Day 1521, Karlstadt offended the Elector Frederick by dressing in a common man's clothes, celebrating the Eucharist in German, and giving both the bread and the wine to the laity. This was offensive because Karlstadt was piling change after change into the service. People may well have feared that such violent and rapid changes might even anger God. The symbol of the common clothing of the working man and using the everyday language that people heard in the market or at work was powerful. Karlstadt further denied himself the title of "Doctor" and asked that he be called "Brother." Everything about the service proclaimed that titles and hierarchy meant nothing, and that simple faith and regeneration of life meant everything.

Karlstadt did not stay in Wittenberg long after Luther's return. In 1523, he left Wittenberg for the town of Orlamünde, to serve as pastor. Here Karlstadt continued the reforming of worship and doctrine that would characterize the Radical movement. Believing that baptism meant that the recipient had repented, he stopped baptizing infants.[6] Assuming that the early Christians had sung psalms without instrumental accompaniment, he had the organ removed from the church. While in Wittenberg, Karlstadt had already written a treatise arguing that the Scriptures should not include the apocryphal books, demonstrating that his reform was not only of the external facts of Christianity, but of its basic document as well.[7]

Karlstadt was not the only figure with Wittenberg ties to turn to the more radical side of the reform movement. Thomas Müntzer (c. 1489–1525), who had studied at Wittenberg University in 1517–1518, was a brilliant and mercurial theologian whose inability to compromise for practical political purposes represented both genius and folly. Müntzer studied at Leipzig and Frankfurt and immersed himself in the Bible, the Fathers, and mysticism. Apparently, in these studies, Müntzer came to believe that the whole decline of the Christian church had come from the ineptitude of its trained and ordained leadership. In trying to solve such a problem, Müntzer turned away from the present model of the church as defined by its leadership and instead saw the church as a voluntary community of professing believers, bound together by the Holy Spirit.[8] In 1520, Luther recommended Müntzer to fill in temporarily for another pastor in Zwickau. Here Müntzer began to preach a socially radical message—that the gospel demands must be carried out in the everyday lives of the believers. When the pastor he was substituting for returned, Müntzer remained in Zwickau, at another church, St. Catherine's, whose membership was more clearly aligned with the messages of common man, being full of weavers and miners. Here Müntzer became even more radical.[9]

Three members of St. Catherine's went on to fame of their own. Nicholas Storch, Thomas Drechsel, and Marcus Thomas Stübner were among the common people in Müntzer's church. Perhaps inspired by Müntzer's preaching, the three talked openly of their theological differences with commonly held opinions. By late 1521, they were required to appear before the town officials to defend their positions on baptism. Instead, the three went to Wittenberg, where they met with Philip Melanchthon, one of Luther's staunchest supporters, and a leader of the Wittenberg reform during Luther's time at the Wartburg. They defended their teaching against infant baptism and at least for a brief time impressed Melanchthon. Soon, however, Melanchthon was warning Frederick the Wise about the activities of the three and cautioning him about the situation in Zwickau. Luther, on his return from the Wartburg, gave the three the name by which they are most frequently termed—the "Zwickau prophets." Luther was making fun of them, but some Christians took them deadly seriously.

In 1521, the town council of Zwickau forced Müntzer to leave. He went to Prague, in Bohemia, the modern-day Czech Republic. There he wrote his *Prague Manifesto*, a harsh attack on the present situation of Christianity, which blamed the clergy and the upper classes for the poverty of the people. Beyond the attacks, Müntzer laid out two further emphases. First, the goal of redemption is the receiving of the seven gifts of the Spirit, from Isaiah 11:1–5.[10] We see again Müntzer's stress on the Spirit and its basic prominence in his thought. Only the elect, those who will be saved, will receive the gifts. Second, to prepare for the gifts of the Spirit, the elect have to go through persecution and fear. The importance of persecution came early to Müntzer, and he was not shy about proclaiming it.

Müntzer preached openly in Prague, but he did not gain a significant following. He went back to Germany and took a position as pastor in the town of

Allstedt. At Allstedt, he was both a brilliant liturgical reformer and a radical theologian, if less openly so. Müntzer's liturgical reforms demonstrated an emphasis on the people's participation. He arranged the service so that key parts would be sung by the congregation. He did not neglect the teaching aspect of the liturgy, demanding that when a psalm was sung in worship, the whole of it was to be sung. In the same way, his Scripture readings were whole chapters, rather than the far briefer readings that were common in his day. He had the Ten Commandments carved on signs and placed at the front of the church. These habits turned the regular worship experience into a kind of grammar school for knowledge of the law, the Psalms, and the Bible in general.

Müntzer seemed successful in Allstedt. He began to settle down and even got married. However, his basic temperament and apocalyptic beliefs could not allow him to guide a gentle reform in a small town. On July 13, 1524, at Allstedt Castle, Müntzer preached a sermon remarkable both for its content and for its audience. The audience included Duke John, the brother of Frederick the Wise, and the duke's son, John Frederick. Various town councilors were in attendance as well. The duke and his son held different opinions about the proper role of the Christian lord and how he should support the church. Thus, they turned to hear Müntzer's ideas to see whether his preaching might clarify their own thoughts.

Müntzer preached a sermon on the second chapter of the book of Daniel. This sermon has been preserved and is known by the title "Sermon before Princes." Müntzer held nothing back and decreed that the princes had a responsibility before God that trumped any other. He considered the many-leveled statue from Nebuchadnezzar's dream (Dan. 2:31–45), likened it to a series of kingdoms, and made the final level of a mix of clay and iron the present age. He then announced that the princes should have a new Daniel, one who would be led not by Scripture but directly by the Spirit. It is clear from the sermon that Müntzer believed that he himself was that Daniel. Müntzer declared that the princes had the duty of cleansing their realms of unbelievers and that they need not worry about consequences, as the unrighteous only have a right to live so long as the righteous grant it to them! The reaction was swift. Five days later, Luther named Müntzer the "Satan of Allstedt."[11] Soon Müntzer was on the road again, only to reappear among the peasants in one of the more famous uprisings in the Peasants' War. We shall return to that story later in this chapter.

Before we leave Müntzer, his theology demands a closer look. Müntzer held radical positions on the church, on suffering, on the use of the Scriptures, and on the coming apocalyptic events. In each of these, he fashioned a position that represented a third path, markedly different from the paths taken by the Magisterial figures we have considered and by Rome. In examining his positions, we can get some clue as to why so many people, especially among the lower classes, were drawn to this strand of the Reformation.

First, Müntzer's notion of the church depended upon the inherent dignity of the Christian believer, rather than upon university education. The simple choice to believe, and to profess that belief openly, was the most significant issue in being part of the true church. While this may seem like something quite small to modern observers, it represented enormous change for the sixteenth century. People in the sixteenth century were members of the church through baptism, which was almost always something done *to* them, before they had a choice in the matter—that is to say, when they were infants. Further, this open commitment to the church led to the second point, the importance and acceptance of suffering. To announce one's membership in the Anabaptist community meant to deny the basis of some of the glue that held late medieval society together. Society did not take this lightly.

In the modern world, tolerance is a virtue. Twenty-first-century citizens of modern democracies argue that belief cannot be forced, that the very idea of compelling someone to change his or her most deeply felt religious beliefs is either misguided or impractical. Sixteenth-century Europe had a different perspective. In the first half of the sixteenth century in Western Europe, radical religious dissent was met with tried-and-true remedies. The medieval tradition had handed down the notion that some heresy was a cancer on the body of believers, a disease in society that would spread if it was not cut out. Frequently, therefore, the penalty for being an Anabaptist was death.

Müntzer did not back away from suffering. In fact, he celebrated it. Part of his critique of the Magisterial Reformers in general and Luther in particular was the very lack of suffering. He called Luther "Dr. Liar" and "Dr. Softlife" for Luther's avoidance of the anguish that true Christians must undergo. For Müntzer, Luther's theology represented a turn away from the gospel. The true gospel must be entered into in suffering. As Christ was crucified, so the believer enters into Christ through suffering—and only through suffering. On the far side of suffering lies true faith. Müntzer argued that the believer must cling to the "bitter Christ," and that Luther had substituted a "honey-sweet Christ." While Luther's version of Christ was more inviting, it was also false.

Müntzer made another step that separated him from Luther and that illustrates the chasm that quickly developed between the Radical and the Magisterial Reformations. This bitter Christ who must be grasped comes with tasks. To follow Christ means to take up the tasks that Christ sets before the believer. To fail to do so is to deny Christ. While Luther drew a sharp division between salvation and good works, Müntzer tied them together in the strongest fashion. When the princes to whom he preached at Allstedt Castle did not accept their divinely given tasks, they chose to deny their Christian calling and took themselves out of the society of the saved.

Müntzer's thought on scripture also represented a departure from Rome, Wittenberg, and Zurich. In his thought, the true believer who has grasped Christ through suffering and has received the gifts of the Holy Spirit does not need Scripture. The Old and New Testaments are only for the testing of the visions of the Spirit, so that the devil does not come in and spoil the gifts. But only the spiritual man can do this. If one has not received the Spirit, nothing else will help. Müntzer wrote that "he [who has not the Spirit] does not know how to say anything deeply about God, even if he had eaten through a hundred Bibles!"[12]

This belief in the priority of direct knowledge from the Spirit over the words of canonical Scripture is called "continuing revelation." It marked Müntzer and others of the Radical Reformation as clearly different from the Magisterial Reformers, who denied the possibility of exceeding the canon. This also allowed for a greater sense of the importance of the common man, for one does not need a university degree or the knowledge of Greek and Hebrew in order to receive direct knowledge from the Holy Spirit.

To finish with our consideration of Müntzer's thought, we must observe the apocalyptic strain in his sense of his own time. He believed that he was living in the last days, that God was finishing the divine work with that age. God was ending history and bringing it to a close in his own terms. Thoughts of the necessity of daily human needs and of providing for the future simply got in the way of the coming kingdom. Because of this, Müntzer became a figurehead in the Peasants' War.

THE PEASANTS' WAR: 1524–1525

The Peasants' War of 1524–1525 was an example of the interpenetration of political, economic, and spiritual thought in the sixteenth century. Though modern historians have demonstrated that there were earlier rebellions, the Peasants' War has raised the question, to both historians and the people living at that time, of what the effect was of the new evangelical teaching on political and legal issues.[13] Did the peasants rise up at least in part because of the message of the gospel? Let us take a closer look at this conflict.

The Peasants' War was a series of uprisings and battles between approximately 1524–1525, initiated not only by peasants but also by those in the population who were open to the emphasis on the common man. The popularity of the Karsthans literature, the widespread belief that God desired better economic and social situations, and the willingness to take specific actions to make these beliefs into realities were all factors that were shared broadly across many classes of society.

One of the ways for exploring the religious foundation of the Peasants' War is to examine the manifestos created by various groups who participated in the war, or who were sympathetic to the cause of the common man. These were generally not the works of great theologians, but were more reflective of the beliefs of the common people who were gathered together in one locale or another. One of these declarations is the Memmingen Articles of 1525. The pastor of St. Martin's in Memmingen, Christoph Schappeler, had sided with the lower classes throughout his career. In early 1525, he wrote the document, possibly collaborating with Sebastian Lotzer, that would colloquially be called the Memmingen Articles. The full title of this reform program was "The Just and Fundamental Articles of All the Peasantry and Tenants of Spiritual and Temporal Powers by Whom They Think Themselves Oppressed."[14] The most cursory glance at the articles clearly demonstrates that they set out an ideal of a spiritual and material kingdom, a melding together of religious and secular concerns. The first article addresses the necessity for the community to have the power to elect and appoint pastors. Further, the article explicitly demands the power to remove pastors who behave improperly. The pastors must preach only the gospel, without human additions. Certainly, Lutheran ideas hover in the background.

The second article clarifies how a pastor and church shall be supported. Following scriptural warrant, the article states the willingness of the people to pay the tithe on grain. This tithe should be handled by elected church officials, who from it will distribute a fair wage to the pastor and use the rest to alleviate the suffering of the village's own poor. A tithe was a kind of church tax; the willingness to pay would have represented an innovation. Previous tithes could be collected involuntarily.

While the first and second articles directly address evangelical reforms, the third through the eleventh clearly move into legal reforms and the reform of customs. The third demands appropriate freedom from unbiblical ownership of the poor by the lords; the fourth insists on the right of commoners to catch wild game. The fifth claims the right to cut firewood on community lands; the sixth declares that the labor obligations owed to the lords should be decreased. The seventh requires that the oppression of serfs by the lords cease; the eighth calls for rent reform. The ninth champions legal reform so that the peasants will be judged by a common law, rather than by an arbitrary bias; the tenth claims that common lands that have been seized must be returned to common ownership; and the eleventh demands that the death tax be abolished. Though the character of these articles is far more secular than the first two, they are made more religious by the inclusion of the twelfth article. The twelfth article states that if any of the articles are demonstrated to be against God's Word, as proven from the Bible, the people will give up that article.

What the Memmingen Articles lay out is an ideal of a commonwealth where the division between secular and sacred disappears. It may not have been practical, but it did represent a visionary effort to claim a certain amount of freedoms and rights, both by linking those rights to the message of the gospel and by allowing that when those rights conflicted with Scripture, they would be abandoned. Several groups adopted the Memmingen Articles, and the concerns that they lift up were widely held by many people who were touched by the Peasants' War.

The Peasants' War, or at least one of the main events of the Peasants' War, began in June 1524. Williams records that "the war was set off on 23 June 1524, when the countess of Lüpfen-Stühlingen tried to send some of her peasants off to gather snails while they were intent on taking in their hay."[15] While the workers were trying to get the basics of life together, bringing in the hay that would feed their animals, the countess demanded that such work stop so she could enjoy snails. Because haying must be done when the weather is dry, time was of the essence. The countess's demand demonstrated that her world and her concerns had no room for her servants' needs. Outrage spread throughout the district by the end of the year. Hans Muller rallied the peasants into a force.

Meanwhile, in the nearby town of Waldshut, Balthasar Hubmaier (1481–1528) was seeking to reform the town after the pattern of Zwingli in Zurich. He had met Zwingli in 1523, and after the Second Zurich Disputation he instituted more radical reforms in Waldshut than Zwingli had managed in Zurich. Hubmaier immediately married, abolished the Latin service, and eliminated all the traditional decrees concerning fasting. The reforms and the rapid pace of reform angered the Catholics and the Austrian authorities.

The combination of the reforming pastor and the enraged workers was the perfect storm. Each fed on the strength of the ideas and moral outrage of the other. Armed peasants arrived at the city in numerous bands and negotiated a treaty with the town. This type of pattern was repeated again and again across Thuringia, Franconia, and elsewhere. The mixture of evangelical reform and peasant economic and legal concerns was only sometimes fully integrated. When evangelical and Radical reformers could harness these concerns, the presence of reforming preachers or prophets gave a spiritual cast to the uprisings. When such was not the case, fewer spiritual concerns were raised. While this volume cannot describe the various battles and uprisings that made up the Peasants' War, it is important to discuss the issue of Frankenhausen. In Frankenhausen, we see the usual partial fusion of radical spiritual concerns and peasant economic interests. But we also see the response of the lords and observe a kind of ending and a new beginning.

The battle that broke out near Frankenhausen included both a famous spiritual leader, Thomas Müntzer, and a strategically brilliant opponent, Philip of Hesse.[16] Müntzer had joined the band of peasants and become one of its spiritual leaders in early 1525. He had even gone so far as to design two war symbols for them, putting a sword on a white flag, and a rainbow on a white banner.[17] He was clearly linking the cause of the peasants to biblical themes of covenant and renewal. As soon as he realized the danger of the new movement, Philip moved and confronted the greatest concentration of the peasants at Frankenhausen. His first military scuffles with the peasant forces proved that the peasants could hold their own against light cavalry. Philip entered into negotiations with the leaders of the band, offering to leave them in peace if they would surrender Müntzer. While they considered the proposal, Philip brought up his main force and his artillery. The peasants, after some time, turned down Philip's offer because of the appearance of a rainbow above the landgrave's troops. This was the very symbol on their own banner. Surely, they reasoned, God was with them.

Their reasoning about God's plans and their military strategy proved equally faulty. Philip's trained troops slaughtered the peasant forces while suffering almost no casualties. Müntzer was captured, and on May 25, 1525, was beheaded. The effects of the battle were so disastrously one-sided that many of the Radicals became not only militarily disillusioned with the chance of defending themselves by force; they also took on the positive idea of a theological virtue of pacifism.

The opening to pacifism that came with the end of the Peasants' War changed the character of Radical religion and Anabaptism. Until the experiment of the kingdom of Münster in the mid-1530s, Radical religion tried to avoid entanglement with politics and military service, and even went so far as to take up the idea of pacifism and deny the cooperation of the spiritual and political kingdoms. We can see this immediately, in the confession of the Schleitheim Articles and in the particular case of a former Benedictine monk, Michael Sattler.

MICHAEL SATTLER AND
THE SCHLEITHEIM ARTICLES

In February 1527, a group of Swiss and German Anabaptists came together at the small village of Schleitheim, in northern Switzerland. Michael Sattler was one of the clear leaders of this group, which produced a confessional document. The Schleitheim Articles would be the working confession of the pacifist movement among the Anabaptists for the next generation, and it would become a confessional norm for the later movement of the Mennonites.

Considering Michael Sattler (c. 1490–1527), historians are unable to pin down exactly what his motivation to join the reforming cause was, and how he took a turn from Magisterial reform toward more Radical ideas. He was born in Germany, around 1490, in the town of Stauffen. He became a Benedictine monk and served as prior, one of the leaders, of his monastery. When his monastery was invaded by a band of peasants in the Peasants' War, his abbot, the overall leader of the monastery, fled. Rather than stay in the monastery, Sattler chose to leave the safety of such an existence and abandoned the order and the Church of Rome. He went to live among the common people, in the region north of Zurich. He seems to have received believers' baptism in June 1526.[18]

After being banished from Zurich, Sattler traveled to Strasbourg. Strasbourg was one of the more tolerant cities, and its reforming leader, Martin Bucer, had a peaceful spirit, even when he disagreed with others. Sattler made friends among some of the reforming leaders there, but after another Anabaptist figure, Johann Denck, was banished, Sattler felt he must leave as well. From Strasbourg, he found his way to Schleitheim in early 1527. This is also the year that Protestants began to execute Radicals, such as Felix Manz, who was executed in Zurich on January 5, 1527. This was not a good omen for Sattler's own career.

In Schleitheim, Sattler met with several other Anabaptists and in a brief time hammered out the confession that has come to be called the Schleitheim Confession, though its original title was "The Brotherly Union." The confession is remarkable in several points. First, it is brief, spanning only seven articles and approximately eight pages in modern translations.[19] Second, though the persecution of Anabaptists by both Protestants and Catholics had certainly begun, the confession is far more concerned about those brothers and sisters who are in the community than it is about outside threats. The confession's goal is to proclaim that the adherents have decided to live "as obedient children of God, sons and daughters, and as those who are separated from the world—and who should be separated in all that they do and do not do."[20]

The seven articles briefly outline pacifist Anabaptism. The first article appoints baptism only for those who have learned repentance, and denies that it can be given to infants, who cannot desire or request it. The second establishes the ban. The ban became a vital sign of Anabaptism. The ban was the practice of excluding brothers and sisters from the community if they fell into sin. The third article institutes the practice of prohibiting eucharistic fellowship with those outside of the separated community. Only those who were clearly part of the Anabaptist society could partake of this meal, and to share with those outside made a mockery of it.

The fourth article establishes the Anabaptist community as truly separated from the world. Believers were to have nothing to do with those outside of the community, not even with Catholics or members of the Magisterially reformed churches. Alarming in its matter-of-fact tone, this article notes that this separation would naturally bring persecution and that nevertheless the "devilish weapons of force" must be shunned. The fifth article represents clearly the distinction between Radical religion and either Catholicism or Magisterial reform. The article is about pastors, their duties, their support, and their replacement. The first part is straightforward, at least for Protestantism. The pastor's duties are defined by teaching, by explanation of Scripture, and by church discipline. The second part clearly differentiates between the Anabaptists and the Magisterial Reformers—the pastors must be financially supported by the congregation. Lacking the possibility of turning toward taxes for support, the Schleitheim articles set out a wholly voluntary polity—the rules for governing the church. Finally, the third part is faithful but chilling in its matter-of-fact tone. When the pastor is driven away, or martyred for the faith, the congregation should ordain another in his place. The Anabaptists expected to be persecuted, and they provided for a path forward when persecution came.

The sixth article defines Anabaptism as pacifist. Christians must avoid the sword. Therefore, Christians cannot take part in war or in the military. However, by extension, Christians cannot be a judge in the court, as that might require punishing criminals by the sword. Furthermore, this rule of the nations was defined as a ruling over the kingdom of the flesh, but the church should be governed according to the spirit.[21] The final article denies Anabaptists the right to swear oaths. These final two articles clearly set Anabaptists outside the boundaries of the wider society, as they were unable to perform many of the duties of citizenship. Anabaptists could not take the oath of allegiance to the city in which they lived, they could not take oaths before giving testimony in court, and they could not take an oath of loyalty to a lord. Essentially, this set Anabaptists outside the normative society.

If the Memmingen Articles could be called a fusion of economic and spiritual concerns, the Schleitheim Confession could not. The Schleitheim document clearly is a confession of faith that defines a church order, describes right belief, and explains the correct relationship between the church and the world. In many ways, the Radical critique of society was more terrifying to the medieval mind than the rebellion of the peasants had been. In the rebellious movements, defenders of the status quo could and did argue that those who participated were simply trying to get more economic goods—and this was nothing new. Schleitheim clearly argued, however, that the wider society was so corrupt that a true believer had to separate himself or herself from it. While people had long accepted the possibility that the normal social life had problems, and that some spiritual elites such as monks might withdraw from society, very few were prepared to accept that the traditions of generations would keep one from the hope of heaven.

Just how upsetting were such beliefs? Michael Sattler soon found out. Sattler left Schleitheim soon after the colloquy and was apprehended with his wife by Catholic authorities near the town of Rothenburg.[22] The circumstances of the ensuing trial were unusual on several counts. First, the local authorities refused to put a university theologian on the panel of judges, though most of the charges were about doctrine and church matters. Second, Sattler refused the benefit of legal counsel. Third, Sattler really did not argue against the charges, but rather against the laws. In other words, Sattler admitted that he had done those things of which he was accused, such as denying infant baptism and denying the mediation of the Virgin Mary, since she was presently asleep, waiting for Christ's return. He then argued that such things could not be against the law since they were scriptural. Finally, when it came time for Sattler to defend himself, the authorities refused to allow him to see a written copy of the charges against him. Sattler was eventually burned at the stake, but not before the application of a particularly brutal set of tortures. He never recanted and was executed by burning on May 21, 1527. His wife also refused to recant, and she was executed by drowning eight days later.

Sattler's death became a model for the Anabaptists and a problem for Catholics. For Anabaptists, Sattler's steadfast refusal to recant demonstrated clearly that God supported him. For Catholics, the simple judicial execution for clear lawbreaking was just, but it created the idea of Sattler as a holy martyr, which the church denied. We will return to martyrdom in the eighth and tenth chapters, but it is significant to note here that Sattler was the first to fulfill the fifth article of the Schleitheim Brotherly Union.

MELCHIOR HOFFMAN, APOCALYPTIC, AND THE KINGDOM OF MÜNSTER

Though many Anabaptists took pacifism and separation from the rest of society as the correct stance after the Peasants' War, this was not a universal attitude. Melchior Hoffman (c. 1495–1543) took a different tack with his apocalyptic prophecies. His spiritual leadership led to his death in jail and to the foundation of the Kingdom of Münster by his disciples, an event that divided Dutch Anabaptism.

Hoffman was not a priest or trained theologian. He made his early living in the fur business. After Luther's fame spread, Hoffman was attracted to Luther's teaching. He made his way to Wittenberg and proclaimed himself a lay preacher while continuing as a businessman. However, he displayed a knack

for getting into trouble and was eventually banished from Dorpat for iconoclasm, from Stockholm for inciting religious unrest, from Kiel for a Zwinglian
eucharistic doctrine, and from Strasbourg for Anabaptism. He was rebaptized
in 1530.

In 1530, Hoffman took on his prophetic and pastoral tasks. His ministry of
baptism led him to baptize a few hundred people and to found several churches
in East Frisia. In 1532, he established a religious community at Emden, the
most significant city in East Frisia. His ministry was not only characterized by
baptism; Hoffman also took on the eucharistic controversies of the time. He
definitively rejected both Catholic transubstantiation and Lutheran consubstantiation, preferring originally a Zwinglian view. He also developed a theology of the heavenly body of Christ, which suggested that Jesus Christ did not
receive humanity from Mary but rather possessed a human body prepared for
him from eternity by God. Hoffman saw himself as a new prophet, as one who
took on the prophetic mantle of the Old Testament prophets, who spoke the
word of the Lord. Hoffman believed and taught openly that Christ was going
to return in 1533, in Strasbourg. He also declared that prior to Christ's return,
all the ungodly would be purged from the earth, causing civil authorities everywhere to watch him carefully. Believing that he had received a true foretelling
of his own need to be jailed before Christ would return, Hoffman returned to
Strasbourg and was imprisoned. His imprisonment was extraordinarily long
for the sixteenth century, and he died in prison in 1543.

Hoffman's influence did not die with his incarceration. His theological
ideas inspired several figures and lived on in the thought of Dirk and Obbe
Philips and Menno Simons. But his greatest notoriety came from those of his
disciples who took up his revolutionary ideas and applied them to the creation
of a holy kingdom, centered in Münster. The excesses of that kingdom, and
its tragic end, caused horror both in Anabaptists and in those who sought to
stamp out all Radical religion.

As we begin to consider the tragedy of the kingdom of Münster, it must be
pointed out that many factors played a role in its story. The city had been evangelized by its pastor, Bernard Rothmann, with Lutheran ideas for years preceding the Anabaptist takeover. Rothmann had been supported by the powerful
guilds, which kept the local bishop from stopping his ministry. Further, there
were basic political power struggles between the upper classes and the working
guilds. But our attention must concentrate on the religious struggle.

Two men who had been greatly attracted to Melchior Hoffman's ideas
arrived in Münster in 1534. Their names were Jan of Leiden and Jan Matthijs.
They came to Münster because of the persecution of Anabaptists that was
occurring in the Netherlands. Further, they came to Münster because
although they believed in the visionary apocalypticism of Hoffman, they

judged that Hoffman was wrong about his prophecy that the new Jerusalem would be in Strasbourg. Instead, they believed that it would be in Münster. They quickly set out to make that idea a reality.

In attempting this, they had help. Hundreds of Anabaptist refugees from the Netherlands had flooded into Münster. Their ideas had proven attractive to the Lutheran pastor Rothmann, who had long suspected that infant baptism was unscriptural. He submitted to adult baptism in 1534 and supported the Anabaptist takeover of the city. The Münster elections of early 1534 brought into the government a strong majority of men convinced of the rightness of Hoffman's ideas. These ideas and those people who held them were known as "Melchiorite," or Melchiorites. This power base allowed far greater opportunity for the prophets to assume political power. They almost immediately seized the opportunity.

Jan Matthijs moved swiftly to force the city to match his vision of a holy Zion. He set up communal ways of life and destroyed the records of landownership. He soon declared that he intended to kill all the godless in the city. By godless, he meant those who had not joined in a baptismal covenant that the Anabaptists had signed. By the end of February, all the non-Anabaptists had left. All this time, Matthijs was inviting Anabaptist refugees from other areas to come to Münster. Soon, however, this became very difficult. Both Catholics and Protestants encircled the city with an army and besieged it. This army was not a token force to be taken lightly; Matthijs himself was killed in an action against them in early April, as Williams describes:

> In order to show their bravery, the men of the city staged occasional sorties against their beleaguerers. On such a sally, on Easter Sunday, 4 April 1534, . . . Matthijs lost his life. There seems to be some indication that he thought God would help him, almost single-handed, to overcome the episcopal troops, and that . . . Beukels [Jan of Leiden] may have encouraged him in this fatuous expectation.[23]

After the death of Jan Matthijs, Jan of Leiden became the prophet of Münster. As prophet, he dissolved the council and replaced it with twelve men he had picked. He called them Elders. Jan and the Elders instituted a harsher form of communal life and set forth a new law code. The law code was the opposite of the basic message of the Schleitheim Articles. Instead of the church withdrawing from the state, Jan's model was a theocracy. There was no difference between ecclesiastical and civil power—and the punishments given for all offenses were harsh. Sinning after (re)baptism was punishable by death.

Jan's most extreme actions were extraordinary by any measure. He proclaimed mandatory polygamy and had himself crowned king of Münster. Polygamy, or more specifically, polygyny—the practice of men taking multiple wives—served several functions. First, theologically it allowed Jan and Roth-mann to argue that Münster truly did follow the practice of the patriarchs of the Old Testament. Second, women outnumbered men in the city by about three to one. This was because some men had refused to convert when their wives did, but also because more men than women were dying in the constant siege of the city. Finally, Jan wanted the widow of Jan Matthijs.[24] He eventually took sixteen wives.[25] The practice of polygamy was not popular, but Jan had grown too powerful to resist. Soon his power (and perhaps his megalomania) increased to the point where in September 1534, he had himself anointed king of Münster.

Our concentration upon the internal politics and spiritual life of Münster has somewhat concealed one extraordinarily important practical detail—Münster still was a city under siege. Occasionally other Anabaptist forces attempted to break the siege, but they were never successful. Food began to run low, morale even lower. The city fell on June 25, 1535, betrayed by deserters. The slaughter was almost total; the besiegers were in no mood to offer mercy. Jan and other leaders were captured, tortured, and executed.

The aftermath of the debacle at Münster set the pattern for Anabaptism in various ways. For some, this was an example from God of the problems with human desires for power. Obbe Philips, one of the leaders of the Anabaptists, wrote a treatise that detailed his own disillusionment. For others, the model of pacifist religion clearly had won the ideological battle. One of those who saw his own calling most clearly in the needs of the scattered Anabaptists serves as our next and final figure.

MENNO SIMONS AND MENNONITISM

One of the figures most influenced by Sattler's beliefs and model was also crucially stimulated by the theology of Melchior Hoffman. Menno Simons (1496–1561) was a Catholic priest serving in Friesland when he became absorbed with the struggles of the Anabaptists. He was moved to pity a group of Anabaptists who had been hunted and scattered in the battles around Münster—so moved that he went to be their shepherd.

Menno Simons was born in the village of Witmarsum. His father made a living as a dairy farmer; the priesthood would have represented a significant socioeconomic step up for young Menno. He was ordained to the priesthood in early 1524 and was assigned to be a vicar in the parish of Pingjum. His first brushes with heterodox theology had nothing to do with Anabaptism. As a priest, he frequently celebrated the Eucharist, but he came to doubt the doctrine of transubstantiation. He later wrote:

> It occurred to me, as often as I handled the bread and wine in the Mass, that they were not the flesh and blood of the Lord. I thought that the devil was suggesting this, that he might separate me from my faith. I confessed it often, sighed and prayed; yet I could not come clear of the ideas.[26]

Clearly, Menno did not believe the clear teachings of the Church of Rome on the presence of Christ in the Mass. He studied the Bible further on his own, read some of the works of Luther, and came to an attitude that was not Lutheran but was far closer to Zwingli's position.

Menno did not leave the Church of Rome over eucharistic differences, however. The sacrament of baptism drew him away. In his readings of the New Testament, Menno became convinced that the church's tradition on baptism was backward. Menno believed that baptism did not cleanse a person of original sin. In fact, the whole world was cleansed of original sin by the sacrifice of Christ; for Menno that was the heart of the gospel. With the issue of original sin removed from the equation, and with the clear testimony from the New Testament of adults choosing to be baptized after coming to faith, Menno developed a theology of baptism that saw it as entrance into the full membership of the church, a step that could only be made by an adult fully aware of the costs of following Christ. Baptism has a covenantal aspect, in which both parties to the covenant, God and the believer, must be fully able to form such a pact.

In 1536, Menno could no longer stand to believe so differently from the Church of Rome while serving as a priest. Moved by pity for a band of shepherdless Anabaptists, he renounced his priesthood and sought to serve this new flock. He received believer's baptism, probably in late 1536, and was ordained as an elder by Obbe Philips in that same winter of 1536–1537.[27] From that point on, Menno's life perfectly illustrated the kind of persecuted existence that the Schleitheim Articles had predicted. He lived as a refugee, frequently moving with his wife to avoid capture, especially after 1542 when the Holy Roman Emperor, Charles V, put a price on his head. He died in 1561 and was buried in his cabbage garden.[28]

In the twenty-five years of his active service to the radical wing of the Reformation, Menno gave significant leadership to the Anabaptist movement. He was not its founder, nor did he ever claim to be. But at a moment of great crisis, when the Münsterite experiment had failed so disastrously, his calm leadership, coupled with his hearty rejection of the militarism espoused by the leadership of the kingdom of Münster, allowed him to assume a controlling stance in the movement. His leadership became so successful that the movement took on his name, and many of the Anabaptists came to be called Mennonites.

What did Menno teach? First, adult baptism was crucial. Children simply did not have the faith necessary to request baptism. Second, in Menno's thought the division between salvation and the works of the saved that was prominent in Luther's theology was unthinkable. As Sjouka Voolstra explains, "Menno defines faith equally as a gift and a power conferred by God. It penetrates the opened heart or the conscience and grants the certainty of salvation. As a consequence, the penitent believer acknowledges that both the Law and the gospel are just and true."[29] Menno believed that the saved believer must do the works of the law. Only this ongoing working-out of faith demonstrates that the faith of the believer is actual and true.

Linked in a vital way to this was Menno's doctrine of the body of Christ. He almost certainly was influenced by Hoffman's ideas of Christ's human body not coming from Mary, but he did not publicly proclaim that so as not to be linked to the excesses of the kingdom of Münster.[30] In any case, this doctrine that Christ had not received humanity in any way from Mary allowed Menno to argue that the perfect, holy body of Christ came directly from God. It was human but was like Adam in that it was directly from God. Thus, as Christ's human body was perfect, so too should believers take on the task of perfection in their own lives of faith.

As a consequence of this, Menno developed a strong doctrine of the ban. As stated before, he did not invent this doctrine. In fact, we see it quite early in the Schleitheim Articles. He wrote a treatise in 1550 that took up the issues of the ban in a series of questions and answers.[31] In it he affirmed that the ban was for a spiritual purpose, and as such was appropriate in all cases. The bond of husband and wife should not be stronger than the community's ban, nor should the bond of parent and child. For Menno, the Christian life had to be a demonstration of following Christ and denying sin. This strict character forced Mennonites to abandon any hope of creating a broad, godly society because the wider societies simply refused the strict morality enforced by the ban. This helped to shape Mennonitism as a spiritual community that defined itself against the wider society, rather than as a part of it.

Finally, Menno Simons directed the Anabaptist movement away from the idea of a human revolutionary character to the ideal of the body of the church. He believed that the Christian life was a struggle, but that the only weapons available to the Christian are spiritual. Revolt must be impossible. With these rules in place, Mennonite religion was clearly on the path toward pacifism. For Anabaptism, power had been turned upon its head—the truest value was placed on being humble and, if need be, persecuted. At the end of Menno's life, his followers and admirers respected his poverty. One of them, Valerius Schoolmeester, wrote, "I have heard it said that the pious Menno left very little and great poverty after his death. I would prefer to hear that than that he had left one or two hundred guilders, or house, or land to his children. It bears good witness to him, with which he puts many others to shame."[32] In Menno, the persecuted man was the model of Christianity.

DISTINCTIVE RADICAL REFORM BELIEFS

As we have seen, the term "Radical Reformation" is very broad and includes a diverse number of figures, with sometimes very different and even conflicting theological beliefs. Thomas Müntzer's belief in the use of the sword of the righteous cannot be reconciled with Michael Sattler's conscientious pacifism; Menno Simons's desire for a community set apart from the wider and sinful society clashes with Jan of Leiden's ideal of a godly kingdom in Münster, where all were to be compelled to the true life. To aim at a summary of Radical or Anabaptist belief to which all subscribed is impossible.

However, that is not to say there were not distinctive characteristics of the Radical Reformation, characteristics that either were so distinctive or so widely held that they make up part of what the opponents of the Radicals identified as Radical religion. In this section, we will examine four of them: their approach to Scripture, their approach to salvation, their emphasis on believer's baptism, and their vision of the nature of the true church.[33] While this does not by any means exhaust the interesting character and content of Radical theology, it does give us a graspable summary that would have been recognizable to many of the members of the communities, as well as their opponents.

The Radical approach to Scripture sought to make the question of its interpretation a community affair. Because of the Radicals' general acceptance of the principles of *sola scriptura* and the priesthood of all believers, this made perfect theological sense. However, in practice this did not always occur. In part, that depended on the personalities of some of the leaders of the Radical movements. Jan of Leiden seems to have had little use for any conflicting scriptural interpretations his subjects would have offered. Further, the emphasis on the ongoing presence and work of the Holy Spirit meant that for some, *sola scriptura* could be extended to the continuing revelation that was being offered to the prophetic figure. That sense of the gift of the Holy Spirit naturally raised the interpretations of such a figure above those of the community.

Though it must be qualified, the biblical principle did function for the Radical communities. Radical ideas of the sacraments depended on a clear scriptural base and argued against Magisterial and Catholic doctrines as being corrupted by human traditions. Radical models of the church were dependent on New

Testament models and specific injunctions found within the Epistles. The communities of believers chose to live their lives by a particular grasp of the Bible, which they frequently paid for in the persecutions of the wider society.

The Radical approach to salvation might justifiably be called a third way between the Lutheran and Reformed emphasis on God's grace, and the Catholic stress on the importance of the works of the believer. Certainly, the Radicals accepted the Magisterial Reformers' emphasis on God's grace and its priority in salvation. God had to save people; people did not save themselves. However, the Radical emphasis on the Christian life caused them to link salvation firmly to sanctification. Thus, though a Radical theologian might well say that believers are saved by grace, he might also say that this salvation can be lost without the proper response to that grace. Once God had offered salvation and the sinner had accepted, the covenant relationship must be maintained by a moral life.

This model of salvation influenced and was influenced by the next two areas of doctrine—believer's baptism and the nature of the church. For most Radicals, the very nature of baptism and the New Testament witness made it quite clear that only a person of actual faith could ask for it or receive it. Mature faith was necessary, because in accepting adult baptism, a person in sixteenth-century Europe was literally gambling with his or her life. Further, believer's baptism allowed one to be baptized into the life and death of Christ. Just as Christ's new life was radically separated from his old, believers were called to begin life anew in a wholly new way. Just as Jesus had said in the Gospel of John that "the servant is not greater than the master—if they persecuted me, they will also persecute you," believers who accepted this baptism had to be prepared to accept the persecution of the world.

Thus, the nature of the church for the Radicals was caught up in discipleship to the living and persecuted Christ. Christians were called to follow him, not to be conformed to the world. Therefore, the community that made up the church had to be very different from the surrounding society. This community had to hold itself to a far higher moral standard, living out in the lives of believers the truth and model of Christian belief. Further, the community intentionally had to be different; it had to separate itself from the society by different patterns of life and by a determined withdrawal from the corrupting influence of the society. The ban existed to separate those who were too caught up in the world from those whose lives followed in Christian discipleship.

The Radical Reformers impacted the sixteenth century like a match dropped into a pool of gasoline. The ensuing blaze both terrified observers and provided light to clarify several theological points. For the Catholics, the Radicals represented the excesses to which the Magisterial reforms would lead. For the Magisterial Reformers, the Radicals' examples pointed out that the sure confidence of their dependence on the Bible, and the priesthood of all believers, might not be the sure barricade against false religion that they had believed. For thousands of simple believers, Radical religion represented the purest reform and the best way of living the Christian life. For all, the shock of the Radical Reformation could not be denied or forgotten.

QUESTIONS FOR DISCUSSION

1. What is historiography? How can the way we think about a thing change our opinion of it?
2. Should the biblical notion of suffering and the model of Christ's passion be normative for Christian communities?
3. Radical communities were frequently separated from the societies that they inhabited. Did this allow them to follow the Christian religion more purely, or did they engage in something that was not Christian but instead elitist?
4. Many Radical communities practiced the ban. Why did they do it? What are the possible problems with this practice? Conversely, can any community claim to be Christian that does not attempt Christian purity?

SUGGESTED FURTHER READING

Primary Readings

Baylor, Michael G., trans. and ed. *The Radical Reformation*. Cambridge Texts in the History of Political Thought. Cambridge: Cambridge University Press, 1991.
Müntzer, Thomas. *The Collected Works of Thomas Müntzer*. Translated and edited by Peter Matheson. Edinburgh: T&T Clark, 1988.
Sattler, Michael. *The Legacy of Michael Sattler*. Edited by John Howard Yoder. Scottdale, PA: Herald Press, 1973.
Williams, George H., and Angel M. Mergal. *Spiritual and Anabaptist Writers*. Library of Christian Classics. Philadelphia: Westminster Press, 1957.

Secondary Readings

Blickle, Peter. *The Revolution of 1525: The German Peasants' War from a New Perspective.* Translated by Thomas A. Brady Jr. and H. C. Erik Midelfort. Baltimore: Johns Hopkins University Press, 1981.
Dipple, Geoffrey. *"Just as in the Time of the Apostles": Uses of History in the Radical Reformation.* Kitchener, Ontario: Pandora Press, 2005.
Estep, William. *The Anabaptist Story: An Introduction to Sixteenth-Century Anabaptism.* 3rd rev. ed. Grand Rapids: Wm. B. Eerdmans Publishing Co., 1996
Gritsch, Eric. *Thomas Müntzer: A Tragedy of Errors.* Philadelphia: Fortress Press, 1989.
Haude, Sigrun. "Anabaptism." In *The Reformation World*, edited by Andrew Pettegree, 237–56. London: Routledge, 2000.

Matheson, Peter. *The Imaginative World of the Reformation*. Minneapolis: Fortress Press, 2001.
McLaughlin, R. Emmet. *Caspar Schwenckfeld, Reluctant Radical: His Life to 1540*. New Haven, CT: Yale University Press, 1986.
Williams, George H. *The Radical Reformation*. Philadelphia: Westminster Press, 1962.
———. *The Radical Reformation*. 3rd ed. Kirksville, MO: Sixteenth Century Studies, 1992.

DOCTRINAL-VOCABULARY DISCUSSION

Sacraments?

The reforms of the sixteenth century dealt with the sacraments. The different sacramental systems that different church bodies and different theologians offered up spoke volumes about what they thought was important and how they viewed Scripture and the traditions of the church.

Sacramentum was the Latin translation for the Greek word *mystērion*, used in the New Testament and meaning "mystery." The sacraments, which thus had a mystical character about them, were a set of rituals of the Christian church. These rituals were set apart from other rituals by three characteristics. First, the sacraments were involved in salvation. Second, the sacraments were seen as vehicles of grace. Third, the sacraments had been instituted by Christ. We should define what "instituted" means, but cannot. That was part of the argument. Did "instituted by" mean that Christ did the ritual in question himself? Did it mean that he was present at the ritual and blessed it by his presence? The earliest Christians practiced the sacraments of baptism and Communion. But over the centuries, the number of sacraments grew. By the sixteenth century, the Roman Church accepted seven sacraments: baptism, penance, Communion, confirmation, ordination, marriage, and last rites, or extreme unction.

When Luther began to question the authority of the Church of Rome, he also doubted whether Rome could "create" a sacrament. He then went back to the Scriptures with a very narrow definition of "instituted by Christ"—that basically Christ had to command the ritual in question. Luther reduced the number of sacraments to these: baptism, because Jesus underwent it and commanded his followers to do it; the Eucharist, because Jesus had done it and commanded his followers to remember him in it; and confession, because Jesus had ordered his followers to forgive one another. Other reformers denied that confession was even a sacrament. Some of the Radical theologians even doubted that there should be sacraments in the traditional sense.

The Church of Rome was not impressed with the arguments for a shorter list of sacraments. At the Council of Trent, the church of Rome decreed that there were seven sacraments and that they were necessary for salvation. Rome demanded participation in the sacramental system as a part of the ordinary path of salvation and as something that believers could do to help in their own spiritual life. Most Protestant theologians took Luther's general tack and argued that, biblically, there were not seven sacraments, and that these represented a Roman "innovation." With the increasing historical ability that came about through humanistic examinations, Protestants were equipped to argue that some of the traditional sacraments were definitely not used by the churches of the apostles.

As in many other cases, sacraments became a sign of division. Without too much difficulty, an observer in the late sixteenth century could watch which sacraments were celebrated by a community, and how they were celebrated, and tell you which of the Christian "churches" he or she was observing. The irony was that the vehicles of grace that were supposed to unite Christians became another way of dividing them.

Calvin and Geneva

Later Swiss Reform

In John Calvin and Geneva, we come to one of the more celebrated and feared combinations in the sixteenth century.[1] Further, we come to a man and a city that wonderfully illustrate the kinds of paradoxes that were common in the reforms of the time. Calvin and Geneva did not like each other, did not always easily cooperate, frequently criticized each other, and yet are joined together as if by iron handcuffs. If Geneva was Calvin's cross, it was also the laboratory where he attempted to build the godly commonwealth. If Calvin was Geneva's aggravation, he was also the figure who was widely responsible for its reputation in the wider evangelical community and the magnet that drew religious refugees that swelled its population and city treasury.

An unhappy pairing—and yet productive! Calvinist or Reformed ideas and church order spread throughout Europe, taking root in Germany, Poland, the Netherlands, France, and eventually England and Scotland. Students would come from far and wide to study at the Genevan Academy. Refugees fled persecution in other parts of Europe and made Geneva not only larger but also far more diverse. Calvin himself wrote almost constantly, but he also had the practical workshop to see how the design of his ideas about city and church would actually work.

In John Calvin, we approach perhaps the foremost theologian of the sixteenth century, one whose works are still read. We will begin with his life, and then turn to Geneva at the proper time. Calvin was not a Genevan by birth, but rather a Frenchman, born in Noyon, France, in 1509. He would always be an outsider in Geneva. In fact, when the town first hired him, the official record did not even record his name, simply calling him *ille Gallus*, "that Frenchman."

Calvin, like Luther, was neither a member of the nobility nor a part of the peasant class. His father, Gerard, was a notary, serving the group of clergy in

Noyon, the cathedral chapter. Gerard had high hopes for the advancement of his family through his son's talents. He does not seem to have been very personally pious. However, Calvin's mother, Jeanne LeFranc, was quite religious, and she took Calvin to religious shrines, and it seems that young John was quite unremarkably participating in the religious world of late medieval French Catholicism.

THE YOUNG CALVIN

Calvin's education prior to his entering the University of Paris remains largely a mystery. We know that he received a better education than most, due to his connection to a local family of the nobility, the de Hangst family. Through the influence of this family, Calvin received both a good early schooling and benefices to support his further education.[2] Benefices were monetary gifts paid by the church to a young scholar of promise so that he would not have to work for money while he studied. At least some benefices were supported from the incomes of parishes that the church allowed to remain unfilled. In using benefices to support himself, Calvin was participating in one of the abuses of the medieval church.

Calvin left his home in Noyon for the University of Paris in 1523.[3] We know more about his Paris education. Though he stepped into a theological cauldron, he also came to know some of the more celebrated scholars of the day.[4] He came under the direction of one of the foremost Latinists of the time, one Mathurin Cordier (c. 1479–1564). This was during his brief stay at the Collége de la Marche from August until late in the year.[5] It was this early instruction that provided Calvin with his excellent Latin style.[6] Calvin was quickly transferred from the Collége de la Marche to the Collége de Montaigu. Its emphases in education are fairly well known. The college had been reformed by Jean Standonck, who used the model of the piety of the Devotio Moderna. If conditions from Standonck's day still applied when Calvin attended, he would have been formed in a model of piety that emphasized meditation, examination of the conscience, frequent Communion, and brotherly support for living the better, more moral life. The required reading would have leaned on Thomas à Kempis's devotional classic, *The Imitation of Christ*, and on Scripture, with a particular emphasis on Paul.[7]

In 1528, Calvin's education took a new road. Calvin's father got into trouble with his employers. Consequently, he directed his son away from theological studies and toward law.[8] Calvin went to study law at Orléans, where the famous jurist Pierre de l'Estoile taught. This choice of school had the happy coincidence of providing Calvin with the opportunity of meeting and studying with Melchior Wolmar. It was Wolmar who taught Greek to Calvin, as Calvin acknowledges in his dedication to his commentary on 2 Corinthians.

Calvin did not remain long at Orléans. Calvin and some friends left Orléans in the spring of 1529 to go to Bourges. It seems likely that Calvin would only have switched to the rival school in order to study with the brilliant Italian jurist (and rival of de l'Estoile's) Andrea Alciati.[9] Alciati was more of a humanist than de l'Estoile, and in Bourges, Calvin would have had the opportunity to come fully under the spell of the new humanistic learning. From Bourges, Calvin returned to Paris in 1531. He did not return to the College de Montaigu, but instead would study at the Collège Royal. Here Calvin's humanism was strengthened by constant study of the works of Erasmus and Lefèvre and nourished by continual contact with the leading lights of the humanist movement.[10] Though there is no evidence that he converted to Lutheranism at this time, it makes sense that this would have been the period of crystallization of Calvin's conversion to humanism.[11] He was surrounded by leading lights of the movement and began his own literary work in a typical humanistic genre— a commentary on a classical Roman philosopher.

In April 1532, Calvin completed his commentary on Seneca's *De clementia*, which revealed all the marks of the humanist scholar he had become. François Wendel comments:

> Everything, even including the limitations of his knowledge, betrays the previous humanist in Calvin. His erudition was immense, but all within the domains that the humanists had made their own—political, ecclesiastical and literary history, philology, exegesis, law and philosophy. He seems never to have been seriously interested in physical or natural sciences nor in mathematics.[12]

Calvin had become a humanist. In examining the Seneca commentary, we find a scholar who though young (Calvin would have been twenty-three) had immersed himself in the classics. Calvin demonstrated a firm grasp of both the Greek and Roman classics, as well as Augustine, especially *City of God*.[13] Calvin was well-versed in Scripture, especially the Pauline Letters, and Ganoczy notes that the commentary demonstrates a certain Erasmian moralism.[14] What we do not find is someone who was particularly Protestant in his sympathies.

For Calvin, it may have been a heady time. He was caught up in the newest academic movement, he had a small but growing reputation, he had a doctorate in law from a prestigious school. All was not wonderful, however. Calvin had published the Seneca commentary at his own expense, and it never sold well. Further, he seems at this time, between mid-1532 and 1533, to have become interested in the reforming ideas that would have circulated in humanist circles. He may have read some of Luther's works at this time; they certainly

were circulating in the city of Paris. Furthermore, the faculty of theology of
the University of Paris and the king of France were locked in a power struggle. The theologians were united in their opposition to humanism and the
Lutheran heresy, but the king supported humanism in several ways.

On the first day of November 1533, Nicolas Cop, the newly appointed rector of the University of Paris, gave an address that stressed the need for reform
in the church. The firestorm of protest that blew through Paris demonstrated
how sensitive a subject this was. Cop fled Paris. Calvin also left Paris. The most
likely reason for this is that the authorities were taking several of Cop's
acquaintances into custody, and Calvin wished to avoid this. However, one of
the two copies of Cop's address that still exist is written in Calvin's handwrit-
ing. Some scholars have speculated that Calvin wrote the address; others
believe that he simply copied it.[15] In either case, his connection with Cop was
too close for comfort, and Calvin felt safer out of Paris.

From that point on, Calvin's progress toward allegiance to the Protestant
cause is difficult to pinpoint. Writing much later in his life, Calvin termed his
conversion a "sudden conversion to docility," an act performed by God. The
translation is problematic. By *subita conversione*, Calvin may have meant "sudden" in the sense of happening in a brief time and lacking preparation. Or he
may have meant that it was not sudden in a sense of time, but rather in the
sense of the action not done by him. Calvin scholars have wasted a forest of
trees and an ocean of ink trying to pinpoint the date of Calvin's conversion.
The task may be impossible. What we do know is that Calvin felt that God
had aligned him with the new evangelical movement, and he sought to take
his part. In 1535, Calvin finished a treatise, which he dedicated to King Francis I of France. It was printed in Basel in March 1536. This little treatise was
the first edition of Calvin's *Institutes*.

In 1534, another event occurred that made Paris a dangerous place for
Calvin or for anyone of Protestant sympathies. The Affair of the Placards took
place on October 17 and 18, 1534. At night, a number of posters that criticized
the Roman ritual of the Mass were posted in a variety of places in Paris and
other French cities. The most upsetting to the king must have been the copy
that was posted on the door of his bedchamber! The most likely author was
Antoine Marcourt, the preacher of Neuchâtel. The king, who had previously
been a supporter of humanism and at least somewhat open to considering
humanist patterns of reform, was infuriated. France was now dangerous for
evangelicals, and the number of arrests and executions rose dramatically.

Calvin was in Basel from early 1535 until probably March 1536. Here he
came to embrace the cause of the new reform with his whole heart. Basel at
this time was full of humanist scholars and evangelical reformers. Nicolas Cop,
after fleeing Paris, had taken up residence there. During this period in Basel,

it is likely that Calvin learned about the execution of his friend Étienne de la Forge, who was burned alive in Paris on February 16, 1535, for his religious beliefs.[16] Erasmus lived in Basel, and he died there the following year. Calvin may have known several other important reforming figures and scholars, such as Simon Grynaeus, Wolfgang Capito, Guillaume Farel, and Oswald Myconius.[17] At this time he began his lifelong concentration on the Scriptures. He continued his study of Greek and Hebrew but also developed an idea of the Scriptures as the necessary tool for the church. The church, for Calvin, was the *schola Dei*, the school of God. The textbook for this school would always be the Scriptures. Further, Calvin identified the living Christ with the gospel. As Ganoczy states, "One thing is certain: for Calvin from this time on, the Gospel is Christ and Christ is the Gospel."[18]

In Basel, Calvin published the first edition of his *Institutes*.[19] This was not actually his first work of theology. In 1534, he had taken up the task of writing against a particular doctrine that some of the Radical Reformers held, namely, the belief in the sleep of the soul. This was the belief that between the death of the body and judgment day at the end of time, the soul simply sleeps. Calvin wrote a treatise against this, called *Psychopannychia*. He believed that the Radical theologians who were proposing such a thing were not paying close attention to Scripture. However, this was not published until much later. In 1536, Calvin's reputation in the evangelical world depended upon the *Institutes*.

If Calvin's Seneca commentary was an economic flop, his *Institutes* was the polar opposite. Simple yet profound, the small volume quickly sold out, consuming the whole printing within a year. Calvin had found his writer's voice. The 1536 edition of the *Institutes* began with a dedicatory letter written to the king of France, Francis I. In this, Calvin made clear that part of his motivation for writing the treatise was to defend the evangelical cause against the vicious attacks of its opponents. In theology, this type of writing is called "apologetic." The apologetic character of the first edition of the *Institutes* was clear both in the dedication and in its organization. The book was brief, arranged in six chapters. The topics were traditional, covering the Ten Commandments, the Apostles' Creed, the Lord's Prayer, and the sacraments of baptism and the Lord's Supper. To these Calvin added two more—a chapter on the false sacraments that Rome held, and a final chapter on Christian freedom, church power, and the role of the magistrate. Throughout, Calvin set forth a model of evangelical faith and demonstrated that it was the true heir of historic Christianity.

In 1536, Calvin left Basel and traveled rather widely, visiting Ferrara and probably Paris. He then set out in the summer for Strasbourg. However, a war between France and the forces of the emperor caused him to detour through Geneva. The chief reforming minister in Geneva at that time was Guillaume

Farel (1489–1565). Geneva was small enough at that time that Farel found out that Calvin was in town. Farel looked on Calvin's arrival as a gift from God's providence. He asked Calvin to join him in the reforming work in Geneva. Calvin politely refused; it is apparent that at this stage of his life, Calvin believed that he would be a Christian humanist scholar and not a preacher. Farel had a fiery temper, and he did not hesitate to use it. He replied to Calvin's rejection that should Calvin refuse to help with God's work in Geneva, God would never give him any peace. Calvin apparently believed him, for the shy, bookish scholar stayed and was hired by the Genevan town council to teach Bible.

THE EARLY RELIGIOUS REFORM IN GENEVA

But before we go further with Calvin, let us bring the narrative of the town of Geneva up to 1536. While Calvin is frequently called the reformer of Geneva, the progress of evangelical belief preceded his arrival in town by years. Geneva had actually long been a political football in western Switzerland, though the city itself was not technically part of the confederation. It had two rulers—the bishop of Geneva and the duke of Savoy. These rulers had been struggling for control of Geneva for generations. Meanwhile, the Genevans looked for a way to establish their own political freedoms. In 1530, the city managed to beat off an attack by the duke's soldiers through an alliance with Bern and Fribourg. By 1536, the city was technically independent but needed the assistance of Bern to avoid being overwhelmed by the troops from Savoy.

The need for Bern's help also provided a door for the evangelical reforms to come to Geneva. Bern had adopted Zwingli's reforms in 1528 and wanted to spread these to Geneva. While the city leaders of Geneva were always rightly cautious of Bern, they did allow Farel to come to Geneva in 1532, where he began preaching. Apparently his preaching attracted considerable numbers of people. This upset Catholic Fribourg, and the city demanded that Geneva expel Farel. Because the city council of Geneva was painfully aware that its independence depended greatly upon the goodwill of Protestant Bern, they did not expel Farel. Bern sensed an opportunity and sent the evangelical minister Pierre Viret (1511–1571) to Geneva in early 1534.[20]

Faced with a growing problem, the city council of Geneva adopted the solution that many Swiss towns had taken: they held a debate. A public disputation was held on January 27, 1534, between Farel and Guy Furbity, a Dominican doctor of theology.[21] While the records of the debate are not entirely clear, the public widely perceived Farel to have won. Fribourg abandoned its alliance with Geneva. Only Bern stood between Geneva and the troops of either the bishop or the duke of Savoy. Faced with a politically difficult situation, the council abolished the Catholic Mass in 1535. The local bishop excommunicated the whole city, and the Catholic clergy left the city.[22] The city council responded by taking possession of the various church properties within the city. They even went so far as to declare themselves wholly independent, with a motto that they minted on their new coins: *post tenebras lux*, "after the darkness, light."[23]

The duke of Savoy could no longer stand it. He began a war to regain custody of Geneva. Bern responded, both at the plea of Geneva and for its own political and territorial reasons. The Bernese army was successful and entered Geneva in early February 1536. When it withdrew, the republic of Geneva was born. Farel pressed the authorities to adopt the reforming movements explicitly. The city voted to do so in late May, choosing to "live henceforth according to the law of the gospel and the word of God, and to abolish all papal abuses."[24]

Thus, when Calvin arrived in Geneva in 1536, some of the particular battles needed for the city and the surrounding countryside to become Protestant had already been won. However, the character of the reform was not yet set. The Genevans had no particular church order, they had no company of pastors, and they had no academy for the training of future leaders of either the church or the republic. They had no confession of faith or catechism, and no summary of the set of Christian beliefs that set them apart from the Catholicism they had just thrown off. In fact, it is abundantly clear that the Genevans were far more certain about what they did *not* want in terms of religion than what they did.

As the Genevans had hired Calvin simply to teach Bible, it hardly seemed likely that he would be the most significant figure in molding their church and their faith. Circumstances intervened. In the war that liberated Geneva, Bern had also taken over Lausanne. Desiring to establish the evangelical cause in Lausanne, Bern arranged for a debate, termed the Lausanne Disputation. It began on October 1, 1536. Bern asked its former residents Farel and Viret to represent the Protestant side. Calvin came along, but not as one of the named representatives.

Against all likelihood, Farel and Viret performed poorly. As happened many times, the deck had been stacked somewhat in the favor of one side or another, this time in favor of the Reformed position. But the stars presented their arguments without a great deal of ability, and they seemed to have trouble answering the question of the relationship of the Reformed faith to the teachings of the Fathers. As we have seen, the relationship of faith to the teaching of the Fathers, the revered theologians of the early centuries of the Christian age, was of considerable importance to the late medieval and early modern mind.

Calvin saved the day. He stood up and denied the charge that the evangelical cause scorned the Fathers. Far from it, he answered. Instead, the evangelicals respected the Fathers more than their Catholic opponents and knew them better. Then, without notes or preparation, Calvin strung together an incredible sequence of passages from the Fathers, complete with citations, showing how the evangelical doctrine or practice more closely approximated the beliefs of the early church than that of the Catholics. The Lausanne Disputation was widely held to have been won by the evangelical cause, and Calvin was no little part of that victory.

Calvin and Farel quickly set about reforming the city of Geneva. The city council was packed with supporters of Farel, whose political party name was taken from Farel's first name: they were called the Guillermins.[25] This should have been great for the two reforming ministers. But it may have made them too confident, allowing them to think that the pace of reform could be almost instantaneous. Between early 1537 and the year's end, the reformers introduced a new order for the church of Geneva and a confession of faith. Both were designed to make permanent changes in Genevan society. Frequent celebration of the Lord's Supper, the use of excommunication at the discretion of the pastors, and the setting up of a consistory were basic parts of the church order. The confession of faith was supposed to be a litmus test: if someone would not sign, he or she would be forced to leave the city.

At least some people in Geneva rejected the newly proposed changes. The city council seems not to have wanted to give pastors the power to excommunicate people so soon after that power had been taken from the bishop. The people who objected protested the power being so concentrated in the hands of foreigners, for the pastors were not native Genevans. The result of Calvin and Farel's ambitious plans for a godly city was that they were weakened politically. In 1538, when Bern demanded that the Genevan church accept the patterns for the Lord's Supper that were followed in Bern, Calvin and Farel refused. The city council made a political calculation about the relative value of a powerful ally versus an annoying pair of foreign pastors without a great deal of difficulty. In April 1538, Calvin and Farel were banished from Geneva.

CALVIN'S EXILE FROM GENEVA
AND THE STRASBOURG MINISTRY

Calvin set out for Strasbourg, a city full of scholars and theologians. The leading minister of the city, Martin Bucer (1491–1551), took Calvin under his wing as a protégé. But there were other significant thinkers beyond Bucer in Strasbourg. Johann Sturm was perhaps the leading educator in Europe, and Calvin would be impressed by his educational theories. Wolfgang Capito lived there at that time; he was a theologian of considerable talent in his own right. The preacher Matthaus Zell and his wife, Katharina Schutz Zell, were important in the evangelical cause in the city. In going to Strasbourg, Calvin gained the opportunities for conversation and being mentored that were denied him in Geneva. He took full advantage of them. In Strasbourg, Calvin developed from a young man of one book and a failed ministry into a mature minister of a successful congregation of French refugees, with more books published, and a greater stature in the theological controversies that embroiled Europe. In Strasbourg, Calvin grew up.

Martin Bucer was directing the reform of Strasbourg when Calvin arrived there. Bucer was far more established than Calvin in 1538, and his mentoring of Calvin seems significant. One thing he did for Calvin was to convince him to take charge of a congregation of French evangelicals. Strasbourg was a German-speaking city, but there was a French congregation there, mainly made up of religious refugees. This congregation received Calvin warmly, and his experience and abilities in directing a congregation grew significantly there.[26]

Just as important as Calvin's maturation as a pastor was his written output from his period in Strasbourg. Simply put, it was amazing. In 1539, Calvin published the second edition of his *Institutes*. This was hardly a quick reprinting of the first edition. The work had grown from the small book of six chapters to a far heftier work of seventeen chapters. Further, its purpose had changed. The first edition was apologetic and catechetical, explaining the purposes of the evangelical cause to its opponents and giving the basics in the faith to a wide audience. The second edition stated that its intention was the preparation of ministerial candidates for the reading and interpretation of Scripture. Calvin had changed the *Institutes* from a general manual of theology to a schoolbook for pastors-in-training. This new version did not turn away from the education of all interested Christians, however. In 1541, Calvin himself prepared a French translation of the work, a practice that was still new at the time.

Beyond his work on the *Institutes*, Calvin began a project that would gain him his greatest fame in the sixteenth century. He began to write commentaries on Scripture, beginning with a commentary on the Epistle to the Romans, published in Strasbourg by Wendelin Rihel in 1540. His contemporaries hailed him as one of the most eminent biblical commentators of their time. This Romans commentary launched a series on the Pauline Epistles that Calvin finished in 1551.[27] Calvin followed this series with published commentaries on almost the whole of the New Testament and much of the Old Testament.[28]

At this time, Calvin was also writing treatises. While his *Short Treatise on the Lord's Supper* took up the issue of how various Protestant bodies should think about the presence of Christ in the sacrament of the Eucharist, another treatise, the *Reply to Sadoleto*, published in late 1539, revealed more about Calvin's situation and his ongoing relationship with Geneva. The treatise is interesting for two reasons. First, it was written on behalf of the city that had banished him. Second, it demonstrates how Calvin was thinking about the nature of the church.

In March 1539, Cardinal Jacopo Sadoleto (1477–1547) addressed a letter to the Genevan citizens inviting them to return to the embrace of the Catholic Church.[29] Sadoleto was a humanist and a man of impeccable moral character. His letter implored the Genevans to return in order to save their eternal souls. He argued that concern for one's soul was the heart of the reason to have religion. He then suggested that the Genevans had been deceived by crafty preachers who were involved in the reforming movements for their own personal gain.

The letter's arrival caused extraordinary consternation among the populace and leadership of Geneva. The council members quickly realized that they no longer had the theologian of the caliber necessary to compose a good reply. Astonishingly, they asked a man whom they had banished from the city, Calvin, to represent the city. To support the cause of reform and to answer the criticism of his ministry, Calvin agreed to write the response.

Calvin worked fast, and his reply appeared in October 1539. He immediately attacked the self-centered character of Sadoleto's appeal—that people should choose a religion completely out of fear for their souls. Instead, he argued for the choice being based on God's truth. Much as he had in the Lausanne Disputation, Calvin took on the charge that the Reformed faith departed from the Fathers, arguing that it did not do so in matters of consequence, and that when it did depart from the Fathers, it was in areas where the Church of Rome had also departed.

Calvin remained in Strasbourg, happily ministering and writing. In July 1540, he accepted citizenship in Strasbourg, something he had never done in his time in Geneva. In August 1540, he married a widow, Idelette de Bure. He was established in Strasbourg and seemed content to stay there. Changes in the politics of Geneva intervened, however. In late 1540, the Genevan government, following a new round of elections, started asking whether Calvin and Farel might consent to return to Geneva. Farel did not return, at least in part because he was back in the employ of Bern, which did not allow him to return. Calvin at first chose not to return; he viewed Geneva as at best a cross, at worst a curse. But his friend Farel convinced him that his presence was necessary for the continued spiritual growth and health of Geneva.

CALVIN IN GENEVA: 1541–1564

In 1541, Calvin returned to Geneva. He would remain there until his death in 1564. He now had significantly more power, for the Genevans had asked him to return. Some of his reforms were quickly passed into law. This is not to say that from that moment on Calvin was the Genevan pope. Far from it. His battles with the Genevans were constant and did not end until 1555. The way that Calvin came to consolidate his power reveals something about sixteenth-century politics and finances.[30] For some years, Calvin's fame outside of Geneva had grown quickly. His writings were widely read, and many people outside of Geneva immigrated there, either to live in a place where they believed they could grow in the Reformed faith, or because they had to flee religious persecution from Catholic authorities in their home countries. The population of Geneva swelled considerably in the mid-1500s.

The refugees did not have the power to vote, but some came with their own considerable financial resources. In the early 1550s, someone in Geneva proposed that citizenship be sold to put the city on a more stable financial footing. When this was done, the overwhelming majority of the refugees voted for the political candidates who supported Calvin. In 1555, the tipping point was passed, and Calvin did not face a serious challenge from the city council for the rest of his life.

We have only begun to scratch the surface of what Calvin's contemporaries either valued or abominated him for in his own time. His theology, and the way that it was put into practice, was the key to understanding Calvin's reputation and impact in the middle part of the sixteenth century.[31] Both of these elements—his theological doctrines *and* the way he put them into practice— are vital elements of the Reformed ideal of the Reformation that Calvin did so much to develop.

CALVIN'S THEOLOGY

The place to begin with Calvin's theology and the way it forms Reformed theological ideals is where Calvin himself began. Calvin began his *Institutes* with these words: "Nearly all the wisdom we possess, that is to say, true and sound wisdom, consists of two parts: the knowledge of God and of ourselves."[32] What Calvin went on to explain was that humans only know themselves truly when they see themselves in the light of the knowledge of who God is. This dialectical character, of knowledge of self only in connection with the knowledge of God, is crucial for grasping Reformed thought. It changes everything a person knows about herself or himself. For instance, when we look at ourselves to see whether we are morally good, we tend to look at other humans. For most of us, that means we look in the mirror and see someone who's pretty good— "I may have some problems with envy, but I've never stolen a car or embezzled money or killed anyone." Calvin's insight demonstrated that this was the wrong comparison to make. Instead of comparing ourselves to other humans, we must compare ourselves to the utter sinlessness and holiness that is God. When we do that, the picture fundamentally changes. Now, instead of seeing a mirror that shows us basically good people, we see people who choose to sin, to waste the gifts of God, to kill themselves with drugs, tobacco, and overindulgence.

If the dialectic of knowledge of God and the self ended there, the picture would be bleak. But Calvin did not end there. Instead, he insisted that humans must accept their stained character and look further at what God does. What God *should* do, according to human standards, is hate all humanity for its sinfulness. What God *does* do, according to Scripture, is love humanity with all the power in the universe. God begs humans to turn to him, God sends the Son to die for humanity, God continually grants graces and favors beyond all deserving to humanity. According to Calvin, God's love must be grasped, but it can only be grasped when people understand that they do not deserve it.

Because humans cannot trust their own minds to lead them into a right relationship with God, they need a true source for religious knowledge. For Calvin, this source was Scripture. He eloquently reasoned that Scripture to the believer was like a pair of strong reading glasses to an old man. Further, Calvin wanted everyone to be reading Scripture. As we have seen, for Calvin one of the most significant metaphors for the church was the *schola Dei*—the school of God. The curriculum for this school was the Bible. So Calvin wrote commentaries— in Latin, the language of scholarship—so that ministers might better understand the Scriptures. He then translated the commentaries into French so that any interested person might do the same. He organized weekly Bible studies on Friday, called the *Congrégations*, which were open to the public. The admonitions from the Consistory, the regulators of morality in Geneva, to the members of the Genevan church were based on Scripture. For Calvin, the Bible was a guide to right spiritual knowledge and right moral action.

The next point that is vital to grasp in Calvin's thought, which later Reformed or Calvinistic theology accepts, is the radical character of sin and grace. For Calvin, sin corrupts everything. It corrupts human desire, it corrupts human possibility. It even corrupts human knowledge. Humans, after sin, are so tainted that they not only do not want what they should want; they do not even know what they should want. This was Calvin's doctrine of the total depravity of the human condition. Many people find this offensive. Calvin did not mean that humans are wholly evil, made of an evil essence. What he did conclude was that the human nature was wholly tainted. For example, consider a twelve-ounce glass of pure water. Nothing is in the glass except water— healthy and safe to drink. Sin is like putting half an ounce of black ink into the water and stirring it through. Chemically speaking, the glass is still almost wholly water. But is there any safe place to take a drink? Similarly, Calvin argued that no part of the human person still persisted in the original righteousness; humans no longer have the possibilities they were originally created to have.

Grace is the free gift of God to help humans. Given this radical character of sin, grace must be every bit as radical. Since humans cannot help themselves, God's grace comes without any merit from humans. God does not give grace because of the inherent goodness of particular people. Instead, God gives grace because of the immensity of divine mercy.

For some thinkers, that led immediately to another question: Does God give grace equally to all people? Calvin's answer was no. God chooses for God's own reasons to give the grace to be saved to some people, but withholds that same grace from others. This was the doctrine of predestination. Calvin actually taught a form of this doctrine called double predestination. In double predestination, God chooses some people to be destined for heaven, and others for hell. This differs from the doctrine of single predestination, in which God chooses some people to be destined for heaven and makes no actual choice about the rest of the people. Logically speaking, there is little ultimate difference between single and double predestination. If one needs God's saving grace, which can only come through God's choice, and God chooses not to make the choice, one is just as damned as if God had given the choice of damnation.

While Calvin had the theological courage to teach double predestination openly, he cannot fairly be painted as a gloomy figure who enjoyed the terror of sinners. He himself called the doctrine of predestination a "horrible decree," and he believed that the only possible reason to teach it was God's choice to include it in Scripture. Since it was in Scripture for people to discover, Calvin reasoned that there must be a spiritually uplifting message in the doctrine. For Calvin, that spiritually heartening effect of the doctrine was the confidence it inspired in believers. Calvin encouraged believers to see that since their salvation was in the hands of God, it could not be taken from them. The damnation of the reprobate was a message for the justified. Those people whom God had chosen for damnation existed for the benefit of the saved. They should see that their God had chosen to be merciful and loving to them, and rejoice at God's amazing love.

While Calvin's doctrine of double predestination did arouse opposition in the sixteenth century, it was not the centerpiece of his thought that later historians have mistaken it for. Calvin believed that it was the message of Scripture and thus should be taught. But he did not concentrate upon it to the detriment of other messages. One critique that theologians leveled at predestination in the sixteenth century was that it would cause people to act immorally. These theologians reasoned that if one were saved, there was no point in acting morally since one could not lose one's salvation. Similarly, they argued that the thoughtful reprobate would not wish to act morally since he or she was going to be damned anyway.

Calvin's answer to this critique was to chain justification and regeneration together inseparably. As we have discussed, in justification God accepts the sinner through mercifully forgiving him or her, making the sinner in some sense righteous. Regeneration was the new life that the Christian lived according to grace. In fact, the discussion of regeneration, the living of the Christian life in the world, precedes justification in the later editions of Calvin's *Institutes*. Calvin believed that God justifies sinners graciously, and that no human action can affect that. Further, he argued that only when the believer knows that God is in complete control of his or her salvation can he or she have any confidence about salvation. On the other hand, Calvin contended that while believers cannot change their salvation status before God, they can respond to the new spirit within themselves and seek to make grateful spiritual and moral progress in this life. This progress would never be a salvific progress, but an effort to become more like Christ, to live the new life, in this world. Calvin saw this as a difficult process that required constant effort and was helped by the ministrations of the church.

Calvin made a significant contribution to the theology of the sacrament of the Lord's Supper. In Geneva, Calvin adopted a mediating position in his theology between that of Martin Luther and Huldrych Zwingli. As is frequently the case with mediation or compromise, neither side was happy. Both German Lutheran theologians and Swiss Zwinglian theologians criticized Calvin for his lack of fidelity to the "true" positions that Luther and Zwingli had staked out. Some of this may have been simple party loyalty, but there were definite doctrinal issues at stake.

Just as the Marburg Colloquy had sought to find a way to bridge the chasm that was growing between the Zwinglians and the Lutherans in 1529, so too Calvin sought to find the way to a solution to the question of how Christ was present in the Lord's Supper that would be sufficient for all Protestants. He first did this in *A Short Treatise on the Lord's Supper*, published in 1541. He participated in the effort of the French and German Swiss churches to find a solution, and he signed the Consensus Tigurinus (the Zurich Agreement), the document that set forth the Swiss understanding of the Eucharist, in 1549. For his signature, he was roundly criticized by the Lutherans. He constantly worked to find language that would clearly set forth what Scripture taught while explaining clearly both what was important to believe and what should never be taught about the Supper.

Calvin's own theology of the Eucharist evolved over time, at least in part in response to the various theological battles that the Protestants fought over it.[33] As noted in chapters 4 and 5, Luther had taught a doctrine of consubstantiation, while Zwingli had taught a doctrine of remembrance. Calvin adopted another position, which does not have a helpful name to set it apart. For Calvin, the Zwinglian remembrance was too mental, too antimystical. However, Calvin did not believe that the Lutheran position could be held without believing things that orthodox theology denies. Calvin argued that if Lutherans believed that the actual body of Christ was on the plates on a thousand physical Communion tables every Sunday morning, then Christ's actual human body was a myth.

For over a thousand years, Christian theologians had believed that the second person of the Trinity was both fully God and fully human. Creedal statements had been developed early in the church's history, at the Council of Nicaea in 325 and at the Council of Constantinople in 381, that established this. Failing to hold these beliefs was considered a clear statement of heresy, which put a theologian outside of the Christian mainstream and liable to the death penalty. In 381, the Council of Constantinople had adopted a statement of belief, a creed, that put it this way:

> And [we believe] in one Lord Jesus Christ, the only-begotten Son of God, begotten of the Father before all worlds, God of God, Light of Light, very God of very God, begotten, not made, being of one substance with the Father, by whom all things were made; who for us men, and for our salvation, came down from heaven, and was incarnate by the Holy Spirit of the Virgin Mary, and was made man, and was crucified also for us under Pontius Pilate. He suffered and was buried, and the third day he rose again according to the Scriptures, and ascended into heaven, and sitteth on the right hand of the Father. And he shall come again with glory to judge both the quick and the dead, whose kingdom shall have no end.

The Creed set out the necessity of both a very divine godhood and a very creaturely humanity in Christ. The human part of Jesus Christ had to be like all other humans in all things except sin. But human bodies cannot be in more than one place at a time. Calvin reasoned that if the human body of Christ was sitting at the right hand of the Father, it literally could not be in dozens upon dozens of church buildings in Europe every Sunday. For Calvin, Zwingli said too little, and Luther said too much.

Calvin's solution depended upon the acting of the Holy Spirit in the Lord's Supper. Calvin believed that the nourishment believers receive in the Supper is wholly spiritual, not physical. Therefore, he claimed that true believers who came to the Lord's Supper were mystically transported up to heaven by the power of the Holy Spirit, where they were nourished spiritually.[34] This doctrine allowed Calvin to say that the true presence of Christ was absolutely made available to believers in the sacrament, while maintaining that Christ's human body had all the properties that other human bodies had. Further, it solved the issue for him of false believers coming to the table. If someone who did not really believe came to the Communion table, he or she would receive bread and wine, but the Holy Spirit would not lift a nonbeliever up to heaven. It was a difficult and sophisticated doctrine, but it allowed Calvin to avoid some of the logical problems inherent in other solutions.

Calvin believed that the Eucharist nourished believers spiritually, so that they could live the Christian life better on this earth. Because of the difficulty of living the Christian life, Calvin sought to give more help through the institution of Christian discipline. Calvin assumed that even believers will act more morally if they are helped, with the assistance of ministers and elders of the community to direct them. So Calvin set up the Genevan Consistory in 1542. The members of the Genevan Consistory were the pastors of the city and some of the elders of the church. This body was not a legal body, and it could not assign legal penalties to members of the Genevan church for their moral and spiritual lapses. It was able to direct members of the church to attend sermons or catechism classes, and it could deny people access to the sacrament of Communion for their choosing to persist in scandalous sin. But it could not have people whipped or banished or executed; these were all civil penalties that the courts of Geneva reserved to themselves.

The Consistory oversaw problems in moral and spiritual order. It heard cases that had to do with people choosing not to attend church, or to hold on to Catholic beliefs. It heard cases that had to do with people opting to go outside of Geneva to Catholic territories to have their children baptized in Catholic ceremonies for family reasons, and cases that had to do with marital strife. No punishments were ever assigned, but rather encouragements were given and specific spiritual duties were assigned, such as attending sermons more regularly.

It would be a gross exaggeration to say that the Consistory always worked as planned, and a fantasy to state that all of the Genevans appreciated its work. Some Genevan citizens clearly hated the institution and saw it as intrusive. However, it is also important to note that the Genevans never voted in a city government that chose to dissolve the Consistory. For at least some of the Genevan populace, the Consistory was part of the moral and social fabric of the city.

This observation leads to our final issue in Calvin's thought. For Calvin, there was always a necessary character in the living out of Christian doctrine. The church does not know Scripture when it does not live by it. Believers do not accept the grace of God unless they try to change their lives in response. For Calvin, there would never be a pure Christian state in this world. However, that lack did not mean that believers should not work at the creation of the most Christian commonwealth possible. Therefore, Calvin saw a use for the Christian magistrate to work hand in hand with the Christian minister, both seeking to restrain disorder and sin.

Geneva acquired a reputation for this effort at becoming the Christian commonwealth, especially among refugees. They came from many countries, frequently in such numbers that they formed their own enclave communities in Geneva. The reason that the modern world has so many of Calvin's sermons is that the French refugees hired Denis Raguenier to write them down as Calvin preached them. John Knox, the great Scottish reformer, came to Geneva and was so impressed that he called it "the most perfect school of Christ."[35] The Scottish reformer meant especially that the city of Geneva had committed itself to the reform of morals that a truly Christian city must.

GENEVA AND EVANGELISM

Part of the reason that Geneva gained such a reputation outside of the tiny republic was that Calvin himself was always looking beyond the borders of Geneva. Calvin never forgot his homeland, never discarded his *Institutes*' original dedication to the king of France. This orientation caused him to form and train pastors for the underground church in France, the church of the Huguenots.

Throughout Calvin's career, an evangelical church existed in France. This church was frequently persecuted by the majority Catholic population, and its members had to fight for their existence. This fight took two forms. The first is rather straightforward: they engaged in armed conflict for their right to exist. But the second is just as important: they fought an ideological battle about the right of a minority to have a different religion from the majority, and they sought to come to an understanding of their own calling to be French Protestants.

Calvin's role in this second struggle was to send a steady stream of trained pastors into France. At first, the missionaries to France had simply been formed by their time in Geneva. Eventually, however, Calvin convinced the city fathers of Geneva to form the Genevan Academy in 1559 for the training of young men and boys in those subjects that would fit them to lead the republic and the church. A great number of the early students of this institution found their way into France, where many were eventually martyred, or executed for heresy, depending upon one's perspective.

We shall consider France more in the tenth chapter. For now, it is important to see other ways in which Calvin exported the Reformed model of the Christian religion to environs far from Geneva. First, Calvin was a tireless letter writer, who engaged in a broad exchange with correspondents all over Europe, both with those of high station and of low. Calvin was consulted, for instance, when the French churches hammered out a confession of faith for themselves, the Gallican Confession. He wrote to scholars, to kings, to nobles, to pastors, and to simple believers. This vast wave of letters affected those who received them, and Calvinistic ideas spread.

Second, the refugees who came to Geneva to escape persecution frequently went home and tried to emulate the religious life of Geneva in their own countries. Clearly this was the case in the Netherlands, in parts of Germany, and in Scotland. The Church of Scotland first adopted as its confession of faith the Scots Confession, composed in 1560. One of the authors of this confession was John Knox, who had been so impressed by religious life in Geneva. Even where Calvinistic or Reformed church bodies did not spring up, Calvinistic ideas acted as significant ingredients in the theology and discussion of church discipline. Such was the case in England.[36] Finally, some of the places where Calvinism took root later exported it on their own. This is how Reformed thought came to North America, to South Africa, and to Korea.

CALVIN'S TRIALS

Calvin suffered through life. Of course, part of that was due to a series of health conditions that his rigorous study habits probably only made worse. As well, Calvin's personal life was not a series of personal triumphs. It hurt his pride and probably wounded his confidence to be banished from Geneva, a town he had never wished to minister to in the first place. The details of his own private life frequently wander between sad and disastrous. He had married Idelette de Bure in 1540, a match that was not based in romantic passion. He had in fact asked a friend to recommend someone who could help him with his life by taking care of cooking and perhaps be generous with his physical ailments. But he grew to love her deeply. However, happiness continued to escape the Calvins. Idelette had a son with Calvin, but he did not survive the first few months of life. Then Calvin lost Idelette herself in 1549 to illness. The simple struggles of life that all humans share were not a matter of academic consideration for Calvin.

Beyond the difficult nature of his personal life, Calvin faced serious opposition in the city of Geneva. Until the consolidation of power in 1555, Calvin frequently lost in his ongoing scuffles with the council and citizenry. Even when he won, his victories left him exhausted and vilified, rather than triumphant. Two such conflicts are worth considering, even in this brief discussion.

In 1551, Jerome Bolsec (d. 1584) challenged Calvin over his doctrine of predestination. Bolsec was a medical doctor employed by a prominent noble in Geneva. He had come to Geneva after a time at the court of the duchess of Ferrara, a noted patroness of evangelical thinkers. In 1551, Bolsec challenged the teaching of predestination at the regular Friday *Congrégations*, the public Bible study. Though the speaker that day was not Calvin, Calvin soon took up the challenge. Eventually, Bolsec was obliged to leave the city. He attempted to settle elsewhere in Reformed territories but was unwilling to sign the confessions of faith of other cities. Eventually, he moved back to France, where he converted back to Catholicism.

Though Bolsec's motives could hardly be termed "unbiased," his biography of Calvin, published in Lyons in 1577, was widely accepted as being true by Calvin's enemies. In it, Bolsec made up a number of lies, including that Calvin was homosexual and was also a sexual predator with women.[37] The logical contradiction between these two claims never seems to have occurred to Bolsec. He seemed incensed that the people of Geneva and other Swiss cities never accepted that he was simply right about the doctrine of salvation, and so he attempted to pay Calvin back after his death.

While the Bolsec affair demonstrated that reputation could be attacked safely from afar, the case of Michael Servetus revealed the nature of the stakes of sixteenth-century theological dispute. This is the single issue upon which many people fasten their dislike of Calvin, seeing in this event the tyranny of Calvin's theocracy in Geneva.[38] To see it so is to fail to understand theology in the sixteenth century, Calvin's role in Geneva, and historical difference.

Michael Servetus (1511–1553) was a brilliant Spanish scholar, a medical doctor, and an avid lay theologian. His greatest achievement was probably the discovery of pulmonary blood circulation. Servetus was a man of great linguistic skills who read the Scriptures avidly. He came to believe that the Trinity was a made-up doctrine, and he developed highly unorthodox views of the person of Christ. Many of these views he published in 1533.

For reasons that remain a mystery, Servetus decided to challenge Calvin personally. Why he did so is somewhat of a mystery because Calvin was hardly the only theologian who disagreed with Servetus. Servetus had openly and knowingly denied the Trinity; all orthodox theologians—whether Lutheran, Reformed, or Catholic—would have rejected this. But Servetus picked on Calvin, occasionally sending him letters and, in a mocking tone, explaining why Calvin's doctrines were false.

Eventually Servetus was arrested by Catholic authorities in Vienne, France. He was tried and sentenced to be executed by burning at the stake, the normal punishment for heresy. However, Servetus escaped from prison. Here we come to another of the mysteries of Servetus—he made his escape through Geneva. After years of personally mocking Calvin, why go anywhere near Geneva? He was recognized in Geneva, arrested, and tried for heresy. Calvin gave significant evidence against him, and as the leading theologian in Geneva, he was the most substantial accuser in the charges of heresy. However, to say that Calvin autocratically demanded Servetus's death is historically inaccurate. First, Calvin did not have the power base in 1553 to demand anything. Second, Servetus received a civil trial, because the sixteenth-century mind saw heresy as something that attacked the civil order. The judge and jury were all citizens of Geneva. In 1553, Calvin did not even have Genevan citizenship but was an employee of the city.

Servetus was found guilty. The council, in seeing the probable outcome of the trial, had sought out the advice of other Swiss Protestant cities. The other cities demanded harsh punishment for Servetus.[39] It is probable that the Protestants did not wish to give the Catholic propagandists a useful topic to use. Everyone knew that Servetus was a heretic, and everyone knew the normal punishment for heresy. To do otherwise was to invite the charge that the Genevans, or Calvin, or the Swiss Protestants were soft on heresy because they were themselves heretics. Servetus was sentenced to be burned; Calvin asked that he be spared that pain and executed by beheading. His request was denied, and Servetus was burned at the stake on October 27, 1553. His execution was unremarkable in the sixteenth century but was a source of embarrassment for Calvinists in the twentieth and twenty-first centuries.

In 1564, Calvin's health was failing. On April 27, he addressed the members of the Small Council, the ruling council of Geneva, for the final time. The next day he addressed the pastors of Geneva. For weeks, he was unable to climb into the pulpit to give his sermons. His friends came to see him for a final time, even eighty-year-old Guillaume Farel, who had shamed him into the Genevan ministry in the first place. His final words before dying on May 27 were "*Quousque, Domine?*"—"How long, O Lord?"[40]

CALVIN'S FOLLOWERS

Calvin's ministry inspired many. Several scholars and pastors came to Geneva to work or to study and were impressed by Calvin. They became the second generation of Reformed leaders and continued the vision of spreading the gospel to the world beyond Geneva. Nicolas des Gallars and John Knox were touched by Calvin, and they spread his particular style of evangelical faith to France and Scotland. But chief among the first followers of Calvin was Theodore Beza (1519–1605). Beza was unlike Calvin in that he was descended from French nobility. He had spent time in Paris, where he had gained a literary reputation. He converted to the evangelical faith and made his way to Geneva in 1548, where Calvin welcomed him warmly.

Though Beza did not always reside in Geneva over the next course of years, he clearly became Calvin's right-hand man. When Calvin formed the Genevan Academy in 1559, Beza was the first appointed teacher of Greek. At Calvin's death in 1564, Beza became the chief lecturer in theology, and it was his brand of Reformed theology, influenced by Calvin, that generations of students heard. Beza wrote one of the most popular early biographies of Calvin after his death, and his praise of Calvin is so high that at times the biography seems merely idolatry.

CONCLUSION

John Calvin does not command the attention as Martin Luther did and still does. He does not seem a French-Swiss Hercules, changing the world as he strides across it on huge legs. Rather, he remains an intensely private person, unknown to most of the world. At least in part, this is because he wanted it that way. Calvin always suspected idolatry and superstition. His last will and testament directed that he would be buried in an unmarked grave, so that there would be no hero worship after his death at the "Calvin shrine." Calvin believed that the message of the gospel, the ministry of the service of the Lord, overwhelmed the personality of the minister or believer. Faced with the reality of God, humans see themselves clearly and humbly. He believed this was as true of pastors as it was of lay believers. Calvin's personality does not often show through in his writing because he intentionally hid it; in his thought, it had no place beside the majesty of the message of the gospel.

Having said that, Calvin and Reformed theology and ministry crashed on the European scene like a tidal wave. Calvin's potent mix of clearly argued biblical theology and unambiguous application to the everyday lives of people appealed to believers across Europe. Calvin's absolute belief in God's sovereign mercy, coupled with inherent realism about human nature and practical remedies for that nature, produced a compelling vision that exported well. In Calvin's hands, the Reformed movement that Zwingli had begun moved beyond Switzerland to take on a theological character not related to a particular region. His ordered reforms proved captivating even to those Calvin would have rejected, including the people who desired to set up utopias on earth. Only in Calvin's vision did they see both the inspiration of plan and the practical and ordered detail that provided the path forward.[41]

Calvin was a second-generation reformer; he did not break new theological or spiritual ground as did Luther or Zwingli or even Michael Sattler. The town he is most famously linked to had already voted in the evangelical faith before he arrived. His gift was in theological persuasion and in the ordered way of proceeding that he set up in Geneva. In doing so, he provided a model that would be copied in countries across Europe and that would ensure the strength of Protestantism throughout the sixteenth and seventeenth centuries.

QUESTIONS FOR DISCUSSION

1. Why did Calvin become a pastor in Geneva? Can successful religious leaders have difficult relations with their churches?
2. What was Calvin's eucharistic teaching about the presence of Christ? Did he effectively mediate between the Lutheran and Zwinglian positions?
3. Calvin believed and taught double predestination, yet he also demanded high moral character and instituted the Consistory in Geneva. How do these different impulses fit together in his thought? Can radical grace and a staunch moralism be held together?
4. Calvin's life was devoted to the creation of a church culture saturated with Scripture. His commentaries, *Institutes*, and sermons were all aimed at helping people engage with the Scriptures. Can a leader accomplish the creation of a biblical culture without allowing readers to come up with their own opinions on Scripture?

SUGGESTED FURTHER READING

Primary Readings

Calvin, John. *Calvin: Commentaries*. Edited by Joseph Haroutunian. Library of Christian Classics. Philadelphia: Westminster Press, 1958.
———. *Calvin's New Testament Commentaries*. 12 vols. Edited by David W. Torrance and Thomas F. Torrance. Grand Rapids: Wm. B. Eerdmans Publishing Co., 1960.
———. *Calvin: Theological Treatises*. Edited by J. K. S. Reid. Library of Christian Classics. Philadelphia: Westminster Press, 1954.
———. *Institutes of the Christian Religion*. 2 vols. Translated by Ford Lewis Battles. Edited by John T. McNeill. Library of Christian Classics. Philadelphia: Westminster Press, 1960.
———. *Institutes of the Christian Religion: 1536 Edition*. Translated and annotated by Ford Lewis Battles. Grand Rapids: Wm. B. Eerdmans Publishing Co., 1975.

Secondary Readings

Benedict, Philip. *Christ's Churches Purely Reformed: A Social History of Calvinism*. New Haven, CT: Yale University Press, 2002.
Cottret, Bernard. *Calvin: A Biography*. Translated by M. Wallace McDonald. Grand Rapids: Wm. B. Eerdmans Publishing Co., 2000.

Dowey, Edward A., Jr. *The Knowledge of God in Calvin's Theology.* 3rd ed. Grand Rapids: Wm. B. Eerdmans Publishing Co., 1994.

Ganoczy, Alexandre. *The Young Calvin.* Translated by David Foxgrover and Wade Provo. Philadelphia: Westminster Press, 1987.

McKim, Donald K., ed. *The Cambridge Companion to John Calvin.* London: Cambridge University Press, 2004.

Naphy, William. *Calvin and the Consolidation of the Genevan Reformation.* Manchester: Manchester University Press, 1994.

DOCTRINAL-VOCABULARY DISCUSSION

Eucharistic Controversies

In the sixteenth century, the sacrament of the Lord's Supper caused many controversies between the various confessional camps. The Lord's Supper was variously known as the Eucharist, Communion, the Lord's Supper, and, among Catholics and some Lutherans, the Mass. Conflicts arose over several points. First was the question of who could participate fully in the sacrament. Second, conflicts cropped up over the presence of Christ in the sacrament. Finally, different beliefs surfaced over the questions of participation, of who had the right or privilege to come to the sacrament.

Who could participate fully in the sacrament—who could receive both the bread and the wine? This matter actually arose before the sixteenth century. In the earliest centuries, the church had given both elements, technically also called both species, to all participants in the sacrament. But over the years, a division between clergy and laity had arisen. By the fifteenth century, the Church of Rome had developed a tradition that only clergy should receive bread and wine, both species. In Bohemia, a controversy arose over this custom, and the practice of distributing both elements to the laity was established. The Church of Rome decreed that this was a heresy, calling it the "Utraquist" heresy—meaning "both kinds." In 1415, Rome attempted to stamp out this heresy by executing one of the leaders of the Bohemian rebellion, Jan Hus (c. 1370–1415). Luther in 1520 argued that Hus had been correct in many things; he pointed out that since Scripture demanded that all people receive the wine, the church did not have authority to withhold it. Most Protestant groups followed this model and gave the cup to the laity. The Church of Rome at the Council of Trent determined that laity should never receive the cup. In fact, the Church of Rome would have denied the question, stating that the laity were fully participating in the Mass without the cup.

The presence of Christ in the Eucharist was another topic of controversy. When Jesus said, "This is my body," did that mean that the actual body of Jesus was on the Communion plate? Three main opinions existed over this. The

Roman position was transubstantiation, defined first at the Fourth Lateran Council in 1215. This belief stated that the actual body and blood were on the plate and in the cup, and that it was not truly any longer bread and wine. The Lutheran position was consubstantiation, which Martin Luther first published in 1520 (without that particular word). This principle stated that both the actual body and blood *and* the bread and wine were on the plate and in the cup. The third major position, held by many Reformed theologians but usually attributed to Huldrych Zwingli, is called "remembrance." Zwingli put more emphasis on the words of Jesus to "do this in remembrance of me" and so called the meal a celebration of remembrance of Christ's gifts to the faithful. John Calvin offered up a fourth position that attempted to mediate between Zwingli and Luther; it saw the true sacrament only being consumed in heaven.

What was at stake in the presence battles? Nothing less than the doctrine of Christ and the witness of the Scriptures. For the Lutherans and Catholics, the remembrance position was simply too "thin." They argued that in this model, believers did not truly commune with Christ. Zwinglians and other remembrance advocates pointed out that the Lutheran and Catholic positions meant that Christ's human body was on a thousand different tables in a thousand different churches every Sunday. They argued that this denied the reality of the human body of Christ, which logically could not be in more than one place at a time. As for the Scriptures, the question was how to understand which words. Were the words "This is my body" meant literally by Jesus? Were they meant metaphorically? Further, should "This is my body" be more important than "Do this in remembrance of me"? Deep and difficult questions were at stake in understanding the biblical issues around this sacrament.

Finally, who had the right or privilege to come to the table or altar? All varieties of confessional bodies practiced excommunication in the sixteenth century. This was a matter of discipline. People who had committed known significant sins and were not reconciled to the church were barred from the sacrament. All bodies practiced this so as to cause believers to realize the magnitude of their sin, repent, and return to the community. All at one time or another probably abused the practice, and those people who were excommunicated frequently made the charge that the issue at hand was not piety but politics.

The ability to approach the Lord through the sacrament of Communion was a clear marker of confessional identity in the sixteenth century. Because so much was tied to this sacrament, the fights were particularly ferocious. If the Lord's Supper had been less central to the piety of the sixteenth century, perhaps the issues could have been more calmly considered. Instead, the doctrine of the Lord's Supper became one of the easiest markers to use to determine what confessional camp one owed allegiance to.

8

English Reform

The Foundation of the Church of England

The German Lutheran pattern of reform depended upon a single prophetic figure, Martin Luther, seen as a giant leading the way toward the purer faith and religion. The Swiss Reformed pattern of reform produced no single figure like Luther, but a variety of theologians who served as focal points of leadership. Both the Lutheran and Reformed reformations depended upon close cooperation between ministers and magistrates. The Radical Reformation did not produce a single leader and did not act in cooperation with the secular rulers, choosing instead to set its institutions apart from the society to demonstrate their calling out of the world. What we have seen so far among the Protestant movements in the sixteenth century is a variety of patterns of reform, adopted for different political and theological reasons.

In considering the reform of the Church of England, we come to another design for reform. The Church of England's reform was accomplished by the monarchs and parliaments of England, without specific concern for popular support. This is not to say that no one in England desired the renovation of the church in its morality or its structures. However, the impetus for the changes came from the kings and queens of England, who made their choices for religious and political reasons, far more than from the bishops, pastors, and theologians who served in England. Diarmaid MacCulloch has noted this character of English reform being in the hands of kings and queens and their counselors:

> Thus one does not find fiery clerical reformers independently spearheading the changes which transformed the English Church. There was no Luther to arouse the nation against the Pope, no Zwingli to turn the eating of a sausage into the downfall of a city's traditional faith, and among the rather thin and muted ranks of English religious

radicalism, no Thomas Müntzer to face death for a revolutionary new Jerusalem.[1]

Because of this ruling factor, this chapter will be organized according to the succession of England's rulers. This is not at all to say that the various theological voices and the work of pastors and bishops had no effect—quite the contrary. But in no other evangelical country did the fortunes of the reform so clearly depend upon the political issues of the sovereign. The chapter begins with the religious state of England in the beginning of the sixteenth century, then considers Henry VIII, Edward VI, Mary I, and Elizabeth I.

RELIGIOUS LIFE IN ENGLAND: 1500

Religious life in England around 1500 was actually quite calm. Religious life in England was roiled by dissent in the beginning of the sixteenth century. Obviously, these two statements contradict each other. They represent the two popular trends among historians of the English Reformation.[2] Both have some reasons to be believed. England was not part of the Holy Roman Empire, and so the electoral issues that frequently shook the empire did not exist. Further, though England had had heresy, in the form of a movement from a group called the Lollard sect, it did not seem central to religious life in England. On the other hand, if people in England were so content with Catholicism, why was there not a general uprising when Henry VIII and Parliament abandoned Rome?

In 1966, Heiko A. Oberman published *Forerunners of the Reformation: The Shape of Late Medieval Thought.*[3] This became one of those books that changed the course of the discipline. Oberman pointed out that instead of neglecting the late Middle Ages, roughly the fourteenth and fifteenth centuries, historians should spend more time on them. This would allow the reforms of the sixteenth century to take a more historically contextualized place in the stream of history. One of the figures whom Oberman briefly considers in that book is John Wycliffe (c. 1330–1384). To understand the history of religious unrest in England leading up to the sixteenth century, one first must understand something of Wycliffe.

John Wycliffe seemed to be the polar opposite of a religious revolutionary. He was an Oxford theologian and philosopher who began his career by commenting upon the inadequacy of skepticism as a philosophical outlook. His theological investigations, however, took him to an unorthodox position, which he was clearly teaching in 1377 and 1378, that saw the Scriptures as the only source of authority for doctrine. Wycliffe added to this the discovery that the authority of the papacy was not well supported in Scripture. It should be noted that Wycliffe made these observations during the Avignon Papacy, discussed in the second chapter. As well, England and France were in the midst of the Hundred Years' War. Wycliffe argued for a view of political power that saw the king above the pope. These positions added up to a simple sum: John Wycliffe was on a collision course with Rome.

Wycliffe was not through. Immersing himself in scriptural study, he came to the conclusion that the monastic orders and the orders of the friars denied the clear teaching of Scripture, and he asked that the English government reform these religious orders. Finally, he began to teach that transubstantiation was both unbiblical and philosophically irrational. Wycliffe was censured by the archbishop of Canterbury, William Courtenay. Though Wycliffe had to retire, he did not stop writing pamphlets and trying to make his own version of Christianity heard.

Wycliffe died in 1384. During his lifetime, his work had been part and parcel of university theology, the area of learned men. However, Wycliffe's ideas found an audience beyond the university context. Jan Hus, the Czech reformer, openly stated that he had read and approved of Wycliffe's teachings. (We examined Hus's reforms briefly in connection with Martin Luther in the fourth chapter.) Hus was burned as a heretic by the Council of Constance in 1415. But Wycliffe's doctrines found a popular audience within England. The people who accepted Wycliffe's teachings, or a popularized form of them, were called Lollards. This term probably came from a Dutch word meaning "mumbler." It was always a term of ridicule, and eventually "Lollardy" became synonymous with heresy in England. Wycliffe's ideas also became an object of suspicion for the English authorities.

The Lollards did not form a clear opposition "church" that could be defined by a set of practices and beliefs to which they would all agree. It was a far looser movement that was basically anticlerical in nature. The Lollards' anticlericalism undoubtedly had some basis in abuse by members of the English clergy, though to what extent that actually moved the laypeople of England is debatable. What is clear is that the anticlerical sentiment that already existed found a set of theological arguments in Wycliffe's thought. Lollards soon turned to the Bible for support for their positions, against the traditional teaching of the Catholic priests and bishops. Again, they were following Wycliffe, who had translated the Bible into English. Because this was a popular movement, frequently held by uneducated people, Lollards advocated translating the Scriptures into English since they could not read Latin. They came to believe that laymen could perform the functions of priests and that the lavish wealth of the late medieval church was part of what was wrong with Christianity.

Lollardy lasted roughly from the late fourteenth century to the early sixteenth century. The English Crown persecuted Lollards vigorously after 1401, when Parliament passed a statute setting burning as the punishment of heresy. Due to this official persecution, most of the time people with Lollard sympathies kept quiet about it; indeed, Lollardy was an underground movement for much of the period of its existence. In part to answer the turmoil that arose from popular strains of Lollardy, English church leaders began to prohibit the possession of translated Bibles, especially those Bibles with Wycliffite prefaces. Prefaces would become an important way to guide the reading of Scripture throughout the sixteenth century as well, and possession of an English translation of the Bible with a preface that sympathized with Wycliffe's theological positions was generally taken as proof positive of Lollardy by religious and secular authorities.

An interesting case that demonstrates many of these issues comes from the story of Richard Hunne (d. 1514). The case involved Lollard sympathy, the conflict about the power of the church and of the crown, the issue of anticlerical sentiment, and the church and crown's treatment of this heresy. Richard Hunne was a prosperous London merchant. He came to the attention of the authorities when he refused to pay the mortuary fees to the priest who buried his infant son in March 1511. The priest, Thomas Dryffeld, demanded the most precious possession of the deceased, as was his legal right under church law. In this case, he demanded the garment in which the baby was clothed for his burial—an expensive garment that he could have sold. Hunne refused, citing civil law that the baby did not own it but that his father did. Immediately, we see the conflict of church and civil law.

The case worked its way through the church courts, and Hunne was found guilty and was sentenced to pay the value of the garment to Dryffeld. That should have ended things, but when Hunne was at worship, Dryffeld's assistant priest, Henry Marshall, called Hunne "accursed." Hunne brought suit for slander. In doing so, he appealed to the Praemunire Statutes, a set of laws stating that it was illegal to appeal the civil law to the church's authorities. These were already ancient laws by 1512 and had never been fully tested in court. Now the issue was king's law versus church law—and the stakes could not have been higher. The church court took Hunne into custody and imprisoned him in the Lollard's Tower of Old St. Paul's Cathedral. His home was searched and an English Bible was found, complete with a Wycliffite preface. Hunne remained in prison, and on December 4, 1514, he was found hanging by his neck in his jail cell, an apparent suicide. However, the coroner refused to find it a case of suicide, since there was ample evidence that Hunne had been strangled and a clumsy effort made to fake his suicide. Eventually, the bishop's chancellor and two other men were indicted for the murder. However, the church court intervened again and managed to avoid the case ever coming to trial. Small wonder that there were violent anticlerical feelings in England and a strong desire to read the Bible without the filter of a priest. English Bibles proved to be very popular.

England provided one of the most significant biblical translators of the sixteenth century, whose work deserves a place next to that of Luther for his German Bible. William Tyndale (c. 1494–1536) was a brilliant translator with an extraordinary knowledge of the biblical languages of Greek and Hebrew and an exceptional ability to turn a memorable English phrase. Tyndale was educated at Oxford and was surprised during his master's studies to find out that the course did not require the study of Scripture. Though Tyndale converted to the Lutheran cause early on, his greatest conversion was to the ideal of a scriptural religion. He was firmly convinced that placing Scripture into the hands of the common people was the best way to achieve a godly church. John Foxe quoted him as saying, "I defy the Pope, and all his laws; and if God spares my life, I will cause the boy that drives the plow in England to know more of the Scriptures than the Pope himself!"[4]

Tyndale set out to translate the Bible, beginning first with the New Testament. His work was done on the Continent, as the climate for reform was inhospitable in England, and many of the bishops there did not trust the idea of a vernacular Bible, possibly linking it to the tradition of the Lollards. In fact, though the English Reformation was quite different from that on the Continent, there was constant interaction between the two. In 1526, Tyndale's New Testament was published in Worms, and copies were smuggled into England. English authorities naturally found out, Tyndale was condemned, and copies of the book were burned. Tyndale spent much of the next ten years in hiding in Europe but continued his work on translating the Old Testament. In 1535, Tyndale was captured by imperial authorities in the Netherlands. In 1536, he was burned at the stake. Though he was silenced, his work lived on. When in 1611 a new English king, James I, decreed that there should be a new English Bible, which would come to be known as the King James Version, the team of scholars depended heavily upon Tyndale's translations.

Beyond the popular Lollard movement, the early sixteenth century saw significant interest in the doctrines of Martin Luther at the university level, especially after 1517 and the indulgence controversy. Though Wycliffe had been a professor at Oxford, the interest in the new "Lutheran" theological ideas centered in England's other premier university, Cambridge. By 1520, Lutheran ideas were reaching England and the popular imagination. Cardinal Wolsey publicly announced Luther's excommunication in London on May 12, 1521. Wolsey ceremonially burned Luther's books and ordered the confiscation of all of his books from any who might possess them.[5] While this is clearly evidence of Wolsey's intention to stamp out Lutheran belief, it also is probably evidence that such belief was growing in England, especially at the White

Horse Inn, where Cambridge theologians would meet to discuss Lutheran ideas. It was so famous for this identification with Luther that it was nicknamed "Little Germany."

The English and Continental reforming movements influenced much of England, but the monarchs also played their role. It is time to return to the kings and queens who ruled over England and over the fate of reform on the island nation. Their own personalities and particular theological and religious tastes would have as great an impact on the pattern of reform in England as that of any individual theologian, bishop, or priest.

KING HENRY VIII

Henry Tudor (1491–1547), who would reign as Henry VIII, deserves a far more significant reputation than he has gained for his many wives. His talents, his desires, and his impact on the form of the Christian faith in England make him a fascinating figure and captivate the historian's interest as much for his great contradictions as for his king-size appetites. He was the second son of the first Tudor king, Henry VII, a fact that is crucial to understanding Henry. Henry was not supposed to be king. His older brother, Arthur (1486–1502), had been first in line for the throne. As heir apparent, an important dynastic marriage had been arranged for Arthur from a young age. In 1501, Arthur married Catherine of Aragon (1485–1536), a Spanish princess. Catherine had very important family connections, not least of which were her parents, Ferdinand and Isabella, the king and queen of Spain. She was also the aunt of Charles V, who would become the Holy Roman Emperor, but that was not at issue in 1501. Unfortunately, Arthur died in 1502, without fathering an heir with Catherine.

Henry thus became the heir to the English throne. The reasons in favor of a marriage between the heir to the English throne and a powerful Spanish princess still existed, so Henry VII desired that Catherine be engaged to Henry. However, under church law, this was illegal. Medieval church law prohibited a man from marrying his brother's widow. This would not have been the case if the marriage had never been consummated, which was what Catherine always argued. A request was made of the pope, Julius II, to set aside the law, to give a dispensation so that Henry and Catherine might be married. He did so, and Henry VIII was married to Catherine of Aragon in 1509, one of Henry's first acts after taking the throne.

As state marriages go, Henry and Catherine were basically happy enough. However, a fundamental problem existed in the marriage—Catherine could not produce a male heir strong enough to survive. In 1516, Catherine gave birth to a child who survived but was a daughter, Mary. Henry needed a male heir. England had recently been through the dynastic Wars of the Roses, and so securing the succession to the crown was of paramount importance. Through a number of pregnancies, still only Mary survived. Desperate, Henry began to wonder whether his marriage was cursed by God. On the other hand, he may only have begun to wonder once he fell for Anne Boleyn.

Henry was not simply a bad Christian, looking for a way out of a dynastically awkward marriage. In 1521, he wrote a book criticizing Martin Luther and defending the seven sacraments. Many historians believe that the book was probably the work of one of Henry's theologians. That did not matter to Pope Leo X, who was thrilled to have a monarch of an important realm speak so strongly against the Lutheran heresy. In October 1521, Leo granted Henry the title "Defender of the Faith." Though a later pope, Paul III, revoked the title, English sovereigns have held the title since 1544, when Parliament granted it to all English sovereigns. In any case, Henry VIII was a thoroughly convinced Catholic, absolutely in favor of many traditional Catholic doctrines. So why did he wish to divorce?

This is one of the most difficult questions to answer in the history of Henry VIII. Did Henry honestly believe that his marriage was cursed, or did he simply look for a convenient excuse? Historians have come down on both sides of the question. Against the sincerity of Henry's claim, he seems already to have been in love with Anne Boleyn, but she was withholding her favors from the married king. Supporting Henry's claim is the fact that the king was an amateur theologian with some knowledge of the Scriptures and theology; he found a passage in the book of Leviticus that supported his theory that he had no child because he had married his brother's wife. Henry stated that he believed Catherine had lied in her statement that her marriage to his brother had never been consummated. Because of this concern, Henry asked Pope Clement VII to annul his marriage to Catherine in 1527.

At any time, asking a pope to set aside the specific work of a prior pope is a serious matter, but that is exactly what Henry was asking Clement to do—to say in some sense that Julius II had been wrong to give a dispensation so that Henry and Catherine could wed. Such things were not normally impossible, especially in cases of dynastic concern. However, political considerations at that moment made the matter far more complicated. When Henry sent his emissaries to Clement to ask for the annulment, Clement was basically the prisoner of the Holy Roman Emperor, Charles V. Charles had sacked Rome in 1527, and the pope was his prisoner. Charles was Catherine's nephew. To annul the marriage, Clement might have had to make some finding that Catherine had lied about her first marriage to Arthur. Further, the effect of this would have been to turn Catherine into a "whore" and her daughter Mary into a "bastard." This was politically impossible, and after long negotiations trying to find a possible solution to Henry's problem, Clement refused.

Faced with a negative answer and realizing that Catherine, who was now forty years old, was not going to bear him the son he needed, Henry took a different tack. He moved forward with his pursuit of Anne Boleyn and secretly married her in 1533. He simultaneously set out a new vision of England, seeing it as an empire, without any superior on earth.[6] Henry had his marriage to Catherine annulled. The English Parliament passed a series of acts, with the key year being 1534. In that year, Parliament passed the Succession Act, the Supremacy Act, and the Treasons Act. The Succession Act recognized the legitimacy of Anne Boleyn as Henry's wife, and her children as his heirs. The Supremacy Act set out the English sovereign as the supreme head of the English church. The Treasons Act made denial of the king's sovereignty of the church a treasonous deed. Henry's new chief minister, Thomas Cromwell, steered these acts through Parliament. Probably Henry did not realize the depth of Cromwell's own evangelical religious convictions.[7] Many more practices were reformed or changed. Henry suppressed the English monasteries, gaining both territory and wealth. He changed the character of the religious calendar, drastically restricting the celebration of holy days. Finally, an English Bible was to be deposited in every church, representing a clear departure from the suspicions of Lollardy that simply possessing an English Bible had aroused two decades earlier.

Though Henry's saga of wives has made him a figure of popular fascination,[8] his engagement with the religious sphere did not end with his marriage to Anne Boleyn. Though it is common to see the acts of 1534 as the beginning of true Protestantism in England, this was hardly the case. Henry was still in many respects a convinced Catholic; he had simply needed a new wife. However, Henry's religious conservatism did not stop him from making some moves that would forward the cause of reform in England. Partly through the influence of Anne, Henry appointed Thomas Cranmer as the ecclesiastical head of the English church, the archbishop of Canterbury, in 1533. Cranmer (1489–1556) carefully shepherded the Church of England on a path toward a more Protestant character, even when that required him to be extremely cautious around Henry himself.

Cranmer originally came to Henry's attention because he was a priest who was supportive of Henry's divorce. Henry appointed him as part of the team sent to Rome to negotiate his divorce. When that failed, Cranmer was sent to Germany to gain an understanding of Lutheranism, to see whether it would have benefits for England. Cranmer himself at this time became a convinced "Lutheran" and secretly married Margaret Osiander, the niece of a prominent German reformer, in 1532.

In 1533, Henry appointed Cranmer as archbishop of Canterbury. As soon as the pope approved the appointment, Cranmer stated that Henry's marriage to Catherine of Aragon was annulled, meaning that technically it had never occurred. This paved the way for the acts of Parliament of 1534 that would place the English church on the road to its own divorce, away from Rome.

If the story of English Protestantism ended in 1534, it would be a much easier story to tell. However, the story did not end with the official acts of Parliament. In 1535, Henry taxed the clergy of the realm, breaking the ancient tradition of clerical immunity from taxes. In 1536, the king suppressed the smaller monasteries and took over their lands and properties. In 1538, he returned to the monasteries as a convenient source of cash and shut down the larger ones.[9] In all of these actions, Cranmer and Cromwell were supportive actors.

Henry's religious acts did not come without political consequences. His schism had made England a kingdom or empire that was without political allies and exposed to attack. France and Spain, enemies for most of a century, had recently made peace, and Henry had reason to worry that they might unite against England. Henry attempted to explore alliances with the Lutherans, which might have given him German military allies. He allowed Cranmer to publish the Bishops' Book of 1537, which included several compromises with the Lutheran positions. This strengthened his appeal to the Lutheran princes and made the prospect of some kind of Protestant league more likely.

Henry himself was changing in some ways, as Christopher Haigh skillfully describes:

> He had not set out to be supreme head of the church, but he found he rather liked it, caring for his subjects' souls as well as their bodies, purifying religion for the good of the realm. In royal injunctions for the church in 1536 and 1538, the king tackled "superstition"—veneration of images and relics was banned, pilgrimage was discouraged—and he ordered every parish church to have an English Bible. When the official "Great Bible" was published in 1539, its frontispiece showed Henry handing out Bibles to Cranmer and the bishops on his right and to Cromwell and the counselors on his left, who then passed "Verbum Dei" to the people—while Christ looked down approvingly from the clouds. That was how Henry had come to see himself, as God's agent bringing true religion.[10]

Henry was the sovereign of a realm that was religiously moving in ways that he approved. His role as sovereign was wed to a role in the church. Church and realm worked seamlessly together in this ideal. That was the good side of the coin. But every coin has two sides. Much as Luther and Zwingli had found that people could take their ideas in ways they had not intended, Henry sometimes found parts of the reform movement that he detested.

In 1539, Henry made clear that his theological convictions had not actually changed with the publication of the Six Articles. In part, this reflected the new political reality that France and Spain were back at war and thus were less likely to attack England. The Six Articles made denial of transubstantiation a capital offense, with the criminal to receive the normal penalty for heresy: burning at the stake. Other traditional Roman observances were also upheld, such as confession and the necessity of celibate clergy. In part, the publication of the Six Articles symbolized a politically defensive move on Henry's part: he had been excommunicated in 1538 and was demonstrating his orthodoxy in significant theological matters. In 1540, Henry proceeded further toward the ideal of Catholicism without a pope. He executed Robert Barnes, a leading English Lutheran, on charges of heresy. Barnes had been instrumental in the negotiations between Henry and the German Lutherans, but when Henry put his foot down, Barnes no longer had any value. In that same year, Henry divorced his German wife, Ann of Cleves, signifying his lack of worry about a French and Spanish alliance, and his independence from the (German) Lutheran heresy. Finally, he executed his chief minister, Thomas Cromwell, that same year. It was a bad time to be a convinced Protestant in England.

In 1543, Henry put forth the Act for the Advancement of True Religion. This was another milestone, for it reversed some of Henry's own earlier Protestant-leaning reforms. The act condemned certain translations of the Bible and listed a set of groups of people who were not allowed to read or interpret the Scriptures to other people. The list included women, craftsmen, apprentices, farmers, and laborers.[11] Clearly, Henry was uncomfortable with the idea of a priesthood of *all* believers, preferring a greater concentration of power in the hands of some sort of elite.

The last years of Henry's reign look like a series of underground battles between the supporters of a more liberal, Lutheran or Swiss-style reform in England, and supporters of a more conservative traditional religion. Henry himself gave mixed signals. Nowhere was this more clear than in the education of his only living son, Edward. Edward had been born in 1537, the son of Jane Seymour. Henry had married Jane in 1536, soon after executing Anne Boleyn for adultery. Jane died soon after Edward's birth from complications due to his birth. Though Henry time and again clearly rejected key Lutheran and Zwinglian doctrines, such as justification by faith and the priesthood of all believers, he allowed his son to be educated by Protestant teachers, who formed the young prince as a confirmed Protestant. Henry's will also clouded the waters. In it, he demanded that should Edward die, the throne would pass to Mary, his daughter with Catherine of Aragon. Then he specified that after

Mary, his daughter with Anne Boleyn, Elizabeth, should come to the throne. In effect, his will adopted a fallback position that overturned his whole effort to divorce Catherine in the first place! Worse, the will set out an odd "seesaw" succession, of Protestant Edward, Catholic Mary, and Protestant Elizabeth. Finally, the fallback position was not merely a small chance, for Edward's health was poor, and most people at court knew it. Henry died in 1547, a religious enigma.

KING EDWARD VI

In 1547, Edward inherited the throne. Edward VI (1537–1553) was only nine years old when his father died, so some of the events that happened in his brief reign as king must be credited to or blamed upon his regents, those adult guardians who made many of the decisions for the young sovereign. These were Protector Edward Seymour, Duke of Somerset; and then John Dudley, Duke of Northumberland. Still, Edward VI's reign represents the missed opportunity for English Protestantism. When Henry VIII died, Protestant theologians in both England and on the Continent rejoiced at the idea of the new king. Edward had been raised a Protestant and had clear Protestant sympathies. Thomas Cranmer's coronation sermon compared Edward to the biblical King Josiah: "Your majesty is God's viceregent, and Christ's vicar within your own dominions, to see, with your predecessor Josiah, God truly worshipped, and idolatry destroyed, the tyranny of the bishops of Rome banished from your subjects, and images removed. These acts be the sign of a second Josiah, who reformed the church of God in his days."[12] This was a clear call on Cranmer's part for Edward to step forward beyond the reforms that his father had allowed, to take up the destruction of "idols," and to get rid of all the lasting effects of the Church of Rome that still existed in England. John Calvin even dedicated his commentary on 1 and 2 Timothy to the duke of Somerset, one of the regents of the young king. In these signs, we can see the sense among the supporters of reform that they believed the time had come to complete the reform in England.

Indeed, many reforms did occur during Edward's brief reign. In 1547, the Six Articles and other heresy laws were repealed. This simple change hastened others, as it allowed several religious refugees who had fled to Europe to return to England and work for their ideas of reform. It was not only English who returned to England. The great Strasbourg reformer, Martin Bucer, found Strasbourg impossible over political events and moved to England, where he became professor of theology at Cambridge. John Knox, who would be the most significant voice of reform in Scotland, was appointed court chaplain. In

1549, the duke of Somerset published a new Book of Common Prayer, written by Thomas Cranmer, for use in the English churches. It had a far more Protestant character and removed some of the symbolic marks of the belief in transubstantiation in the service of the Eucharist. In 1550, altars were removed from the churches of England and replaced with Communion tables—the Eucharist was being transformed from a sacrifice into a supper.[13] Clerical marriage became openly admitted, and Archbishop Cranmer openly acknowledged his own wife.

The most significant changes of the Edwardian age were doctrinal, both in statements of belief and in the worship practices of the faithful. In 1553, Cranmer fashioned a confession of faith, like the Augsburg Confession, for the English church. This was the Forty-two Articles. The Forty-two Articles were far more thoroughgoing in their changes of traditional practices and doctrines than many things Henry VIII had allowed. To support this doctrinal change, the English church needed bishops who believed in the changes. During Edward's reign, many Protestant bishops were appointed to take the place of Catholic bishops. Beyond that transformation, worship was being renewed. Sermons took a more prominent place in worship, and the importance of Bible reading and of hearing the Bible read increased greatly.[14] Much of the decorative art that supported the theology of the Church of Rome was removed, hidden, or destroyed during this time.

It certainly seemed that Protestantism reigned supreme. However, far too much depended upon the health of a sickly young king. Too many of the reforms were too new to stand on their own without both the legal arm of the king to enforce them and the spiritual model of the king (or at least his regents) to pattern them. Further, though some of Edward's bishops desired a more thorough change in the English church, resistance to those very changes persisted among some of the lower clergy and in some areas of the kingdom. This was particularly true in the northern reaches of the kingdom and in Cornwall, which had rebelled against the enforcement of the 1549 Book of Common Prayer. The cause of Protestantism needed Edward, but fate or providence or simply poor health intervened. Edward died, probably of tuberculosis, at the age of fifteen. The year was 1553, and the question that Henry VIII had so desperately wanted to avoid, that of the succession to the throne, was again in play.

Henry had stipulated that after his son, his first daughter, Mary, should succeed to the throne. Mary was a convinced Catholic and was bitter over the Protestant churchmen who had helped her father to set her mother aside. The duke of Northumberland, who was the most powerful of Edward's advisors, had Edward write his own will to continue Protestantism. He arranged to have the throne pass to Lady Jane Grey. Grey was the great-niece of Henry VIII, and a Protestant. However, popular opinion swelled around Mary, whose claim to the throne was far stronger, as she was Henry's daughter. Mary took the throne in 1553 and quickly had Northumberland executed for his part in the plot.

QUEEN MARY I

With Mary on the throne, England could again become a Catholic country. Or could it? She quickly maneuvered a series of changes to the laws regarding religion in England. She restored the Mass, required the clergy to be celibate, reestablished England as a country that acknowledged the supremacy of the pope, and reinstated the heresy laws that her half brother had erased. Catholic cardinal Reginald Pole returned from the Continent to assume the archbishopric of Canterbury and to serve as the pope's legate, his closest representative in England. Mary did compromise on one point and did not restore all the monasteries, which would have been financially disastrous for the crown. Christopher Haigh claims that Mary enjoyed widespread popular support: "At the parish level, Catholic worship was restored with eagerness and success: Reformation had been imposed from above, but Counter-Reformation was not."[15]

However, not all was well with the return to the true religion that Mary led. As usual in England, the issues were at least as political as they were religious. First, Mary was every bit as desperate for an heir as her father had been. His will clearly positioned his daughter Elizabeth, a Protestant, as the next in line to the throne, unless Mary could provide an heir. Of course, Mary wanted her husband to support her Catholicism. To that end, she quickly married, but this turned out to be a disaster.

Riots broke out at the announcement of the planned marriage of Mary to Philip of Spain, the son of her cousin Charles V, the Holy Roman Emperor. The English people and many of the English nobility mistrusted an alliance with Spain, and many worried that this would relegate England to becoming dependent on Spain. Mary did not help matters when her marriage treaty gave the title "King of England" to Philip. Mary was not deterred from her goal, but the marriage in 1554 immediately soured the popular support that had helped her gain the throne in the first place.

Mary's next missstep seemed at first like a step of strength. The heresy laws had been reinstated, and prominent Protestants had been imprisoned, including Bishop Hooper and Archbishop Cranmer. Now heresy trials began in earnest, with the traditional punishments. With the full support of Cardinal Pole, Mary began to execute heretics. In February 1555, the Bible translator John Rogers was burned at the stake, the first of Mary's victims. In the remaining four years of her reign, Mary executed approximately three hundred more men and women for their beliefs.[16] This campaign of punishment, whether a reign of terror or the determined act of a sovereign to stamp out heretical belief, earned the queen the nickname of "Bloody Mary."

While Mary undoubtedly wished to constrain heresy and to consolidate her reign through a union of the people of England with the true Church of Rome, her punishment of heresy during her reign had the unintended consequence of creating martyrs. Lacey Baldwin Smith has noted the paradoxical character of Mary's campaign against heresy, noting that since even the weak members of the heretical party refused to give up their beliefs, some power passed from the reigning Catholicism to the outlaw Protestantism: "As a result the initiative suddenly and invisibly passed into the hands of the Protestants, even before the Catholics were aware of it."[17] Some of the martyrs gave marvelously powerful examples to those who shared their same religious beliefs. Thomas Cranmer remains one of the most potent examples. To save his own life, Cranmer had signed a recantation of his beliefs. Later, in an attack of conscience, he reversed himself. Condemned to be burned at the stake, Cranmer held his right hand first in the flames, so that he could burn away the physical remains of his giving up his faith, crying out against his "unworthy right hand" and ruining Mary's victory.[18] Cranmer and the other Marian martyrs demonstrated the power of their own beliefs far more eloquently than Mary and thus won far more sympathy from the general populace.

In late 1555, Philip returned to Spain. He had grown tired of his diplomatic marriage, and his own realm needed him. Mary had been unable to bear a child who would solidify the Catholic monarch's grasp on the throne of England and was exhausted by the continued effort. In 1558, abandoned by her Spanish husband and by the English people, Mary died.

The reputation of the Marian martyrs—or heretics, depending on one's point of view—was helped by a brilliant propagandist, John Foxe (1516–1587). Foxe popularized the martyrology, a form of writing that had seen precious little attention in the long reign of Christianity in Europe. A martyrology is an account of a martyrdom, normally by someone sympathetic to the cause of the martyr. Martyrdom is always in the eye of the beholder![19] To someone supportive of the victim's beliefs, the victim is a martyr. To someone who detests or who is against the victim's beliefs, the victim is frequently simply a criminal. To Foxe, the English Protestants were definitely martyrs, and his writings show them as such. Foxe began to write an account of Christian martyrdom at the suggestion of Lady Jane Grey. His first edition was brief and did not include the victims of the Marian era. His expanded edition, completed in Latin in 1559, was printed in English in 1563. This was after Mary's death, making Foxe an issue for Elizabeth rather than Mary. Though Foxe's book frequently is simply called either the *Book of Martyrs* or *Acts and Monuments*, the full title leaves no doubt about Foxe's beliefs: *Actes and Monuments of these lat-*

ter and perilous Dayes, touching matters of the Church, wherein are comprehended and described the great Persecution and horrible Troubles that have been wrought and practised by the Romishe Prelates, especiallye in this Realme of England and Scotland, from the yeare of our Lorde a thousande to the time now present. Gathered and collected according to the true Copies and Wrytinges certificatorie as well of the Parties themselves that Suffered, as also out of the Bishop's Registers, which were the Doers thereof, by John Foxe. By including the English victims alongside the more commonly accepted martyrs of the church, Foxe was recasting the Marian era as a return to the times when Roman emperors persecuted Christians and Christians gave testimony to the power of the faith in Christ with their very lives. According to Helen Parish, Foxe made "clear the structure of his history: the division of humanity since the time of Cain and Abel into the true church and the false, and more particularly the persecution of the true church by the false."[20] The *Book of Martyrs* remained one of the most widely read books in England and had a profoundly negative effect on English ideas of both Spain and of Catholicism.

QUEEN ELIZABETH I

Mary's death reversed the fortunes of her half sister, Elizabeth (1533–1603). Though at times Mary seems to have been fond of Elizabeth, at other times she found her politically dangerous. Mary had Elizabeth imprisoned in the Tower of London in 1554 on suspicion of her being involved in a rebellion that arose out of the furor over Mary's marriage to Philip of Spain. There was discussion of executing her, but some of Mary's advisors thought such a move would be politically disastrous. After two months, Elizabeth was allowed out of the Tower of London, but she remained under house arrest. Mary did not trust Elizabeth over her Protestantism and over the convenience of her position: Elizabeth had a very strong claim to the throne and could easily be used by rebels against Mary to legitimize a coup. Mary's death allowed Elizabeth to assume the throne, which she held for forty-four years. The length of this reign, and Elizabeth's practical character in all matters of governing, including those of religion, finalized the form of English reform. Her influence was so great that historians of the English church frequently talk of the "Elizabethan settlement" as the time of the final molding of the Church of England.

Elizabeth's own religion remains a question. Some historians suggest that she had a personal liking for Catholicism. However, Catholics in England had never accepted the legitimacy of her mother's marriage to Henry VIII, so they saw Elizabeth as a bastard and thus unable to inherit the throne. That same position was taken by Francis II of France and Mary, Queen of Scots, who immediately declared their own claims to the English throne. Elizabeth was a the daughter of a Protestant mother and had been raised a Protestant. She had resisted the calls of her sister to convert to Catholicism when it would have protected her life to do so. So was she a thorough Protestant to lead the Protestant kingdom? The consensus of most historians is "Not exactly." When she was crowned in January 1559, Elizabeth inherited a country with several competing religious ideals. But she also inherited a political situation that drove her to Protestant confession in order to remain on the throne.

Elizabeth tried to find the middle way between traditional Catholicism on the one hand and radical Protestantism on the other. Indeed, the Church of England came to follow a theology called the *via media*, a Latin phrase meaning "the middle way." One way to think of the English via media is Calvinist theology with Catholic liturgical practices. While her advisors were always Protestants, she frequently disappointed the dreams of the more radical Protestants among her subjects.[21] Nevertheless, Elizabeth's efforts to solve the "religious question" represented a gamble for a queen who only months before was living only by the grace of her Catholic half sister, who regarded her religion as heresy.

It is very easy in this day to look back and see the conflict in England in the late 1560s and onward as being between Catholics and Protestants. But in reality, the issue was more complex than that. There were certainly devout Catholics in England, who would have liked nothing better than to maintain religious allegiance to Rome and continue to worship in the manner of their grandparents and all the generations before them. Some Catholics believed that a great deal of English independence was appropriate; others believed that such a stand was nothing other than schism by a nicer name. Further, the Protestant "party" in England was not a single grouping but a divided collection, united mainly by its rejection of Catholicism. The two most divided emphases within this assembly were the movements of the Calvinist Puritans and of the Anglican Protestants. The Calvinists tended to desire a more thorough rejection of traditional worship, which they saw as idolatrous. Therefore, they would have done away with the Mass, purged the clergy of traditional clerical garb, done away with all religious statuary, and concentrated upon the exaltation of the biblical Word, both in psalm singing and in preaching. The Anglicans believed that this went too far. They wished to hold on to many of the traditional features of English Christianity, while setting that framework upon a more Protestant theology.

In 1563, Elizabeth put forward a new confession of faith for the Church of England. This was the Thirty-nine Articles, a confession of faith that many denominations in the worldwide Anglican communion today still profess. The

Thirty-nine Articles were closely modeled on the Forty-two Articles that Cranmer had offered in 1552.[22] Still, there were Catholic elements allowed, including the use of some traditional clerical garb. Scholars disagree about whom Elizabeth was trying to win over with these vestiges of tradition—Continental Lutherans or English Catholics.[23] In either case, Elizabeth's was the mind that held sway in England. She rejected an excessive emphasis on preaching and disliked married clergy, while she enjoyed church imagery and sophisticated choral music instead of simple metrical psalms.[24]

Of course, though she reigned for forty-four years, everything was not rosy for Elizabeth. Parliament was frequently worried about the succession and pressured her to marry. Elizabeth always managed to avoid such entanglements, most likely because she identified marriage with a loss of her own power. Beyond the question of an heir, there were problems with the Church of Rome and with Spain. In 1569, a group of English lords led a rebellion against Elizabeth, called the Northern Rebellion. Pope Pius V supported this rebellion and excommunicated Elizabeth in 1570. This was only one plot that was supported by papal funds against Elizabeth. Her successful uncovering and surviving of these plots led her and the English people to adopt a deep-seated antipathy for Catholicism that would last for centuries.

Philip II of Spain also harassed Elizabeth in a number of ways. Soon after her coronation, Philip asked to marry his sister-in-law. Elizabeth negotiated this for some time, but it is unlikely that she ever seriously considered repeating her half sister's mistake. Philip saw himself as God's champion for the Catholic faith.[25] While at times that championing was aimed at enforcing religious conformity in Spain through the Spanish Inquisition and the fighting of Protestant heretics in the Netherlands, at other times Philip turned his eye toward England. In 1568, Philip attacked English privateers Francis Drake and John Hawkins. Drake and Hawkins had been attacking Spanish ships returning to Spain from the New World. In 1586, Elizabeth's spymaster uncovered another plot against Elizabeth, known as the Babington Plot. The furor over this legitimated Elizabeth's prior banishment of all Jesuits from the kingdom in 1585, as many believed that all Jesuits were simply spies and plotters against the throne. Mary, Queen of Scots, who had been imprisoned in England after fleeing from Scotland, was implicated in the Babington Plot and in 1587 was executed. In her will, Mary left her claim to the English throne to Philip II of Spain. In 1588, Philip made open war against Elizabeth with the Spanish Armada. Philip's attack was probably less motivated by Mary's will than by England's support for the Dutch rebels in the Netherlands, and because the execution of Mary, Queen of Scots, left little option for a Catholic monarch to take the throne of England. The attack was a military disaster for

Spain, however, and the English saw divine providence supporting their queen and their religion.

When Elizabeth died in 1603, her realm was firmly Protestant in its own unique way, as well as firmly anti-Catholic and anti-Spanish. Her choice to avoid marriage ended the Tudor line on the throne of England, but her reign had given the new patterns of reform time to take hold and to become the normal state of affairs. In this, Elizabeth was as important as any monarch in the setting of English reform.

THEOLOGY OF THE CHURCH OF ENGLAND

The via media that characterized the English ideal of theology did several things. First, it allowed believers, both lay and clergy, to interpret doctrinal statements and patterns of worship in the manner that they saw fit. Frequently, the wording of confessional documents was intentionally left somewhat vague so as to be acceptable by a broad swath of people. In the main, England was left with a moderate Swiss theology that accepted a number of traditional practices that Calvin and especially Zwingli had rejected. Traditional clerical garb, or vestments, was one of these areas. Though this raised a furor at times, the Church of England finally decided that vestments were an issue of adiaphora, of "things indifferent."

Though the Church of England claimed the via media, it did not stay close to Roman belief and practice. Article after article of the Thirty-nine Articles demonstrated the choice to stay closer to the Reformed or Lutheran position than the Roman tradition. Scripture was the only rule sufficient for salvation, rather than Scripture and tradition together. Three prior confessions were given as authoritative: the Apostles' Creed, the Nicene Creed, and the Athanasian Creed. Significantly, the Thirty-nine Articles makes these authoritative not because of the power or holiness of the church, but because they could be "proved by most certain warrants of holy Scripture." Two sacraments were allowed, the doctrines of purgatory and of supererogatory works were discarded, justification was declared possible only through the merits of Christ, and the church was stated to have no power to teach against Scripture, or even to teach one part of Scripture against the meaning of another. Transubstantiation was denied, and believers were to receive the body and blood in the sacrament of the Lord's Supper, but only spiritually, not in some locally present manner such as by consubstantiation. Priests were allowed, but not commanded, to marry. The Thirty-nine Articles preserved the power of the sovereign by making the calling of general councils impossible without the consent of the monarch.

Another remarkable aspect of English Christianity was the toleration of dissent. (This toleration did not extend to all believers; after repeated plots, Catholics were generally banished from the public sphere. England exercised its official anti-Catholic policy mostly against the clergy, especially members of orders such as the Jesuits. Catholics who were members of the laity were generally not executed for their beliefs, though they might be fined.) Christians other than Catholics found remarkable tolerance in England. An example involves those of a "Puritan" sentiment. The long discussion of the proper way to reform Christianity in England, and the frequent movement of religious refugees back and forth between England and Continental centers of reform such as Geneva, Strasbourg, and Zurich, ensured that there would be those who believed that the final settlement did not go far enough. Frequently called "Puritans," these believers sought to clear away all marks of the Catholic past. They wished to cleanse away church art, get rid of bishops in favor of a presbyterian system like that of Geneva or Scotland, and take away sophisticated church music in favor of simple psalm-singing. For some time, these dissenters coexisted within the Church of England, finally either accepting its patterns or emigrating to other lands.

Across four sovereigns, and across more than seven decades, the reform of the English church lumbered forward. At times it seemed to quicken its pace, only to slow again or even move backward. The pattern of reform in England never had an "inevitable" character about it in the manner of a Lutheran explosion. Perhaps that is its own genius—that instead of taking the stamp of a single thinker or school, it was the product of conflicting views of true religion and the mixing together of ideas that were frequently kept apart in other realms. By the end of the sixteenth century, however, England itself began exporting Protestantism to its own burgeoning empire, and it spread these ideas far more broadly than many nations in which the process of reform had been much simpler.

QUESTIONS FOR DISCUSSION

1. The English Reformation explicitly joined the roles of the church and the kingdom. We have seen several models of church-state relations. What should their relationship be? What advantages come from close attachment, and what benefits come from more independence?
2. What was the effect of the idea of the Church of England as the via media?
3. The English Church was full of martyrs. What is the consequence of Christian martyrdom in a time of reform?
4. How important was the back-and-forth character of English religious politics in establishing the character of the English model of reform?

SUGGESTED FURTHER READING

Primary Readings

Bray, Gerald. *Documents of the English Reformation*. London: James Clarke Co., 2004.
Cranmer, Thomas. *Writings and Disputations of Thomas Cranmer Relative to the Sacrament of the Lord's Supper*. Edited by John Edmund Cox. Vancouver: Regent College Publishing, 2001.
Tyndale, William. *The Obedience of a Christian Man*. New York: Penguin Books, 2000.

Secondary Readings

Collinson, Patrick. *The Reformation: A History*. New York: Modern Library, 2004.
Duffy, Eamon. *The Stripping of the Altars: Traditional Religion in England, 1400–1580*.
2nd ed. New Haven, CT: Yale University Press, 2005.
Haigh, Christopher. *English Reformations: Religion, Politics, and Society under the Tudors*.
Oxford: Oxford University Press, 1993.
MacCulloch, Diarmaid. *The Reformation*. New York: Penguin Books, 2005.
———. *Thomas Cranmer: A Life*. New Haven, CT: Yale University Press, 1998.
Todd, Margo, ed. *Reformation to Revolution: Politics and Religion in Early Modern England*
London: Routledge, 1995.

DOCTRINAL-VOCABULARY DISCUSSION

Where Is the Church? Ecclesiological Struggles and Solutions

The religious struggles of the sixteenth century in Europe were remarkable
for several reasons. Among those reasons were the competing claims of Christianity. For most of Western European history, to be Christian had meant to
be Catholic. This unity of organization had allowed theologians to ignore certain questions. One such question was the nature and definition of the church
itself. But with competing claims, the doctrine of the church, called ecclesiology, took on much greater importance.

The word "ecclesiology" comes from the Greek term *ekklēsia*, which is used
in the New Testament. This term originally meant "assembly" and was
widened to include the group that assembled. From time immemorial, to be
Christian meant to be somehow related to the church. Now, with competing
churches, both new questions and opposing answers arose.

One question involved the definition of the church. Several answers were
put forward. For Catholics, the church was defined by the hierarchy. One was
in communion with the church when one was in communion with the pope.
Obviously, few Protestants gave this option much weight. Radicals defined the

church as a voluntary society of baptized disciples who willingly accepted the discipline of the body. Lutherans and Reformed theologians tended to speak of the invisible and visible churches. The invisible church, known only to God, consisted of the saved. The visible church was defined by a set of "marks," which included preaching of the Word of God and right administration of the sacraments.

These marks were more or less efforts to set out the minimum requirements for the existence of a Christian church. This was now a far more significant question than it had been in the fourteenth or fifteenth centuries. Believers needed some guides to know when it was important to leave or to stay within a presumed church. Different theologians generated different lists of the "marks." Calvin defined the church by the right preaching and hearing of the Word of God and the right administration of the sacraments. John Knox, who had been so impressed with Geneva, still felt it necessary in the Scots Confession to add the third mark: church discipline. In either case, most issues were left up to the community, guided by Scripture. With brief definitions, a church could have bishops, or not. It could celebrate the Lord's Supper weekly or daily or monthly.

Predictably, history became a battleground of ecclesiology. Roman theologians found a sore point for Protestants in their debates when they asked, "Where was your church before Luther?" Most Christian theologians were unwilling to suggest that God would have allowed the church in the world to die. Catholics simply pointed to an unbroken institutional history to demonstrate that theirs was the true church. Reformed and Lutheran theologians generally argued that the church had suffered a terrible decline after the first few centuries but that there was always a living remnant. In their view, the present day was like the revival of a patient who had been in a long coma. Lutheran theologians in Magdeburg had struggled mightily with this question, and one of their contributions to the debate was a history, usually termed by its shorter name, the *Magdeburg Centuries*. This multivolume work put forth the historical claim that the Church of Rome was not the true church. Interestingly, the *Magdeburg Centuries* seems to have been the first published effort to break history down by centuries. Occasionally Radical theologians would even state that God had allowed the church to die, only to revive it in the sixteenth century.

The competing ecclesiologies and churches were not examples of greater freedom, however—quite the opposite. A person was making a clear claim about truth, society, and faith when he or she joined a church. Leaving a church for another in the early modern period represented a major break with one's past life, and no one undertook it lightly.

In all cases, theologians, pastors, and laypeople had to think about what the nature of the church was—ecclesiology—in ways that they had never had to before. The result was not always clear, never predictable, and somewhat chaotic. But it began a process of people thinking about what actually defines the church—and that process is still playing itself out.

9

Catholic Reform

Early Modern Catholicism

It is far too easy to accept the categories of the sixteenth century for our own use, and to allow our thoughts in the twenty-first century to mimic those from the sixteenth. Thus, for many of the figures we have encountered, traditional Catholicism was reform's opposite, or even opponent. However, that was not necessarily the case. Our consideration of humanistic reform, including the figure of Erasmus, should remind us that prominent Catholic thinkers desired reform as well. Catholicism reformed in the early modern period, and its reforms were both subtle and profound.

What was the character of this reform? For decades this was a contentious question in the historiography of the period. Frequently a reader could tell the confessional position of an author simply by considering the terminology used. Protestant scholars tended to use the term "Counter-Reformation." This term tended to represent the movement as inspired against the Protestant gains, as a way of defending Catholic territories and doctrines. It also gave the sense that any reforming tendencies that existed within Catholicism were only a response to Protestant movements.

Catholic scholars, on the other hand, tended to use the term "Catholic Reformation." This usage emphasized the character of the reforms undertaken as truly Catholic, and removed the sense of the movement as simply a reaction. Further, it was a broader term, which could encompass the kinds of reforms that were taking place even in the fourteenth and fifteenth centuries, as well as cover the wide variety of reforms that occurred in the sixteenth century and beyond.

Of course, both terms have some value. Some Catholic reforms were internal and had no relationship to Lutheran or Zwinglian or any other Protestant reforms. Other reforms were absolutely and unabashedly trying to fight the

189

Protestant scourge as a plague. The fact of both ideas of reform explains the contentious debate among scholars trying to define the character of reforms. One of the most influential scholars of the period, John O'Malley, SJ, has recently argued that neither term truly fits the wide variety of impulses that were involved in the early modern period. He has argued for the term "early modern Catholicism."[1] This chapter uses all three terms. Although there will always be overlap among the terms, the following signification will be adopted: "Catholic Reformation" will represent those efforts that were not self-consciously aimed at answering or countering Protestantism. "Counter-Reformation" will signify those movements and efforts that clearly sought to oppose the Protestant threat. "Early modern Catholicism" will draw on both, as well as movements that were not always seen as reforms.

STAGES OF REFORM

Reform was not something new in the sixteenth century. As we saw in the first and second chapters, there had been several movements of reform prior to the sixteenth century. The Devotio Moderna, the new religious orders and new religious observances, and the efforts of the conciliarists to bring a new sense of order and purity to the head and members of the church all serve as clear signs that the ideal of reform remained strong in the medieval church. Elizabeth Gleason has suggested three stages to the sixteenth-century Catholic reform movement: the first lasted from the late fifteenth century to about 1540, the second covered the 1540s and 1550s, and the final stage began with the final session of the Council of Trent in 1561. This stage covered reforming impulses that lasted well into the seventeenth century.[2]

More important than the dates of these stages, Gleason argues, was the character of these phases. The first phase was characterized by efforts that originated from the parish or diocesan level.[3] That is to say that the centralizing force of the papacy was not the driving force behind most of these. The second period marked the end of the tolerant atmosphere of the Renaissance church. This middle phase saw the beginning of the Council of Trent, Pope Paul III raising several reform-minded thinkers to the College of Cardinals, and the crackdown on heresy beginning.[4] It was during this phase that Queen Mary I of England and Cardinal Pole took on the Protestant heresy in England. The Jesuit order was also approved at this time, receiving papal sanction in 1540. The third phase followed the Council of Trent. Though this phase can certainly be called the Counter-Reformation, given the large number of canons and decrees of the council that specifically denied Protestant doctrines, it also can appropriately be called the Catholic Reformation, and even early modern Catholicism, since many of the constructive attempts to build a more effective church at this time would impact the church for centuries.[5]

EARLY EFFORTS AT REFORM

While Catholic reform began prior to the rise of Protestantism, and indeed prior to the sixteenth century, this volume concentrates on the sixteenth century and into the seventeenth century, so we will begin with the early efforts at reform in the sixteenth century. First among these were the new religious orders. These new orders changed the face of Christianity in their realms, taking on poverty, the comfort of the miserable, and offering up a new vision of the regular saying of Mass. The earliest new order was the Theatines, founded by Gaetano di Thiene (1480–1547), a nobleman from Venice. Though he had been working toward a lucrative career in the institutional church, di Thiene experienced a religious conversion around 1516.[6] He became active in the Roman chapter of the Oratory of Divine Love. There he gathered to himself several like-minded men who were dedicated to improving morality in Rome and beyond. In 1524, Pope Clement VII established this group as a new order in a papal bull, *Exponi nobis*.

The Theatines committed themselves to social work, to reviving a sense of strict morality among the clergy, and to preaching. The order was known for its strict vows of poverty. One of their ways of doing this, explains Michael Mullett, was "by holding no property, abstaining even from begging and relying entirely on voluntary charity for their maintenance."[7] They founded churches and regularly recruited the nobility into their ranks, setting out a vision of the religious life that denied the concentration on the creation of worldly wealth that was a constant factor in secular life in the sixteenth century.

Another new order was the Barnabites, or the Clerks Regular of St. Paul. The order was founded by Antonio Maria Zaccaria (1502–1547), along with Bartolomeo Ferrari and Giacomo Antonio Morigia. Zaccaria had studied for a career in medicine at Padua. However, when he went to Cremona to practice medicine in 1524, he appears to have come under the guidance of a Dominican friar, and he never took up the medical career. Instead, he was ordained and began to serve as a priest. In Cremona, he and his colleagues gathered a group of men with a strong social vision, as seen in their preaching in prisons and visiting hospitals.[8] The order was accepted by Clement VII in 1533, before it technically started functioning. In 1535, Pope Paul III officially recognized them, giving them their official name. They received the nickname "Barnabites" after they took over the church of St. Barnabas in Milan in 1545. The Barnabites were also remarkable in Zaccaria's vision of a three-pronged structure of priests, women religious, and dedicated laypeople. The order was active throughout Italy and was vigorous in its offering of traditional Catholic services, as its members preached, heard confessions, and visited hospitals and prisons.[9]

The Capuchins and Discalced Carmelites also arose during this time.[10] These two orders differed from the Theatines and Barnabites in that they were not in the fullest sense "new orders." Both of them came from the efforts of members of the Franciscan and Carmelite orders to purify themselves and their order and return to a presumed prior stricter level of observance. The Capuchins were attempting to return to the simple purity of St. Francis's primitive rule, which allowed no possessions. They were recognized by Pope Clement VIII in 1528. Though they grew relatively quickly, there was a moment when they were almost suppressed. In 1542, their general, Bernardino Ochino, left Italy and fled to Geneva to convert to Protestantism. They survived the papal scrutiny that followed and became a force in sixteenth-century Catholicism. They tended to live in small hermitages near the towns where they served, and they followed Francis's rule of begging for their food. Their ministries were concentrated in preaching, frequently outside churches; they were known for caring for plague victims. They were another order that advocated frequent Communion.[11]

The Discalced Carmelites arose in Spain. "Discalced" means "without shoes"; as a sign of observance, members wore sandals. The Discalced Carmelites were extraordinary in that it was a women's movement, in the Carmelite convents, that led the process. The leader was St. Teresa of Avila (1515–1582), whom we shall consider further later. In 1556, Teresa had been a Carmelite for twenty years; however, the Carmelites were not truly observant as an order separated from the world, as Gleason explains: "A nun's family rank followed her into the convent, sometimes together with several servants to wait on her."[12] Teresa organized a reformed convent in which all nuns had to work at manual labor and all were expected to be frequently in prayer. In all, Teresa founded sixteen convents. She also befriended a younger friar, St. John of the Cross (1542–1591). In John, Teresa found a kindred spirit, both as a mystic and as a reformer. The first monastery of Discalced Carmelite friars was founded in 1568. The Discalced Carmelites were known for their piety, their strict observance of their rules, and their contemplative prayer.

While this brief consideration of the new orders does not cover them in their entirety, it does show the breadth of efforts at reform that had very little to do with the Protestant issue. But new orders were not the only efforts at reform. Other Catholic figures took the initiative outside of new religious orders in the early period. One kind of effort that is too frequently set aside as a footnote in the Luther affair was the endeavor to answer Luther and other Protestant thinkers, which was taken up frequently by individual volunteers.

Johann Eck (1486–1543), presents a paradigmatic instance. Eck immediately took up the challenge of answering Luther. Luther himself made the charge that Eck was simply endeavoring to gain glory for himself. This is an understandable charge from Luther, who was frequently the target of Eck's attacks. However, Eck's efforts provided more theological substance than that. First, Eck seems to have been one of the first theologians to understand just how far-reaching the implications of Luther's early positions would lead. At the Leipzig Disputation in 1519, Eck certainly laid verbal traps for Luther. But Luther recognized those traps and chose to step into them. This was especially clear when Luther reevaluated the doctrines of Jan Hus and found them to be Christian.[13] That observation leads to the second fruit of Eck's attack on Luther: in concert with Luther, Eck began to establish how far Luther was from a certain understanding of Christianity, one that Eck believed was mainstream.

Finally, though this first period is not characterized by papal initiative, one significant reform proposal did come about through the efforts of the pope. We might, however, characterize this proposal as the "great reform that wasn't." In 1536, Pope Paul III put together a commission to address abuses within the church. The list of individuals he placed on the commission reads like a "who's who" of Catholic reform-minded cardinals of the time. Jacopo Sadoleto, Reginald Pole, and Giovanni Carafa all were on the commission. Cardinal Contarini chaired the group and in 1537 presented to the pope its report. Titled *Consilium de emendanda ecclesia*, the report seriously took up issues that affected the church and the papacy. Elizabeth Gleason characterizes it in this way:

> The *Consilium*, in effect, criticized the whole system of papal government because it enabled abuses to exist, and called for conceiving papal power in spiritual rather than political or economic terms. Had it led to a reexamination of the power and role of the pope in the church, this proposal would have been a major document of Catholic reform. But it was clearly nothing of the kind, notwithstanding claims for its importance made by some historians. Looked at more closely, it reveals an uneasy and ambiguous coexistence of ideas, not a consistent concept of reform.[14]

What was the problem? First, the problem was not with the proposals themselves. The cardinals identified a number of very real abuses and did not sugarcoat their words. They noted the ordination of clergy, the abuse of benefices, the lax attitude toward what university professors of philosophy taught, and the dangerous books being printed. The attack on the ordination of the clergy noted that there were no accepted high standards of either education or morality for the clergy, especially priests. This practice denigrated the sacrament and made a mockery of the idea that priests were transformed by ordination. Significantly, it was not merely Protestants who saw the dangers involved in the abuse of benefices. The consideration of the lack of oversight by bishops of the teaching of philosophy in the universities observed that both the students in the universities and the people of the towns, in front of whom many disputations were held, could be harmed by a lax attitude toward Catholic truth. The declaration that princes needed to monitor the printing of books recognized the new reality of a culture of reading that was making the impact of books wider even than the number of literate people in the empire.

Most significantly, the cardinals pointed out the way that economic concerns had become so much a part of the normal order of affairs within the church that it was impossible for the church to be a spiritual institution, since it was surrounded and supported by very worldly practices. This insight alone, had it been acted upon, would have absolutely transformed the church of the sixteenth century. The way that money had become a prerequisite for getting much of anything done in the church scandalized some people. However, for others, this economic character of the church made things predictable and assured the Vatican of a steady stream of income, without which its power and ability to persuade governments toward its positions would have been greatly weakened.

Pope Paul III shelved the document. Historians argue about why he did so. He may simply have been unable to grasp the idea of a church that radically differed from the one in which he had come to power. His family ties may have kept him from seeing any value in changing the church.[15] He may simply have felt that the proposed remedies to the illnesses could not do enough. Whatever the case, the pope did not act seriously upon the report.

Since it was a secret report, that should have ended the affair. However, a copy was smuggled out, and Luther published it in 1538. This created two problems. First, Luther's publication came with his own set of comments. While the report had asked for abuses to be addressed, it had not asked for any basic doctrinal changes in the church's teachings. Luther ridiculed that. Second, it was a public relations disaster. The pope had commissioned a report on how to better the church, cardinals had met and diligently prepared that report, and the pope had shelved it. For Protestant polemicists, the affair proved the reluctant nature of Rome to make any serious effort at reform. For Catholic thinkers, however, the fact that the pope had commissioned the study in the first place signaled that the papacy's lack of enthusiasm for reform might be changing.

REFORM IN THE MIDDLE OF THE CENTURY

In the middle decades of the sixteenth century, Catholicism became more engaged with the issues presented by the Protestant protests. Many thinkers believed that the issue was how to stamp out the "Lutheran" threat, or how to answer it so well that believers would be persuaded to return to the fold of the true faith. Other theologians were not so certain. Some tried to reach out to Protestant leaders, to sit at colloquies in order to consider whether some of the theological differences might be hammered out with theological understandings that were acceptable to both sides. These colloquies were quite different from some of the disputations we have already encountered. At Lausanne, Leipzig, and Zurich, the point had been to defeat one's enemy. Therefore, as much as possible, each side tried to "rig" the outcome. Now theologians embarked on a different endeavor—to come to understanding and, if possible, agreement. This was more like the effort of the Lutheran and Zwinglian forces to come to an agreeable theological formula at the Marburg Colloquy in 1529. Many theologians on both the Protestant and Catholic sides were unsure just how wide the gap between them was and whether it could be bridged. The theologians on both sides who favored the effort at discussion and possible reunion had a desire for ecumenism. "Ecumenism" comes from a Greek word used in the New Testament that means "the entire world." Ecumenical theologians were trying to patch together the entire church into one body, and one of their tools was the colloquy.

One of the more significant colloquies came during this second period. It was called the Regensburg Colloquy, though sometimes is referred to as the Ratisbon Colloquy. While there were genuine ecumenical interests at stake, it would be an overstatement to see this as purely a spiritual issue. Holy Roman Emperor Charles V convened the colloquy, in part because of his political and military situation. France threatened him, as did the Turks, who were already in Hungary. Charles again needed the support of Lutheran princes, so he attempted to gain it through doctrinal agreement. The colloquy began on April 27, 1541.

The theologians who attended represented some of the most celebrated minds of the time. The Catholics were led by Cardinal Contarini, who had led the group of cardinals who gave the *Consilium de emendanda ecclesia* to the pope four years earlier. He was joined by Johann Gropper, Johann Eck, and Johann Pighius. The Protestant side also embodied more than its share of theological acuity. Philip Melanchthon and Martin Bucer led the Protestant side. Bucer especially was known for his desire to harmonize between warring Christian factions.

Miraculously, the participants were able to hammer out a compromise on the issue of justification. They did so by turning away from both the Lutheran position on justification by faith alone and the Roman position on justification by grace and works—turning to a third position, called "double justification." This allowed both sides to read the document according to their own principles. The Catholics read double justification to mean that grace is infused in the believer and further grace comes through sanctification, somewhat as Gropper had been teaching. The Protestants read double justification to mean that one is justified by grace imputed to the believer, and then the believer, as a result of justification, begins to live out his or her sanctification.

Miracles did not always have a long shelf life in the sixteenth century. Almost immediately, the joy over coming to agreement on justification gave way to frustration over other matters. The Protestants, Bucer especially, were unwilling to accept transubstantiation or the primacy of the pope. The colloquy ended without the sweeping agreements necessary to forge military alliances or church reunions. Further, both Luther and the curia, the papal court, rejected the double justification doctrine. For Contarini, this was the omen of bad tidings, and he died under house arrest the next year, held on suspicion of heresy. For Protestant and Catholic ecumenists, this took away any optimistic notions of agreement as simply a matter of finding the right words. For some Catholics, this was the motivation to hold a true council, which was convened at Trent in 1545.

IGNATIUS OF LOYOLA AND THE SOCIETY OF JESUS

Another reform movement within Catholicism centered on the religious genius of Ignatius Loyola (c. 1491–1556), founder of the Society of Jesus, commonly called the Jesuits. The order that Loyola founded would revolutionize missionary evangelism, sending Christian messengers into parts of the globe that had never heard of Christianity. The Jesuits would found schools all over the world, competing with Protestants for the minds of students. Finally, the Jesuits would frequently be the enforcers of religious orthodoxy, serving in reforming councils and as vigorous preachers against Protestantism. The complexion of early modern Catholicism, as well as modern Catholicism, is unthinkable without acknowledging the impact of the Society of Jesus.

Ignatius was Spanish, born to a family of the nobility at the castle of Loyola. He was not brought up, like so many other reformers, to be a scholar. Instead, he opted for the life of the soldier and was accepted into the service of the duke of Najera in 1517. In 1521, at the battle of Pamplona, he fought against the French and his right leg was shattered by a cannonball. This proved to be providential for the young nobleman's spiritual development. His leg was badly wounded, but his immediate medical care was poor: the leg had to be broken and set again, probably twice more. The enforced convalescence gave Ignatius little to do but read. Having nothing else to read, he perused Ludoph's *Vita Christi*, a popular life of Christ, and another medieval spiritual classic, the *Golden Legend*. In contemplating these books, Loyola transformed his own desires from wanting earthly glory into wanting spiritual glory.

Ignatius spent the next years working through the depths of the meaning of his conversion. He experienced visions while in a cave at Manresa in 1522. His interior reflections and considerations of these visions and other spiritual realities were the raw material out of which he would create the basic text for Jesuit spirituality, the *Spiritual Exercises*. In 1523, Ignatius left Manresa for Jerusalem so that he could begin to convert others to his faith. As a Spaniard, Ignatius naturally thought of converting the Muslims, who had inhabited parts of Spain until the year after his birth. He wanted to go to Jerusalem to convert them. However, he quickly found that he did not have the education necessary to convert anyone, so he attended a boys' school in Barcelona. The picture of the thirty-year-old soldier sitting with young boys and learning his Latin is humorous, but it also gives an idea of how committed Loyola was. From there he went to the University of Alcalá. While studying in Spain, he came to the attention of the authorities and was briefly imprisoned by the Spanish Inquisition. A significant part of Ignatius's spirituality was bound up in "interior prayer." This form of silent prayer that sought out God in the inner recesses of the believer's soul was not traditional Catholic practice and seemed frightening to a society worried about various heretical sects. After his acquittal, in 1528, he left Spain for the center of the theological world—the University of Paris.

At the university, Ignatius met the friends who would join with him in his religious fervor and would eventually become the first Jesuits. Six friends gathered around him, and in 1534, they took a vow to go to Palestine and to work for souls. John Patrick Donnelly, SJ, notes that "all seven were well educated by the standards of the times; their leader, St. Ignatius of Loyola, was probably the least gifted as a scholar."[16] Their dream of going to Palestine, however, was frustrated by a war between the Venetians and the Turks. Instead, they chose another path and put themselves in the service of the pope. Eventually they chose the discipline of taking on a rule and were recognized as an order by Pope Paul III in 1540.

Ignatius was to Catholic reform what Calvin was to Protestant reform. A brilliant organizer, he also imprinted his own spiritual and doctrinal stamp upon the Jesuits and, through them, upon the church. While Luther and Calvin had seen the basic problem of the time as theological, Loyola saw it as an issue of discipline. He believed that Catholics had fallen away from pure faith by not participating in pure obedience to the hierarchical church. While there are many ideas within the Society of Jesus that allow and even demand flexibility, Ignatius must frequently be counted on the side of the traditionalists. He appended his "Rules for Thinking with the Church" to the *Spiritual Exercises*, and the meaning of these rules was clear. The thirteenth paragraph leaves no doubt:

> To keep ourselves right in all things, we ought to hold fast to this prin-
> ciple: What I see as white, I will believe to be black if the hierarchical
> Church thus determines it. For we believe that between Christ our
> Lord, the Bridegroom, and the Church, his Spouse, there is the one
> same Spirit who governs and guides us for the salvation of our souls.
> For it is by the same Spirit and Lord of ours who gave the ten com-
> mandments that our holy Mother Church is guided and governed.[17]

For Ignatius, straightforward obedience to the church was the same as obedience to the Spirit of the Lord Jesus Christ.

While the original group of friends had been unable to go to Palestine, missions to foreign countries remained a priority of the fledgling order. In 1541,
only one year after their founding, Francis Xavier departed to India, from which
he would set up mission networks throughout Asia. Matteo Ricci (1552–1610)
took the Christian gospel to China. The Jesuits reached Japan, and their mission blossomed there until the Japanese government turned against Christianity late in the sixteenth century. The Jesuits took Christianity to both North
and South America. In North America, Jesuits were frequently among the first
Europeans to reach new lands, and occasionally they paid with their lives for
their missionary zeal. This was the case with Isaac Jogues, who was killed by
the Mohawks in 1646. In South America, the Jesuits utilized a different mission
strategy; they set up settlements called "reductions" and brought the natives to
these sanctuaries, where they could be evangelized and protected from enslave-
ment by Spanish and Portuguese plantation owners.[18] As a missionary franchise
alone, the Society of Jesus changed the face of the globe.

Frequently the Jesuit missionaries would go out alone, rather than having
the companionship of other members of the order. They endured physical tortures, it is true, but also tolerated isolation from other Europeans and the
onslaught of pressure from the cultures they encountered. These last two are
two sides of the same important coin. For a sixteenth-century European,
Christianity was part of European culture. It was very difficult for anyone in
the sixteenth century to differentiate between what was simply European
habit and what was a necessity of Christian doctrine or practice. This was why
so many early missionary projects included efforts to get the native peoples to
adopt European clothing and European worship habits. When a Jesuit was on
a long mission, he did not have the support of the culture that had nurtured
him, a culture that already was tied to Christianity.

The Jesuit missionaries not only lost the support of their own culture but also
frequently were faced by cultural pressures they could not have foreseen. The
natives of Brazil may have seemed just as savage and uncivilized to the Jesuits as
they did to the Spanish and Portuguese who argued that they must be enslaved.
The Chinese and Japanese, on the other hand, were decidedly not uncivilized.

Here Jesuits were faced with cultural and technological accomplishments that rivaled those of their own culture and sometimes clearly exceeded anything that Europe had to offer. In the face of this, it may have been easy to "go native," to accept the culture and beliefs of the new society, rather than to try to bring Christianity to it. In fact, Jesuits were occasionally accused of this. But in the main they were able to maintain their own sensibilities and interpret the gospel of Christianity in a variety of new cultural and societal contexts.

How did they do so? Different reasons can be offered. First, there is the character of the men who chose to join this order. Second, many of the Jesuits had attained extraordinary educational levels for the time. A Jesuit of the sixteenth century, however, would probably look to Loyola's *Spiritual Exercises* for the answer. What were the *Spiritual Exercises?* Though the book was not published until 1548, Loyola was giving the exercises to his friends in Paris long before publication.[19] While the *Exercises* are deservedly famous, they are not well understood. First, the book is not meant to be read. Instead, says John O'Malley, it was "to be used as a handbook designed to help somebody guide another through a program of reflections and meditations that would lead to a deeper sense of purpose in life and to a deeper commitment to the ideals of Jesus."[20] The *Exercises* were a manual for giving retreats. The retreats were set up in four "weeks," but the time frames could be flexible. H. O. Evennett writes that "the Spiritual Exercises are a special experience to be undergone, a shock-tactic spiritual gymnastic to be undertaken and performed under guidance, at some particular moment—perhaps of inward crisis—when new decisions and resolutions in life are called for or held to be desirable."[21] Armed with the spirituality formed through the intense directed deliberations, Jesuits impacted the world in many ways.

So far, we have considered primarily the Jesuit's missionary activity. This is appropriate, because the Jesuits were travelers who desired to spread the gospel. Francis Xavier left for India before Paul III had even formally approved the order.[22] However, the Society of Jesus did not remain only a missionary order. Education became another specialty of the order. In 1548, the Jesuits opened a college for lay students in Messina. By 1579, there were 144 Jesuit colleges! That number had increased to 372 by 1615.[23] The colleges were free, but they required some ability in Latin, so it was not as if they were for the sons of peasants.

The impact of such an overwhelming enterprise made itself felt in a number of ways. First, it stretched the Jesuits: at times there were more requests for schools than the Jesuits could find prepared members of the Society of Jesus to staff. Second, it helped provide a steady stream of young men eager to join the order. Third, it made the Jesuits into a sort of order of "schoolmasters to the world." They trained the next generation of leaders and lower nobility, and did so with a common model for instruction, their *Ratio studio-rum*, produced in 1599. This guide for education regulated Jesuit schools for three hundred years.[24]

Finally, the Jesuits guarded orthodox teaching. From the middle of the sixteenth century, writes O'Malley, "countering the Reformation would in many parts of Europe become an essential constituent of Jesuit self-definition."[25] It is popular to call the Jesuits the "shock troops" of the papacy, so popular that many Jesuit scholars spend time showing the many ways in which that name is patently false.[26] Others simply accept the cliché as true.[27] No matter which approach is more historically accurate, the collision of the Jesuits with Protestantism is hardly a matter of debate. Jesuits acted as some of the most influential theologians at the Council of Trent, where basic Protestant doctrines were declared heretical. Jesuits frequently held powerful positions as advisors to Catholic monarchs, but not to Protestant lords. The Jesuit order had grown astonishingly quickly and was well-positioned to influence the course of both religious and political decisions, though the difference between them was difficult to tell in the sixteenth century. The order changed the faces of Catholicism and of global Christianity.

LATER REFORMS

The pace of Catholic reform and Counter reform quickened in the second half of the sixteenth century. While the face of the Catholic Church continued to change from the 1560s until well into the seventeenth century, with a great number of items worthy of consideration, this volume will concentrate on two. The first is so unknown outside of theological circles that its meaning remains a mystery to most nontheologians. That is the Council of Trent, which changed the institutional face of the Catholic Church and was its last universal council until the late nineteenth century, with the Vatican Council. The second item has the opposite problem—people think they understand it just by hearing its name. This is the Inquisition. Both are worthy of examination, and both give us windows into the minds of the people of the sixteenth century, who sought to renew their ancient faith and thus make it even truer to the design of its Lord.

THE COUNCIL OF TRENT

The Council of Trent (1545–1563) changed the character of the Catholic Church more profoundly and more permanently than perhaps any other particular sixteenth-century individual, event, or process. Counted by Catholics as the nineteenth ecumenical council, meaning it was a universal council and represented the entire church, it did much to establish the spirit of Catholicism well into the twentieth century. The council itself was the product of a long and stumbling journey. The Germans had asked for a council for decades. Reformers of all stripes, including figures who generally opposed each other, such as Luther and Charles V, asked the popes to convene a council to answer the huge questions that faced the church. So why did it take so long to occur? Luther's theses on indulgences had become public in 1517. Why did almost three decades pass before the convening of the council?

Politics must take the blame for this. Had a council been called and convened earlier, it is possible that the sixteenth century might have turned out very differently for all Christians.[28] However, both political situations between nations and the empire and the political calculations of the popes conspired against this. For instance, at times Charles V was eager for a council. At other moments, he was actively engaged in war preparations against other Christians and rather uninterested in councils. Likewise, the popes prior to Paul III had the example of the Council of Constance, which had deposed three (claimed) popes, as a warning. Councils sometimes acted as if the council was above the pope in power—a position that no pope accepted. Calling a council was not something to be taken lightly.

When Paul III did call for the council in 1542, there was still some sense that the council could repair the breaches within the body of Christians in Western Europe. By its third session, the council had given up any such belief and was concentrating upon renewing the Catholic Church and on battling the Protestant threat. The council met in the small Italian town of Trent. This was a compromise location, within the Holy Roman Empire to make the Germans feel better, but in a village that was basically Italian to allow the pope and his Italian supporters to keep watch on its proceedings.

The council actually met in three different assemblies: from 1545 to 1547, from 1551 to 1552, and from 1561 to 1563.[29] Protestant observers were actually invited to the second meeting but were not offered any role other than to observe. The first meeting began in December 1545 with a vote that strengthened the Italian delegation immensely. In some prior councils, the delegates present had voted by nations. Thus, the delegates from France would have one vote, the delegates from Germany would have one vote, and so forth. Each individual voted in order to have his nation cast its vote a particular way. But an early vote at Trent set out a different procedure—individuals would have their own votes. This enormously strengthened the Italian delegation, which was the largest by far.

Then the council got down to business. One of the first things decided was the "symbol of faith." What confession or creed would the church accept?

What short set of doctrinal statements set out the basics of Catholic belief? The third session of the council set out the Nicene Creed as the true symbol and in fact included the whole text of the creed in its decree.[30] At its very next session, the council took up the basic question of Scripture. Protestants had roared out that only Scripture could be authoritative for doctrine and discipline. Trent took very little time to answer back. First, the council denied the sufficiency of Scripture alone. It said that Scripture must be accompanied by unwritten traditions that are kept by the church. Therefore, the church has two sources of authority—Scripture and tradition. Second, the council decreed that only the Roman Church had the right to interpret the Bible and that anyone interpreting against the sense of Holy Mother Church was liable to penalties.[31] Because questions had arisen about what exactly Scripture was, the council set that down as well. The council set out the number and names of the books of the Bible, including some that Protestants had rejected. Then it denied one of the most basic advances of the sixteenth century—the recourse to the Scriptures in their original languages. The council stated that the old Latin Vulgate was to be preferred in all cases, and that no one should dare to reject it.

The first assembly also took up the core issue of justification. After the Regensburg failure, there was little doubt that this was a key topic to answer. A comparison of the decrees from the fourth session, on Scripture, with the decrees of the sixth session, on justification, make clear how much effort the delegates spent on this matter. The fourth session took up only two decrees, each rather brief in itself. The sixth session was divided into sixteen chapters, after which are appended thirty-three canons, enumerating the different ways that one can break the sense of the decrees on justification and earn being anathematized. Justification was the crux of the conflict between Protestants and Catholics, and the theologians at Trent took up the issue very thoroughly.

The delegates at Trent debated justification hotly. Girolamo Seripando (1493–1563), the general of the Augustinian order, argued forcefully for the doctrine of double justification that had been considered at Regensburg. Such a position would have been more open to the positions of some Protestants, and Seripando was probably influenced by his own reading of Augustine. Seripando was no closet heretic and would be made a cardinal in 1561. But at Trent, he lost. In point after point, the decree on justification reads as a rejection of Lutheran or Zwinglian positions. Human merit toward justification was affirmed; the position that no one can know whether he or she is in a state of grace was acknowledged. The human will must do what it can in order to turn itself toward God's grace. Finally, the decree claimed that there was no possibility of justification for anyone who did not faithfully and firmly accept this particular doctrine.[32]

The seventh session of the first meeting of the council took up the sacraments. While this was oddly brief, it was also pointed. There are seven sacraments, no more and no fewer, and the Lord Jesus Christ instituted them all. Further, they are necessary for salvation. To say otherwise is to risk anathema. The seventh session also took up the reform of the clergy, to which we shall shortly return.

The council did not meet again until 1551. By that time, very few thinkers still held out the strong hope that the breach between the Protestants and Catholics could be fully healed. The invited Protestant observers had nothing to do at the council and were simply ignored. In the thirteenth session, this phase of the council took up the presence of Christ in the Eucharist and affirmed transubstantiation. It denied Lutheran consubstantiation theories, Zwinglian remembrance theories, and Calvinist theories of the presence. The fourteenth session dealt with penance and last rites or extreme unction, and it defended their sacramental character.

The council met one last time, from 1561 to 1563. This meeting was not "outward looking" toward Protestantism as others had been. Rather, it was far more about the necessity of finishing the character of the church. In the twenty-first session it decreed that the church had the power to determine the sufficiency of Communion in one kind for the laity. The council reaffirmed the truth of the sacrifice of the Mass, as well as purgatory and the usefulness and propriety of indulgences.

So far as we have covered it, the Council of Trent must be considered a Counter-Reformation instrument. In answer to the issues raised by Protestants of various types, the Catholic delegates joined together in rejecting either the formulation of the issues or the answers given. However, the Council of Trent was also an instrument of the Catholic Reformation. Beyond all the denials of doctrinal formulations of characteristic Protestant positions, the council adopted a number of reforms that were wholly centered on the reform of Catholicism. For instance, the sixth session of the council did not only consider justification. It also mandated that all clergy should reside in their churches. That meant the end of absenteeism, or at least the beginning of its end. Further, the seventh session, which considered the sacraments, also commanded that a man could only hold one cathedral church, that benefices should only be given to those who were qualified for the benefices, and that hospitals should be faithfully managed. The cure of souls, that is to say, the taking care of the spiritual needs of the people, was to be diligently discharged.

In this, the Catholic Church faced some of the same problems that Protestant bodies did. Where could the church find the well-trained men to staff a number of congregations, as well as supply the need for evangelizing the newly found worlds? The council answered this question with straightforward simplicity, by charging that all cathedral and metropolitan churches and churches that were larger than those should make provision for establishing regular education for the priesthood.[33] In short, the council mandated the formation of seminaries. Further, it created decrees of reform on the morals of the clergy and on the preaching of sermons. Many of the abuses that had arisen through centuries of neglect were addressed carefully and systematically for the first time. The council attended to the needs of the faithful in traditional ways, but in a profoundly more thorough manner. Though the decrees of the council were not immediately and evenly applied everywhere in Europe, the "Tridentine" church (the church formed by Trent) had a clear compass.

Did the council take away the power of the popes? Far from it—the sixteenth-century popes managed to channel the outcomes of the Council of Trent in a manner that strengthened, rather than weakened, the place of the pope in the church. Some issues were reserved to the office of the pope. Other concerns that the council had identified were unfinished when the council's last session was over, and these were handed over to the pope. One such matter was the Index.

When the Council of Trent established the Vulgate as the true text of the Bible, it also decreed that no printer could print books dealing with sacred doctrinal matters that had not been examined and approved by an agent of the church.[34] But obviously, this led to the further question of what things the church normally approved and what things might it in all cases reject. In 1557, Pope Paul IV began the process of establishing an index of books that Catholics should not own. This was published in 1559 as the *Index librorum prohibitorum*—the Index of Prohibited Books. From the first edition, the Index provoked sharp dissent. Outside the Roman Church, critics noted that Catholics refused even to think about other ideas; inside the church, detractors argued against the inclusion or exclusion of certain books. In all cases, what the Index represented was an intensely conservative mentality, designed to protect the faithful against outside dangerous influences. The Index would last, in one form or another, until 1966. But Pope Paul IV had not drawn up the Index by himself. In 1557, he turned to the Office of the Inquisition.

THE INQUISITION

In the popular imagination, the Inquisition frequently seems to be a symbol of everything that was wrong with church power. Visions of thumbscrews, the rack, and thousands burned at the stake make for excellent stories and even movies. But as so frequently happens, the historical truth is somewhat more complex. First, the Inquisition was not technically a Reformation-era invention. Inquisitors and inquisitorial power had existed since the Middle Ages. However, the Inquisition developed its institutional form and procedures during the sixteenth century. Second, the Inquisition took on different particular national forms, which tended to keep separate records. Thus, the Roman Inquisition was actually quite different from the Spanish Inquisition.[35]

What was the Inquisition? In its simplest form, this was a formalized way for the Church of Rome to investigate suspected cases of heresy or witchcraft. Therefore, one of its forms in the Spanish Inquisition, the rooting out of Jewish or Islamic beliefs and practices, was not technically something that the Inquisition was supposed to investigate. However, like any historical institution, the Inquisition developed over time in response to a wide set of historical circumstances.

In Spain, the situation differed greatly from most of the rest of Latin Europe. Spain had Muslim communities and in part had been ruled by Muslim rulers until late in the fifteenth century. Anthony Wright explains, "The Inquisition in the Spanish kingdoms was the creation, in effect, of the fifteenth century, when initial reform of the Spanish Church was combined with the beginnings of the final stage in the reconquest of the Iberian peninsula for Christianity."[36] The Spanish crown had only recently conquered the last Moorish possession in Spain, so Muslim rule was a very recent memory. Further, the Jewish and Muslim populations of Spain had frequently been coerced into converting to Catholicism. Sometimes this was because of social pressure; at other times, people converted in order to save their lives. Jewish converts to Catholicism were normally called *conversos*; Muslim converts to Catholicism were called *moriscos*.

Both *moriscos* and *conversos* were continually suspected by crown and church authorities of secretly preserving their old faith.[37] Servants were questioned on the habits of their *morisco* or *converso* masters. Did they refrain from eating pork? Did they say the correct prayers? Did they attend mass regularly? Failure to be a zealous Catholic was dangerous for such people. Thus, the Spanish Inquisition took on a special characteristic of racial purity, rather than simple doctrinal purity. Only secondarily did the Spanish Inquisition turn to the "Lutheran" problem, after 1520.[38]

The Inquisitions did put people to death. Technically, the Inquisition made accusations and carried out trials. The civil authorities carried out any executions. The Spanish Inquisition executed approximately three thousand people, the Portuguese Inquisition about one thousand. The Roman Inquisition itself executed perhaps fewer than 150 people in all.[39] While those numbers are grotesque, they hardly equal what French Catholics did to Huguenots in 1572 alone in the St. Bartholomew's Day Massacre. And as Monter notes, secular authorities were willing to execute approximately forty thousand people for witchcraft between 1580 and 1650.[40] Thus, the Inquisitions did put people to death, but they also achieved their stated purposes. In realms where the Inquisition was most active, Protestantism and religious dissent were thoroughly suppressed.

THE FLOWERING OF MYSTICISM

No consideration of sixteenth-century Catholicism would be complete without mention of the explosion of mystical thought at the time. From Teresa of Avila's *Interior Castle*, which sought to explain how a person could rise up to union with God as a process, to John of the Cross's lyrical love poetry to God, the century saw some of the greatest mystics in the history of the church. As Teresa and John are the recognized leaders and knew each other in the Discalced Carmelite Orders, we shall concentrate upon them. But by no means were they the only mystics or the only religious people interested in the mystical way of union with their Lord who saw mysticism as the most fitting way to revere God.

Mysticism is as ancient as Christianity. When in the first century Paul wrote, "I know a man who was caught up to the third heaven, whether in or out of the body I do not know, but God knows" (2 Cor. 12:2), he was writing about a mystical experience. Also, St. Antony had mystical experiences, as did St. Augustine; St. Bernard of Clairvaux was another famous mystic. Women, too, were part of the mystical tradition, which included such figures as Julian of Norwich and Gertrude of Helfta. But what is mysticism?

Whereas the practice of doctrinal theology seeks to know God or know about God through reason, the mystical approach to God seeks to know God through experience. An analogy might help. You can study a historical figure such as Abraham Lincoln. You can read all his writings, research his presidential decisions, and even look into the lives of the people who surrounded him. If you did this for some time, you might become an expert on Lincoln, but you would not actually know him. On the other hand, we know our best friends, but we rarely study their writings or their historical contexts. Instead, we have an experience of them that is rich in its own way. That lived experience of the living God, frequently termed "union," is the basis of the mystic's effort. Frequently this experience of God comes as ecstatic visions, or trances. While the rational theologian seeks to understand what God did or who God is, the mystical theologian seeks to become ever more in the presence of God, to feel God's presence.

Teresa of Avila and John of the Cross were two such people. Both were involved in the purification of the Carmelite order that resulted in the foundation of the Discalced Carmelites. Teresa herself was probably a *converso* and suspected because of it. She was also suspected for her practice of "mental prayer," a contemplation that did not involve spoken words. Prodded by her confessors, Teresa began to write about her visions. Her book *The Interior Castle* details her advice to the sisters of the convent as to how they might deepen their own knowledge of Christ. She presents a series of seven stages, described as a set of rooms or mansions in a castle. The mystic will rise up to the seventh through long contemplation.

Teresa used four distinct concepts to describe the spiritual life. She spoke and wrote of habitual contemplation of God as an overall term that covered the entirety of the deep inner life. She also wrote of three stages that she illustrated in her own life, which built upon one another. The first was partial consciousness of union with God, which she experienced for twelve years. She noted that frequently after it had happened, she would become aware of the touch of God in her contemplation. The second stage was the habitual union with God in identifying her will with the Lord's. She experienced this for eleven years and noted that in it her will was no longer truly her own. Finally, she described spiritual marriage, which she acknowledged that she felt for ten years. In this, the bride that was her soul was swallowed up in the bridegroom that was God. Obviously, Teresa was explaining a level of identification and union that went beyond words, that went beyond explanation. But her words, and the realities to which they pointed, enflamed many to set out on the mystical road to follow her.

John of the Cross knew Teresa and devoted himself to many of the same causes that she led. John joined the Carmelites in 1563 but was soon disappointed with the lazy ways in which many of his brothers fulfilled their vows. Following Teresa's lead, he founded a house of Discalced Carmelite friars in 1571. The Carmelite Order was not pleased with this. In 1577, the order imprisoned John. After nine months he escaped and was safe only after the two orders were officially separated.

Also like Teresa, John expressed his love for God in a mystical sense. But unlike her, he did not write guides to the devotional path, but rather poetry. His poems were accompanied by his explanations of the meaning of the poems. While the poems themselves were lyrical, sensual, and exotic, the explanations were heavily influenced by scholasticism. John saw three stages in the mystical life as well, but he described them somewhat differently than Teresa had. For John they were purgation, in which the soul is cleansed; illumination, in which the soul is enlightened; and union, in which the soul becomes one with the Lord. John's poetry still speaks of a yearning for the heart's deepest desire that leads many to consider the religious life.

CONCLUSION

The flowering of mysticism in the sixteenth century cannot be seen as representing either the Catholic Reformation or the Counter-Reformation. Rather, it reflected what O'Malley calls early modern Catholicism. In recognizing it so, we also see a kind of profoundly traditional trajectory, which allows some variation of emphasis. Mysticism did not depend upon some innovation, but rather took the ingredients already present in the tradition of the church and fused them together in slightly new ways.

In the same way, the spirit of the early modern Catholic mind depended upon a well-established tradition, but it appropriated that tradition and its fruits in more institutionally clear manners. Trent did not change at all the ideal of a Catholic priest. What Trent did was create a clearer path to the training of that priest and a clearer manner of regulating that priest's ministry. By clarifying the boundaries, Trent both provided a strong institutional framework and a space for doctrinal and spiritual development within those boundaries.

This proved to be the character of Catholic reform. An intense appreciation of the riches of the tradition inspired Catholics to meet the new challenges by returning to both institutional and popular practices. Instead of attempting to go past the history and routines of the medieval period to get to the foundation of the early church, Catholicm embraced the value of the medieval interpretation of the apostolic age as useful and valuable. The focus on the patterns of the past stamped early modern Catholicism with an indelible character that challenged the models of Protantism with a vibrancy of its own.

QUESTIONS FOR DISCUSSION

1. What do the terms "Catholic Reformation" and "Counter-Reformation" signify? Could both have some claim to historical truth?
2. To what sources did Catholic refomers turn when they wished to reform the church? How did this affect Catholic reform?
3. Considering the varieties of reforms at the Council of Trent, from clerical morals to the doctrine of justification to the decree on Scripture and tradition as dual sources of authority, compare the Tridentine Catholic Church with the Church of the fifteenth century. What remains the same, what has been intensified, and what has been changed? How would these factors determine Catholicism?
4. How does the flowering of mysticism fit into the patterns of religious reform in Catholicism in the sixteenth and early seventeenth centuries?

SUGGESTED FURTHER READING

Primary Readings

The Canons and Decrees of the Council of Trent. Translated and introduced by H. J. Schroeder, OP. Rockford, IL: Tan Books, 1978.

Ignatius of Loyola. *Ignatius of Loyola: Spiritual Exercises and Selected Works.* Edited by Parmananda Divarkar and Edward J. Malatesta. Classics of Western Spirituality. Mahwah, NJ: Paulist Press, 1991.

John of the Cross. *The Collected Works of St. John of the Cross.* Translated by Kieran Kavanaugh and Otilio Rodriguez. Washington, DC: Institute for Carmelite Studies Publications, 1991.

Teresa of Avila. *Teresa of Avila: The Interior Castle.* Edited by Kieran Kavanaugh and Otilio Rodriguez. Mahwah, NJ: Paulist Press, 1979.

Secondary Readings

Evennett, H. O. *The Spirit of the Counter-Reformation.* South Bend, IN: University of Notre Dame Press, 1970.

Kamen, Henry. *The Spanish Inquisition: A Revision.* New Haven, CT: Yale University Press, 1999.

Leonard, Amy. "Female Religious Orders." In *A Companion to the Reformation World,* edited by R. Po-chia Hsia, 237–54. Malden, MA: Blackwell Publishing, 2004.

Luebke, David, ed. *The Counter-Reformation: Essential Readings.* Malden, MA: Blackwell Publishing, 1999.

Mullett, Michael. *The Catholic Reformation.* New York: Routledge, 1999.

O'Malley, John. *The First Jesuits.* Cambridge, MA: Harvard University Press, 1993.

———. "The Society of Jesus." In *A Companion to the Reformation World,* edited by R. Po-chia Hsia, 223–36. Malden, MA: Blackwell Publishing, 2004.

———. *Trent and All That: Renaming Catholicism in the Early Modern Era.* Cambridge, MA: Harvard University Press, 2000.

Po-chia Hsia, R. *The World of Catholic Renewal: 1540–1720.* 2nd ed. London: Cambridge University Press, 2005.

Wright, A. D. *The Counter-Reformation: Catholic Europe and the Non-Christian World.* 2nd ed. Burlington, VT: Ashgate Press, 2005.

DOCTRINAL-VOCABULARY DISCUSSION

Confessionalism

At the beginning of the Reformation period, Christians knew that they were Christian simply because of the things they did. Not being faced with another organized religion that claimed to be "Christian," the great majority of the Christian population did not give great thought to the intellectual aspect of the faith or spend a great amount of time considering specific doctrines. The

reformations of the sixteenth century changed all that. Confessionalism marks
out the later periods of the Reformation. Reformation scholars tend to see the
period from 1560 to 1650 as the period of confessionalism, but the early effects
were felt far sooner, and the aftershocks of this trend still affect Christian patterns of life today.

Confessionalism was the identification of patterns of Christianity by the
doctrinal decrees and polity rules of a confession or set of confessions. These
"patterns of Christianity" had a wide range of meanings. Of course, they covered disputed areas of belief. But they also dictated the relationship of the
church to the state, the practice of certain family and community laws, and the
meaning of church discipline. By the end of the sixteenth century, four main
"confessional" groups made up much of the map of Latin Europe. These were
the Lutherans, the Reformed or Calvinists, the Anglicans, and the Catholics.
The confessional documents that most set these groups apart were statements
of belief. Lutherans were defined by the Augsburg Confession. Reformed
Christians generally held to the First and Second Helvetic Confessions and
the Canons of Dordt. Anglicans defined themselves by the Book of Common
Prayer and the Thirty-nine Articles. Catholicism identified itself by the canons
and decrees of the Council of Trent. Other groups, such as Anabaptists,
became known for their lack of confessional status.

The disputed areas of doctrine were always covered in the confessions.
Eucharistic beliefs, the doctrine of Scripture, and the pattern of salvation were
standard topics. But just as important for the setting out of social rules were
the community rules and roles that the confessional groups accepted. For
instance, the relationship of the church to the secular authorities clearly dif-
ferentiated the confessional bodies. Reformed and Lutheran bodies tended
to cooperate with authorities, Anglicans by definition were ruled by the head
of the state, and Catholic popes and bishops cooperated with princes, but
through agreements (concordats) that strongly resembled treaties.

Communal and family laws and practices also varied. In Reformed lands, discipline marked the churches and was entrusted to presbyteries and consistories.
Reformed churches adopted boards of deacons to care for the poor and the hospitals. Lutherans adopted poor boxes, as well as councils of deacons to adminis-
ter the money from the poor boxes to the deserving poor. Catholics and
Anglicans depended on the structures that they had inherited from the Middle
Ages to tend to these matters. Reformed, Lutheran, and Anglican clergy could
marry; Catholic priests could not. This difference tended to concentrate ministry in a clerical class in Protestant confessions, and frequently families of ministers arose, with generation after generation entering the ministry.

As noted earlier, strains of confessionalism arose early in the sixteenth century. Swiss Protestants were generally not considered to be in conformity with

the Augsburg Confession, especially by Lutherans, so they were not protected by agreements between the emperor and Lutherans. As well, in 1537, John Calvin and Guillaume Farel put forward a confession of faith in Geneva that residents all had to sign as a condition of living in Geneva. Although these factors showed up early in the Reformation era, their impact endured long into the modern period. Until the middle of the twentieth century, it was a mortal sin for a Roman Catholic even to attend a Protestant worship service.

A further important note must be raised before leaving confessionalism. Many modern scholars see confessionalism and confessionalization, the process of the establishment of confessionalism, as inextricably bound up in the rise of the modern state. Confessional churches tended to be "state churches"; they were functionally given their legitimacy by the stamp of the ruling authority. Of course, this pattern of analysis had a hard time with the Radical churches, as they avoided entanglement with the ruling authorities. There is an enormous literature on confessionalism around this topic, but it does not directly bear on how confessionalism changed the theologies and practices of the Christian churches.

While the value of all Christians knowing the basic doctrines of the faith should not be denigrated, confessionalization truly brought with it both good and bad points. On the good side, more Christians, especially among the laity, had some intellectual understanding of what their faith proclaimed. On the negative side, when religion became defined as a set of beliefs, it was not long before the people began to accept the corollary belief that religious practice was not the center of Christianity. That would become the cross of the late seventeenth century, when movements of pietism sought to address the imbalance between doctrine and lived religion.

10

Religion and Violence

In writing a history of the Reformation, the question is not "Why have a chapter on religion and violence?" Instead, it is more properly "How can you avoid discussing religion and violence?" In the twentieth century, it became inappropriate to link religion, especially Christianity, to violence. However, that is a relatively modern development. Soon after the cataclysmic events of September 11, 2001, I was asked to speak on a radio program on the topic of religion and violence. Many of the callers rejected the idea that Christianity had any tolerance for violence, believing that violence had only ever been linked to Islam. I countered with history: What about the Crusades? What about the wars of religion? What about the acceptance of capital punishment in America, an industrialized nation that proclaims itself "under God," when so many other countries reject it? Callers had a difficult time with the concept and generally discarded the notion as preposterous.

This is the first reason to talk about religion and violence—because we, as twenty-first-century people, cannot avoid it. In the beginning of the twenty-first century, to deny any link between religion and violence is to make a statement of opinion rather than of fact. Religion is frequently linked to war, both explicitly and implicitly. Crusading language is used by secular leaders as well as religious figures. Part of the value of considering religion and violence in the sixteenth century comes from the lessons we may learn from a time long past, a time whose dead may not have to be avenged.

The second reason to discuss religion and violence arises when we simply accept the different value structures of the sixteenth century and thus construct a truer picture of their motivations and desires. Humans are prone to believe that everything was just the way it is—that values remain constant. The historically informed thinker knows better.

In the sixteenth century, most rulers, most theologians, and most common people believed that a society functioned best when it was built upon the true religion. For centuries the "true religion" in Western Europe had been Christianity. That is not a historical claim about what was "true religion," but rather a historical claim about what the overwhelming majority of people believed. They believed that some form of Christianity was the truth, as opposed to the failure of small minority groups such as the Jews or Muslims to believe the gospel. Further, people accepted that when the true religion was threatened by heresy, false belief could be rooted out by punishment. The people of Europe did not rise up in general clamor against the persecution of the Cathars, a group of French heretics, or the Lollards, a mostly English heretical group. Instead, they believed that attacking heresy was like pulling up weeds in the garden—a healthy procedure for the society.

The sixteenth century changed that. In general, Christianity retained its place as the true religion, but the vital question became "What *is* true Christianity?" For the first time in centuries, Europeans were faced with competing organized factions, all claiming to be the true representation of God's will for Christians. Because people generally believed that God was active and would punish a realm that did not follow the true religion, this choice represented a variety of frightening issues. First, there was the choice—which group to believe? Second, once the first choice was made, what should be done about those in the other group? Could they be left alone? Must they be given rights? Could they be stamped out? The sixteenth century's struggle with these questions led to a variety of answers and a particular shape to the beliefs of the late sixteenth and early seventeenth centuries.

This chapter will not go into exhaustive detail on every religious war or every religiously motivated persecution. Rather, it will highlight some of the most significant wars, massacres, and martyrdoms. Sometimes it will simply offer reminders of a particular conflict that appears in earlier chapters and will not retell the entire story. The purpose of setting out this catalog is to demonstrate the breadth of the phenomenon of religious violence in the sixteenth century. Beyond that, it will allow us to consider what was happening in these events of religious violence, and what values were being pursued. Finally, we will find that it was through religious violence that the beginnings of religious tolerance theory began. This chapter will first cover religious wars, then martyrdom and religious persecution. After those are set out, we will have a better platform on which to consider the responses to these phenomena.

THE RADICAL OR ANABAPTIST WARS

We have already spent significant space on the Peasants' War of 1524–1525 in chapters 4 and 6; considerable space was granted to the Kingdom of Münster in chapter 6. We need not rehearse the entirety of that material here. What is more valuable here is to consider what these two discussions enlighten for us. Several points will come quickly to the surface.

The Peasants' War of 1524–1525 had the character of an economic and political revolt, tied to a religious upheaval. The people who were attracted to this movement took Luther's idea of the priesthood of all believers seriously. And "people" is the right word, rather than "peasants," because they were not by any means all serfs or peasants; this was a movement that mixed the orders of society. The movement drew up several manifestos of desired changes in the ways of life; the Memmingen Articles is one such document. The movement was somewhat leaderless; Thomas Müntzer was a religious leader for some of the bands, but he was hardly universally accepted and was not particularly skilled at war craft. The series of battles and rebellions eventually touched upon approximately a third of Germany and united the princes against it. Though Martin Luther originally had some sympathy for the peasants, he eventually turned against them over what he believed were their excesses and urged the princes to set things right. The princes were able to smash the revolt at Frankenhausen in 1525, though by the reckoning of some historians the aftermath of the Peasants' War would last into 1526.

The Kingdom of Münster represents an experiment in Anabaptist spiritual kingdom building. In 1534, disciples of Melchior Hoffman came to Münster and managed to take over the city. The Anabaptists set themselves up as a kingdom set apart, with their own laws. Eventually the laws of the kingdom became extreme, including mandatory polygamy following the patterns of the Old Testament patriarchs. Catholics and Protestants took on this threat and destroyed this kingdom in 1535.

We can learn several points from these observations. First, many people in the sixteenth century were willing to believe in the immediate rule of God over the human realms. A sizeable number of Christians thought that the message and commandments of the gospel were to be put into practice without delay. These people believed that the models of communalism from the Bible and other specific biblical practices such as biblical morality should be instituted at once. We should be no more surprised at or suspicious of the motivations of the peasants than we are of the nobility. Certainly, the peasants mixed economics and religion and stood to gain by a revolution. But the nobility were just as willing to see God's will in their own power structures, and they defended their privileges with ferocious will. The various interpretations of the meaning of biblical injunctions and God's will created a collision course when applied in real-world situations.

Second, even theologians who seemed to be leading movements could be surprised at the turns of events. Certainly Melchior Hoffman did not claim that Münster was to be the new Jerusalem. It was his disciples, contradicting him, who did so. Martin Luther seems to have been honestly surprised that anyone could take his claims of Christian freedom and apply them to the earthly realm. He denied the validity of the scriptural claims that the peasants made and eventually called for the princes to force them into submission.

Finally, the intensity of commitment to the various positions taken suggests a corresponding magnitude in the seriousness of the issues. Men and women were not risking their own lives lightly. These were far from academic discussions. For many men and women in the sixteenth century—whether peasant, university-trained scholar, or lord—the issue of needing to live in accord with the will of God as revealed either in the Scriptures or in visions or in an authoritative tradition exceeded other needs.

THE SCHMALKALDIC WAR

In 1530, German Lutherans presented their faith to the Imperial Diet at Augsburg in the Augsburg Confession. While this confession was acceptable for a brief interim period by both Catholics and Lutherans, neither side believed that issues were solved. Between 1531 and 1536, the Protestant princes of Germany allied themselves through membership in the Schmalkaldic League. The league's primary purpose was the defense of the members' territories against imperial attack. Catholic forces saw the league's purpose as offensive, however.

In 1546, the Schmalkaldic War began when Duke Maurice of Albertine Saxony betrayed his Protestant allies and attacked Ernestine Saxony, ruled by Duke John Frederick. Because Maurice had been Protestant prior to his attack, he was seen as a traitor by the members of the Schmalkaldic League. Holy Roman Emperor Charles V joined in on Maurice's side; the rest of the Schmalkaldic League came to the defense of John Frederick.

Though the Protestant forces enjoyed early success, at the Battle of Mühlberg, April 24, 1547, imperial forces won a decisive victory over the League. Duke John Frederick himself was wounded and taken prisoner, and another prominent League leader, Philip of Hesse, also surrendered to the emperor. Protestant prospects could hardly have looked more bleak following this demoralizing loss.

However, imperial forces did not conquer everything. Two fortified cities, Bremen and Magdeburg, remained free and continued to oppose an imposed

Catholicism. Finally, imperial forces were simply unable ever to conquer either city. Frustrated in his intention of complete and total military victory, Charles V proposed an agreement called the Augsburg Interim. This was an agreement that was to hold until the Council of Trent should decide issues more finally. The agreement allowed the Protestants to maintain married clergy and Communion in both kinds. However, many Protestant leaders denied its validity. First, they believed that it amounted to creeping Catholicism. Second, they questioned whether it was ever proper to accept a settlement based on coercive force.

The city of Magdeburg forced the issue. Its theologians rejected the Augsburg Interim, crying out that the Interim was the work of the devil and the antichrist.[1] The city held out against a siege and an imperially enforced ban for so long that it was able to negotiate a better settlement with Duke Maurice. In 1551, the city surrendered to Maurice, in return for keeping its religion. In the meantime, the pastors of the city had fashioned a theology of resistance. They had put forth the idea that, at times, God called upon true Christians to resist impious tyrants.

Maurice of Saxony, the traitor to the Protestant cause, eventually turned traitor again. In 1552, he led Protestant forces against the empire. In 1555, the warring was brought to an end by the Peace of Augsburg, the result of another imperial diet. The Peace of Augsburg represented agreements on several issues; for our purposes, the religious are the most important. First, it gave toleration to Lutheranism. Henceforth, both Catholicism and Lutheranism, as defined by adherence to the Augsburg Confession, would be allowed. Calvinists and Anabaptists did not receive any particular protections. Second, the question of religious uniformity in any particular land was answered according to the religion of the prince, and the Peace of Augsburg allowed for those who did not wish to follow that religion to emigrate. Finally, the Peace set out a new idea of empire, as Carter Lindberg explains: "The Peace did recognize that an alternative confessional commitment did not in itself mean disloyalty to the Empire, a point which Luther and Melanchthon among others had vociferously argued since 1530."[2] We shall return to the significance of the Peace of Augsburg when we examine the Thirty Years' War, and in the conclusion to this chapter.

THE FRENCH WARS OF RELIGION

In France of the sixteenth century there was an odd mix of a fiercely Catholic country, whose king held the title of "the Most Christian King" granted by the pope, jumbled together with a sizeable minority of French Calvinists. These French Protestants came to be called "Huguenots." Though hard numbers are

hard to come by, when the French court was required to make a public confession of Catholic faith in June 1562, exactly 31 of the 143 members of the
court chose not to be present—a figure representing more than 20 percent of
the court. While all absentees cannot legitimately be presumed to have been
Huguenots, not all had other pressing business for the crown that took them
away from that confession.[3]

In 1551, King Henry II of France decreed the Edict of Chateaubriant. Basically, this made Protestantism wholly illegal in France. Specific penalties were
set for holding Protestant beliefs, and specific considerable rewards were
established for informing on another person's Protestantism. Nevertheless,
Protestantism in France survived. Partly, this was due to Geneva: Calvin was
always fixed on sending missionaries to his native country, and many ministers
trained in Geneva were sent to France. To some degree, however, Protestantism simply endured because its adherents believed that it was the truth and
were willing to pay the price for that belief.

Protestantism and Catholicism existed together, but in an uneasy existence.
This was not simply because of the illegal status of Protestantism. Raymond
Mentzer notes:

> The conflict was first and foremost an encounter between communi-
> ties of believers, people who worshipped and prayed together. It was
> rooted in collective practices of piety and went well beyond quarrelling
> over a body of beliefs. Antagonisms between rival religious cultures
> focused on everyday conduct and ideas regarding appropriate devotion.
> Protestants vehemently rejected, for instance, the "idolatries" of the
> mass and the veneration of the saints and their relics, while Catholics
> took offence at Reformed sermon services and the singing of the Psalms
> in the vernacular. Each side viewed the other as having profaned the
> Lord and polluted the community. The ensuing cleansing and purify-
> ing process was at best contentious and frequently lethal.[4]

Though Henry II had made Protestantism illegal, it was growing. In 1559,
Henry died of a wound suffered in a tournament. This brought his son, Francis II, to the throne. For Protestants, this was disastrous. Francis had married
Mary, Queen of Scots, who was a niece of the Guise family, one of the most
militantly Catholic families in Europe. The Guise family came into power at
court, determined to stamp out the heresy infecting the kingdom. They also
controlled the young king, who had ascended the throne at age fifteen.

Desperate, the Huguenots attempted to kidnap the king at Amboise in
1560. The plan was apparently to free him from the Guise influence, but the
plan failed, and the conspirators were met by royal troops. The duke of Guise
had several hundred Huguenots executed as traitors.[5] Seemingly, the anti-
Huguenot faction had things well in hand. However, Francis II died in Decem-

ber 1560. This allowed Henry II's widow, Catherine de Medici, to declare herself regent for her son, the new king, Charles IX.

Catherine's policy was to try to accommodate all factions. She decreed the Edict of Saint-Germain in January 1562, which gave legal recognition to Protestants. This was the first time Protestantism was explicitly legal in France. It also was too much for the Guise family. In March 1562, troops loyal to the Guise family caught unarmed Huguenots worshiping in the town of Vassy. They shot them, and the massacre of Vassy started the first French War of Religion.

The wars stretched from 1562 to 1598 and flared up again in the 1620s.[6] The details are not wholly important for our discussion. Neither side could ever gain the full advantage needed to force the other to acquiesce to its demands. Huguenots could not hope to force Catholicism out of France, but they dreamed of a permanent legal status. Catholics hoped to banish Protestantism, but they could not accomplish it militarily. Along the path of the eight civil wars between 1562 and 1598, a number of things occurred that would have seemed wholly bizarre at the beginning of this period. The French Catholic king Henry III was assassinated, not by a Huguenot but by a Catholic monk, because he did not seem harsh enough against the Huguenots. Huguenots wrote tracts defending their right to resist tyranny, and Catholics used those beliefs in their own desire to avoid allegiance to a king who might allow Huguenots legal status.

Finally, in 1589, political considerations forced the hand of the king, Henry III of France. Faced by the Catholic League led by the Guise family that wished to end his reign and his life, he made a treaty with the leading Huguenot general, Henry of Navarre. When later that year Henry III was assassinated, a truly vexing problem arose. Henry of Navarre was the first in line for the throne, but he was a Protestant! As Holt points out, "According to the Salic Law, Navarre ought to be recognized as Henry IV; yet according to the Catholicity of the crown, a Protestant was ineligible. Both were perceived by many Catholics as equally binding fundamental laws of the realm, so how could one possibly choose between them?"[7]

Henry solved the problem by converting. By becoming Catholic, he was both the next in line to the throne and not barred by confessional flaw. But was his conversion genuine? Famously, he is supposed to have said, "Paris is worth a mass." Such a statement would have meant that his conversion was only for political gain. It is unlikely that such an astute politician as Henry would have said such a thing, especially where anyone could hear him. But still, was his conversion motivated by religious feeling? Historians argue. His actions from that point certainly point toward an authentic change. However, until that moment, his life had been totally linked to the Huguenot cause. The question remains, but Henry's further actions are clear.

In 1594, Henry of Navarre was crowned king of France as Henry IV. Desiring to end the civil wars, in 1598, Henry decreed the Edict of Nantes. This edict allowed Protestants the right to worship, set up civil courts where their concerns could be heard, and allowed them the right to civil offices and places at universities. Mentzer summarizes: "While the edict did not give Protestantism complete parity with Catholicism, it did provide a coherent framework for adherents of the two faiths to live together in a semblance of peace."[8] The edict would be the law of the land, though continually contested, until it was finally revoked by King Louis XIV in 1685.

What came out of the French Wars of Religion? First, the eventual ending of the conflict by royal will strengthened the idea and practice of the power of the monarchy, even in matters of religion. Second, the French learned the difficult lesson that it had proven impossible to compel belief by military power, by massacre, or by assassination. Though neither Huguenots nor Catholics trusted the other, their taste for all-out war over the issue of religion was greatly lessened by the beginning of the seventeenth century.

THE THIRTY YEARS' WAR

The Thirty Years' War represents another attempt at the compulsion of belief, this time in the lands that make up modern-day Germany. The war was far too long and far too involved even to list its major events in this chapter. However, it was crucial for several reasons. First, it was another step in the marriage of religion and violence. Second, it tended to strengthen certain state and religious alliances, while weakening others. Finally, its ending brought about a solution that infused sacred power with the power of the ruler in a way that was foreign to the European mind prior to sixteenth century.

The war stretched from 1618 until 1648, giving it its name. It began almost exactly one hundred years after Luther's Ninety-five Theses, and that was not an accident. In October 1617, Protestants celebrated a grand Reformation jubilee. Catholics took offense, and the pope immediately ordered a "counter-jubilee."[9] The two sides became ever-more suspicious of each other and waited only for a match to strike the flame. The match was struck in Prague. In 1618, the new king of Bohemia was Ferdinand II, a devout Catholic. On his election in 1617, Protestants in Bohemia had worried about their religious freedoms, which had been granted in the first decade of the seventeenth century. When Ferdinand sent counselors to arbitrate a dispute over the ownership of two churches, the citizens of Prague reacted violently. They threw the counselors out of the window of Hradcany Castle, some seventy feet up. This event became known as the Defenestration of Prague. The two men lived; according to Catholics, the angels cushioned their fall, but Protestants said they landed in a pile of manure. Furious, Ferdinand, who would soon become Holy Roman Emperor, attacked.

The war did not end until 1648, with the Peace of Westphalia. In the thirty years of its duration, most of the nations of Europe became entangled in its web in one way or another. No one won. Germany and Bohemia were devastated. While the war seemed to be between Protestants and Catholics, it was also between the Habsburgs and their rivals. Thus, for a time during the war, France supported the Protestant cause, in order to weaken the Habsburgs.

The Peace of Westphalia brought the hostilities to a close. It changed the map of Europe, but that is a political matter, not a theological or religious topic. For religion, the Peace of Westphalia demanded that all parties accept the terms of the Peace of Augsburg of 1555, with the addition of Calvinism to the allowed religions of Lutheranism and Catholicism. The religion of any particular realm was again decided by the principle of following the religion of the ruler. This principle became known by a Latin phrase, *cuius regio, eius religio*. Literally translated, it meant, "Whose region, his religion." That meant that the ruler of a region set the accepted religion for his subjects. As well, the right of emigration for those who could not accept their ruler's religion was maintained, and private worship according to conscience was allowed.

The *cuius regio, eius religio* principle represented a new stage in European belief. First, instead of two competing confessions, Westphalia recognized three. Second, it created a problem that had not functionally existed in Europe for centuries. Certainly, it was clear what religion to follow in every land. But what about when a ruler converted? Further, what happened when a succession of rulers held differing religions? These were not theoretical concerns; Henry of Navarre had famously converted, as had other rulers. England had already seen a succession of rulers with different beliefs. Third, secular rulers now had, theoretically, huge and unfettered religious power. Prior to 1500, a king's conversion was likely to earn a papal ban. Life for Christians had changed, and all the kinks had certainly not yet been worked out.

THE PHENOMENON OF MARTYRDOM

Martyrdom returned to the religious scene in Western Europe with a vengeance in the sixteenth century. Further, martyrdom was an equal opportunity experience in the era. Catholics, Lutherans, Calvinists, and Radicals all experienced the pain and opportunity of martyrdom. Opportunity? Yes, for

Christian thought had always regarded true martyrdom as a chance to proclaim the faith. The basic meaning of martyrdom comes from a Greek word meaning "witness." The Christian martyrs throughout the history of the church had witnessed to their unshakeable faith in their Lord, Jesus, by enduring torture and death rather than giving up their belief in him. This had been the case with the famous early martyrdoms of Polycarp, around 155, and Perpetua, in 203. The stories of their great faith in the face of unspeakable torment were seen as proof positive of the validity of the beliefs, and in fact their martyrdoms paradoxically helped to spread Christianity.

Christian martyrdom had become far less common in Western Europe in the centuries prior to Luther. It is in the nature of martyrdom that it arises in a society with deep social and religious differences.[10] Prior to Luther, the great majority of the populace was Christian and accepted the nature of the "Christian empire" as the way things were. Occasionally heresies arose, but they did not excite the sheer numbers that were moved by the various reforming movements in our period.

Now matters were different. The deep religious differences caused the ruptures in society in precisely the way that shocked people into action. In fact, all kinds of people moved to take action. Too frequently, when we look at martyrdom, we concentrate upon the actions of the suffering martyr. But to understand the complex of martyrdom, we must grasp at least two actors. First, there must be someone willing to die for a belief. But just as important, there must be someone willing to kill for a belief! Without the persecutor, or executioner, as the judicial case may be, no martyrdom can occur.

Martyrdom is also a matter of perspective. From the point of view of the community that the martyr represents, the act is unjust—a ritualized murder. From the point of view of the community that the power structure represents, the act is simply an execution of a criminal. For Mary I of England, the people sent to the stake were criminals; for the Protestant community, they were heroes of the faith.

Martyrdom struck all religious communities.[11] Further, the phenomenon of martyrdom drove all religious confessions to memorialize their heroes in popular books. These "martyrologies" had enormous propaganda value, as well as demonstrating the truth of the faith to the various communities. John Foxe (1517–1587), Jean Crespin (c. 1520–1572), and Thieleman van Braght (1625–1664) all wrote long compilations of accounts of martyrdom, demonstrating the evils of the persecutions and the faithfulness of the victims. Frequently, the collections of accounts began with martyrs of the early church and continued into the present day, so as to link more firmly the present-day figures with the ancient heroes of the faith.

THE ST. BARTHOLOMEW'S DAY MASSACRE

While martyrdoms normally concentrated upon the individual, occasionally there were also massacres. We have mentioned the massacre at Vassy, which started the French Wars of Religion. Another famous incident has come to be known as the St. Bartholomew's Day Massacre. On August 24, 1572, French soldiers, militia, and ordinary citizens began a slaughter of Protestants in the streets of Paris that would last throughout the week.[12] When the carnage was over in Paris, others took up the pattern in other parts of France. By the end of the killing, thousands of Protestants were dead. The incident remains unique for several reasons.

In 1572, religion divided the country of France. While the highest nobles and the great majority of the people were Catholic, a sizeable minority of the populace and a number of lower lords were Protestant. These Protestants were known as Huguenots. As we have already seen, the two sides had attempted unsuccessfully to resolve their differences through wars. In August 1572, a different tack was tried. Margaret of Valois, the Catholic princess, was to marry Henry of Navarre, a Protestant prince. Margaret was the daughter of Catharine de Medici, the queen mother. It seems that Catharine's plan was to achieve peace through marriage.

Not all parties in France and especially not everyone in Paris rejoiced at the news of the coming wedding. First, the Guise family, famous for its zealous Catholicism, was upset and plotted for ways to overthrow the power of Huguenots at court. The family's hatred centered on Gaspard de Coligny, a highly placed Huguenot official in the military (his title was admiral, but that was not a naval rank), who had been allowed back to court in 1571. Likewise, many Parisian priests clamored in the streets against the Protestant scourge. At least some of them advocated the "cleansing" of Paris and France of the abomination of heresy.

Coligny and most of the leading Huguenot nobles came to Paris for the wedding. Coligny was also planning to speak to the king, Charles IX, about abuses of the treaty that had ended the last French war of religion. Less well-known to the common people, Coligny was also supplying military help to the Netherlands in their battles against the Spanish under the duke of Alva. This was seen as a religious as well as a political act: the forces struggling against Spain were generally Calvinist, and the Spanish were Catholics.

On August 22, 1572, someone attempted to assassinate Coligny. The attempt failed, but Coligny was seriously wounded. Historians do not know exactly who made the attempt. Instead of leaving Paris, however, Coligny and the leading Huguenot figures chose to stay. The night of August 23, it seems that the king commanded the execution of Coligny.[13] Historians still do not know why. Perhaps the king believed that the Huguenots were enraged at the treachery and would attack him, but this seems like a small threat against the French soldiers and mercenary troops that surrounded the king. Perhaps the king and Catherine de Medici had always planned such an event, and the marriage was a ruse to draw Huguenots to a place where they could all safely be dealt with. Again, this seems rather unlikely, as it goes against Catherine's rather cautious nature. In any case, soldiers went to Coligny's residence, killed him, and threw him out the window. They then carried out the assassinations of several more leading Huguenots.

Perhaps the killing could have ended there. It did not. Barbara Diefendorf links the following slaughter to five words:

> The words were spoken by the duc de Guise upon leaving Coligny's lodgings. Encouraging his troops to carry on with their task, Guise reminded them that they killed by the king's command. The five words, "It is the king's command," overheard by others in the confused excitement of the darkened street, spread like wildfire. Taken to mean that the king had commanded the death of all the Huguenots, these words transformed private passions into public duty. They authorized actions that many people might otherwise have held in check and allowed them to view themselves as soldiers and citizens fighting to protect their city and king, and not as murderers and rabble, wantonly sacking and killing.[14]

What followed was one of the worst popular massacres in early modern history. At times the reasons for attacking a "Protestant" seem through the eyes of the historian to have been jealousy or greed; it was not a good week to be wealthy in Paris. The cruelty rose to ever-new heights, with pregnant women being bayoneted through the stomach and women's hands being hacked off in order to get bracelets. Thousands were murdered in mob violence in Paris over the next week.[15] However, the carnage was not finished. Over the next several weeks the pattern of mob rule and mass murder was repeated in the provinces of France, and many more thousands were killed.[16]

Reactions were mixed. Protestants saw this as a devastating blow. In Rome, the pope viewed it as a victory against the dangerous Huguenots and had a commemorative medal struck to memorialize the day. Eventually the pope would at least come to view the man most suspected for attempting to kill Coligny as an assassin. French Catholics seem to have believed that this action had been a purification of their society.

Supporting that understanding of Catholic reaction, historians have found in some of the accounts of the violence a ritualistic aspect. Some of the horrific actions seem to have been deeply attached to the rituals of Christianity.

When a group of citizens burned a bookbinder in a pile of his own books, they were reenacting the traditional punishment for heresy—burning at the stake. Similarly, the account is given of a young daughter of a Huguenot family. While naked, she was dipped in the blood of her murdered parents and was threatened with the same treatment if she ever became a Protestant. It is rather easy to see this as a kind of baptism, one that concentrates upon the rejection of a specific sin.[17] Catholics were not simply evil murderers but were accepting the roles that Parisian Catholic preachers had been exhorting them to from the streets—to cleanse the city of Paris by any and every means necessary.[18]

CONCLUSION

In the end, religious violence in the sixteenth century cannot be neatly summed up with a tidy catchphrase. It is tempting to say that Europe learned the futility of religiously motivated violence and gave it up—until we note that the witch hunt lasted far longer, and that various crusading motifs were part and parcel of the religious and political rhetoric for years to come. Further, the case of the Spanish Inquisition, considered in chapter 9, demonstrates indisputably that sometimes religiously inspired violence gained exactly its stated goal. The Spanish attacked heresy and were generally able to stamp out any sprout of Protestantism that appeared.

More accurately, the sixteenth and seventeenth centuries were a time of great turmoil about the proper relationship of religion and violence. During this period, calls for religious toleration became far more common, and at least the theory that loyalty to a different confession did not automatically make one a bad citizen of the realm was entertained. Violence in the name of religion was still acceptable but was becoming more nuanced. The lessons of the Thirty Years' War and the French Wars of Religion established that in some circumstances, force could not successfully be used to compel unanimity of belief.

Several conclusions can be drawn about the relationship of religion and violence in the Reformation. First, religious choice frightened the majority of people it faced. Sixteenth- and seventeenth-century people were not twenty-first-century members of liberal democracies, where more choice is always a good thing. The Reformation did not bring about "religious freedom" in anything like the modern sense of that term. Lutheran reforms, the Radical reforms, Calvinist reforms—all of these presented people with a particular choice. But that choice was posed as the difference between right religion and error. No one was trumpeting the virtues of having several "churches" available to give people more choice. Instead, having rival expressions of Christianity in a realm posed enormous psychological and spiritual problems. Social groups relieved the stress created by those problems through several outlets, but as often as not, violence played a role.

Second, competing religions in a particular realm raised the clear and urgent question of the purposes of God. People assumed that God was active in the world. They could ask real questions rather than theoretical ones. Was God behind the uprising of the lower classes in the Peasants' War? Conversely, was God offering the good German society an opportunity to prove its own faithfulness by stamping out this heretical offense? Would God punish Germany if it tolerated this new religion? The French citizens of Paris had been told repeatedly by priests that the cleansing of their city and their land of Protestantism was the only way to evade God's righteous punishment of an impious toleration.

Third, the overwhelming majority of people in that time did not protest religious violence. Almost everyone protested being the victims of religious violence, but very few protested religious violence in itself. The exceptions are instructive. Sebastian Castellio (1515–1563) argued for religious tolerance after the execution of Servetus in Geneva in 1553. However, Castellio's motives are clouded by his personal animosity for Calvin. His hatred for Calvin makes his defense of Servetus somewhat less noble and more self-serving. Erasmus defended toleration and seemed sincere. His model of world peace demonstrates his abhorrence of violence of this kind. But Erasmus was almost a man without a country, a man of the world who could see things from a more global perspective. If Erasmus was truly against religious violence, he is perhaps the exception that proves the rule—people generally accepted it. There were other supporters of religious toleration, but their number pales in comparison to those who did not object to the union of religion and persecution.

Finally, with the exception of mob violence, most of the wars and most of the acts of violence were prosecuted by rulers. In the time of the Reformation, the general mind-set of the European world shifted from the idea that true religion reinforced the state to the practical idea of a single religion, chosen by the ruler, reinforced by the state. Warfare and persecution for the sake of religion had concentrated religious power in the hands of secular rulers. This union would be part of the legacy of the Reformation and would inspire the linkage of religious power and nationhood that is frequently seen as part of the beginning of modernity.

QUESTIONS FOR DISCUSSION

1. What was at stake in religious violence during the Reformation period? What did people think they were protecting or eradicating?

2. What are "rites of violence"? Does this method of analysis make greater sense out of the bloodshed that sometimes occurred in the Reformation?
3. Does *cuius regio, eius religio* solve the religious question? Why or why not?
4. Religious options frightened the people of the sixteenth and early seventeenth centuries. Why was that the case, and why for many people is that no longer the case today? Could a set of circumstances occur that would bring modern society back to that state of affairs?

SUGGESTED FURTHER READING

Blickle, Peter. *The Revolution of 1525: The German Peasants' War from a New Perspective.* Translated by Thomas A. Brady Jr. and H. C. Erik Midelfort. Baltimore: Johns Hopkins University Press, 1981.

Diefendorf, Barbara B. *Beneath the Cross: Catholics and Huguenots in Sixteenth-Century Paris.* Oxford: Oxford University Press, 1991.

Knecht, R. J. *The French Wars of Religion, 1559–1598.* 2nd ed. New York: Longman, 1996.

Monter, William. *Judging the French Reformation: Heresy Trials by Sixteenth-Century Parlements.* Cambridge, MA: Harvard University Press, 1999.

Stayer, James M. *The German Peasants' War and the Anabaptist Community of Goods.* Montreal: McGill University Press, 1991.

Sutherland, N. M. *The Huguenot Struggle for Recognition.* New Haven, CT: Yale University Press, 1980.

11

Other Movements of Reform
and Later Consequences

After tens of thousands of words, after dozens upon dozens of names, what can be left to say that has not already been said? In a word—plenty. This volume has been an exercise in giving an orientation to students who wish to know more about the reforms of the sixteenth and early seventeenth centuries. The necessity of more explanation has limited the number of topics covered in this volume as well as the depth of treatment. This is all well and good. Gaining a broad sense of some of the religious and theological issues that literally turned Europe inside out between 1500 and 1650 is a worthy goal in itself.

However, introduction is not exhaustion. In this next-to-last chapter, our purpose will be twofold. First, we will mention some topics that were not discussed, orienting the reader to some of the themes and questions for further study. Second, we will briefly consider the developments that followed the reforms of the sixteenth and seventeenth centuries. We will examine how the new confessions took on their own characteristics and began their own traditions of development.

There is a famous altarpiece, an oil painting that appeared on an altar, called the Eisenheim Altarpiece. Completed around 1515 by the artist Matthias Grünewald, the painting depicts Jesus on the cross, and at his feet stands John the Baptist, who is pointing at Jesus. Behind John's pointing finger are the words "He must increase, while I must decrease." Grünewald meant that John's point in life was to direct others beyond himself—to Jesus the Christ. But that is also the point of this book—to point beyond itself, to send readers toward engagements with history and theology that are more profound and more sophisticated.

REFORMATION IN OTHER LANDS

Our consideration of the sixteenth century has been geographically lopsided. While Germany, France, Switzerland, and England have been addressed, and Spain and Italy frequently mentioned, other countries are missing. Did the Reformation, or Reformations, simply miss them? Far from it. Significant variations occurred in a variety of realms. Geographically speaking, there were as many "Reformations" as there were domains. Beyond that, the tides of reform frequently affected lands that we do not ordinarily connect with the Reformation. In this section, we will quickly sketch two areas. Scotland and the Netherlands offer different models of reform and took different ideas of reform from the kingdoms around them.

Scotland

Scotland's path to reform could scarcely have differed more from that of England. This is not to say that England did not impact Scotland; many of the developments in Scotland's reform were directly influenced by English political events and religious sentiments. In the centuries before the Reformation, Scotland's nobility had achieved such a level of interpenetration of the church that it was impossible to conceive of the church outside of the political realm. Further, the lords had managed to appropriate so much of the church's revenue for their own uses that it was almost impossible to undertake any kind of reform that cost any money. Scotland's parishes were chronically underfunded.

While reforming ideas and the influence of the new theological currents arrived in Scotland fairly early, the Catholic hierarchy managed to quash its influence rather effectively in the early part of the century. This was done by fear and persecution—for example, Patrick Hamilton was executed for Lutheran ideas in 1528 at St. Andrews, and George Wishart was burned in 1546, also at St. Andrews. The execution of Wishart for his Zwinglian ideas enraged his supporters, who murdered Cardinal David Beaton, archbishop of St. Andrews, the instigator of Wishart's execution.[1] When that uprising was crushed by French troops, one of those caught was the rebels' preacher, John Knox. Knox (c. 1514–1572) spent the next eighteen months as a French galley slave, gaining both a brush with death and a burning hatred for the French and their Catholicism. Eventually Knox was released from this torture and made his way ultimately to Geneva, where he was formed in the Reformed theology of Calvin's time. It was Knox who said of Geneva that it was the most perfect school of Christ since the days of the apostles. It was therefore Geneva's model, rather than Wittenberg's, that informed Scottish reform.

We have already noted that it was French troops who helped break through at St. Andrews Castle. The French were always involved in Scottish politics in the sixteenth century, frequently as a balance to English concerns. Mary, Queen of Scots (1542–1587), was the daughter of Mary of Guise. The Guise family was ardently pro-Catholic and one of the leading powers in France. When Mary came to the throne in 1542, she was still in diapers. Her mother, Mary of Guise, was one of the true powers in Scotland for years to come. Mary I eventually married Francis of France, heir to the French throne. Eventually this French influence proved to be too much for some of the Scottish nobles, and four signed a bond in 1557 pledging themselves to the cause of reform and to establish the "MAIST BLISSED WORDE OF GOD."[2] Though the movement was not originally a popular success, it provided a beginning place from which further reform could occur. Civil war broke out, and the anti-French contingent eventually won.

In 1560, with a treaty in place, the Scottish parliament met; it was to gain the name the "Reformation Parliament." Though it was expressly prohibited from considering religious issues, the members ignored this. John Knox, working with five other ministers, completed a confession of faith, titled the Scots Confession, in only four days. The document shows the effect of having been hurriedly written, but perhaps because of that it has a certain vigor that is less apparent in some of the other sixteenth-century confessions whose authors enjoyed more leisure. The Scottish Parliament ratified the Scots Confession in 1560, and Scotland's road to reform was set.

The Netherlands

The pattern of reform in the Netherlands demonstrates how fluid the religious situation could be in the period of reform. While Lutheranism was the first influence to gain a foothold in the southern regions of the area,[3] Calvinism became more dominant, was part of an initially failed rebellious movement against Catholicism and the Spanish Habsburgs, and eventually triumphed not in the southern regions where reform currents first flourished, but in the northern parts of the area.[4]

Reforming thought was initially very popular in parts of the Low Countries. By 1520, editions of Luther's works were being printed in Antwerp, and the Augustinians of Antwerp decided that Luther's ideas were orthodox and supported them wholeheartedly. Antwerp was one of the major ports of the Low Countries and a trading center. Its nature as a transportation and trading hub facilitated the distribution of copies of Luther's works.[5] This interest in Luther's works and interest in the Bible fused with popular anticlericalism of the region and helped to create a negative attitude toward biblicism and Lutheranism in the minds of some of the religious authorities.

The Low Countries at this time were mostly a possession of the Spanish Habsburgs. Charles V, Holy Roman Emperor, had staked part of his own authority on defending Catholicism. The reaction against Lutheranism was decisive. The Augustinian house in Antwerp was dissolved, and in 1523, two Augustinians were burned at the stake in Brussels. Some of the Lutheran evangelicals were driven underground. But Lutheranism was not the only brand of Protestantism to come to the area. Eventually the Netherlands became one of the most religiously diverse lands in the whole of Europe.

In the 1530s, Anabaptists came to the area from Germany, many of whom were wandering Melchiorites. In any case, the Anabaptists who came brought a theology and practices that differed considerably from the generalized "Lutheranism" that had gone before. Joke Spaans describes how they organized themselves:

> Instead of the rather general criticism of the sacraments found in the adherents of the new evangelicalism, the Anabaptists from the beginning divided into several branches, following specific "prophets" and accepting only those doctrines they considered Biblical. . . . Those who were rebaptized formed tight, self-reliant cells, in which teaching was done by those most able, and support of the needy was modeled on the sharing of goods in the primitive Christian communities. A strict discipline kept them separate from the evils of the world and provided a shield of secrecy.[6]

The Anabaptists found a generally tolerant community in the Low Countries and were frequently not persecuted to the full extent of the law. Their presence radically changed the character of their competitor confessions. When they began to flourish in the area, Calvinist communities were forced to be even more characterized by stern discipline so as not to be held up to unfavorable comparisons with the Anabaptist emphasis on obedience to scriptural law.

In 1550, Charles V decreed his Perpetual Edict, sometimes termed the "Bloody Edict." This edict clarified those activities that constituted heresy, as well as prescribing the punishments for heresy. In part, this was to attack the newly strengthened heresy of Calvinism. Calvinist influence originally simply wandered into the Netherlands accidentally from surrounding countries. But soon after, a Calvinist minister, Pierre Brully, was dispatched from Strasbourg in 1544 to organize small groups of French-speaking Reformed Christians into ordered churches. He was taken into custody by the authorities in 1545 in Tournai and was executed.

This pattern of support from outside of the Netherlands became normal for Calvinism in the Low Countries. England, Geneva, parts of Germany, and even France under Coligny sent aid to the Calvinists as they battled the Spanish. In the 1560s, Calvinists began to push for more rights, both with calls for more religious liberties, and by more openly practicing their religion. In 1566, a group of high nobility, supported by this groundswell of support, pressed the regent of the region, Margaret of Parma, for suspension of the heresy laws. For whatever reason, she promised moderation.[7] This year came to be known as the "Miracle Year" of the Calvinist reform of the Low Countries. Churches grew, new congregations sprang up, and Protestantism became the dominant form of Christianity in several locales within the region.

Official reaction from the Spanish king, Philip II, was swift. He sent the duke of Alva with Spanish troops into the Low Countries to enforce his religious policies of strict Catholic orthodoxy. In 1568, Alva triumphed, and the leader of the Calvinist forces, William of Orange, was humiliated. The prospects for Protestantism looked bleak, and the Dutch Calvinists were reduced to a pirate force called the Sea Beggars. Because of Spain's power and the lack of probable success for the Sea Beggars, even Queen Elizabeth I of England, who had no special love for Philip or Spain, denied them access to English ports. On April 1, 1572, the Sea Beggars made land in the Dutch port of Den Briel. Unfortunately for Alva, the port had been left defenseless. This became the toehold that William of Orange and his forces needed, and by summer most of Holland had been won for Calvinist forces.[8]

Eventually, the Low Countries were partitioned by the Pacification of Ghent in 1576. This formula directed that the area that became Belgium would remain Catholic and in Habsburg hands, while Holland would become officially Calvinist. However, this was a different form of Calvinism than had been practiced in Geneva. Though officially the Netherlanders were even more strict, and required discipline to be part of the "marks of the church," they also practiced extraordinary religious tolerance. A new form of Calvinism had sprung up, with its own beliefs, practices, and heroes.

Other Lands

Processes of reform and reactions to reform thought and practice made their way across the countries of Europe. Even such a bastion of Catholicism as Italy was not spared. Reform-minded priests gathered in Italy and considered ways of strengthening the faith through reform. Some of those priests became leaders in the Roman hierarchy; others eventually fled to Protestant countries.

This patternless pattern held for Romania and Hungary, Transylvania and Poland. The ideas of the Reformation, whether Lutheran, Calvinist, or Radical, respected no territorial boundaries. The ability to predict what happened in the sixteenth century by looking at the dominant forms of Christianity in the twentieth or twenty-first century simply does not exist. Both ongoing

expansion of Calvinism and the Catholic efforts at restoration affected confessional allegiance for decades to come.

MISSIONARY OUTREACH

An item that we have not covered that could take up volumes is the evangelizing missions that the European Christian world took up in the sixteenth
century.[9] All American schoolchildren are familiar with the rhyme "In 1492,
Columbus sailed the ocean blue." Columbus was not looking for the American continents, but he found them. While this discovery enriched the various
European powers because of the vast natural wealth they took, it also opened
up to European minds the concept that there were great numbers of souls who
had never heard the gospel of Christianity. This knowledge inspired missions
not only to the newly discovered countries but to eastern lands as well.

In the early phases of the missionary impulse, most of the new Protestant
denominations were hobbled by a lack of institutional structures. To put it
another way, many of these confessional groups were trying simply to hold
their own in Europe, without worrying about taking the gospel to foreign
lands. While there are notable exceptions, such as the Moravian missions, the
great missionaries of the sixteenth century were the Jesuits, with Protestants
coming later to the enterprise when colonial efforts took hold. The Jesuits, as
we saw in chapter 9, took the gospel message to China, Japan, and India. However, their missions to the Americas were more like those of their Protestant
counterparts and can be counted as part of the colonial venture.

Frequently, any successes of these efforts at spreading the gospel were tem-
pered by contact with the colonialism of the Europeans. The European missionaries had difficulties separating their own cultural trappings from the
message of Christianity. Therefore, they expected that the Native Americans
would necessarily accept European forms of dress, speech, and other aspects
of culture along with Christianity. When some of the native peoples chose not
to do so, friction occurred.

Further, many of the missionaries accepted a European evaluation of the
Native Americans as savages and as having a somewhat lower intrinsic value
in even God's eyes. This led to ideas of the native peoples as naturally fit for
slavery. While the Jesuit Bartolomé de las Casas famously argued against the
exploitation of native peoples for the enrichment of Europeans, his voice
remained far outside the mainstream opinion. Missions to newly discovered
peoples in the Americas remains a deeply troubling aspect of the history of
Christianity's expansion in the early modern age.

EUROPEAN CHRISTIANITY IN NORTH AMERICA

While it has been popular to write analyses of the Reformation that stay wholly within the boundaries of Europe, going beyond the borders makes sense if one believes that the Reformation truly changed the world. When we look at European Christianity in North America, we find it impossible to understand without the framework of the Reformation. In popular American imagination and myth, the Pilgrims arrived at Plymouth in 1620 in order to establish a society rooted in religious freedom. In actual fact, the Pilgrims who arrived in Plymouth were English dissenters who wanted nothing more than to have their own authority, so that they could exercise the true religion freely and keep other influences out.

Further, the relationships of the various European religious communities in America were direct outgrowths of their European origins. Congregationalists and Presbyterians frequently were able to cooperate, while Catholics were often ostracized, even in Maryland, the colony that Lord Baltimore had set up with Catholics in mind. Theologically, the American experiment remained a laboratory test for the European confessions.

WOMEN AND REFORM

Another topic that we have not covered but that has been treated extensively in the past decade is the effect of the Reformation movements upon women, and how women were active as agents in the reform factions. Studies suggest that the Reformation era had enormous consequences for women. The reforms after the Council of Trent changed how convents could be run as well as their amount of contact with the outside world.[10] The roles that were open to women changed with various patterns of reform. A whole new ideal, that of the pastor's wife, opened to women, and the models for a "good pastor's wife" were hammered out at this time. Women were not only acted upon by the changes of the sixteenth and seventeenth centuries, but they also acted. Catherine de Medici was enormously important in the religious controversies in France but has normally only been studied as a political actor. Katharina Schutz Zell was the wife of Matthaus Zell, a preacher in Strasbourg. Yet she was a preacher in her own right, and her impact has only recently been carefully studied. Further, the women who chose martyrdom for their beliefs must be counted as actors in the dramas of the Reformation, but they frequently have not been given the same amount of careful study as their male counterparts. In these and many other ways, new research into the place of women in the early modern age is suggesting a far richer picture than we previously recognized.

THE REFORMATION'S IMPACT ON OTHER BRANCHES OF KNOWLEDGE

The Reformation impacted branches of human knowledge beyond religion and theology. Scholars of the history of politics have long acknowledged the Reformation's impact, without always agreeing on the character of that impact. Did the Reformation bring about tolerance and open the door to the modern nation-state? Or did the Reformation concentrate religious power in the hands of divine-right princes? Economic theorists have long noted that the choices made by Protestant theologians in their reading of the Scriptures changed the way that adherents to their confessions made economic decisions. Max Weber theorized about this in his famous book *The Protestant Ethic and the Spirit of Capitalism*. While many modern economists have criticized Weber's conclusions, very few argue that the religious reforms of the sixteenth and seventeenth centuries had no effect on the economic realm. Even historians of science have noted that the different kinds of religious claims of authority offered up potentials that may have spurred or squelched scientific discovery.

All of these represent areas that this book could not take up but that are very real and worthwhile areas of study that continue to offer up intriguing questions about the human condition and the impact of the Reformation. The Reformation, or Reformations, forced enormous reevaluations of what it meant to be Christian, what it meant to be religious, and even what it meant to be human for many of the inheritors of Western culture. But the story did not end there.

LATER DEVELOPMENTS

Though the reforming movements started within Catholicism, by the middle of the sixteenth century they had become independent Christian bodies, because of both internal and external factors. Internally, these confessional groups or churches were forming their own traditions, which drove them into their own distinctive models of worship, of belief, and of spirituality. Externally, Rome rejected many of these movements, either implicitly or explicitly. Movements that sought to reform centuries of tradition formed their own dearly held traditions. These traditions helped to set the spiritual landscape of Europe that became the context for considering religion and all the issues that religion touched in subsequent centuries. We shall briefly examine four of these issues: international Calvinism, Protestant scholasticism, Catholic restoration, and the question of religious toleration.

International Calvinism

While Lutheranism was the name that many people assigned to all forms of Protestant thought, Calvinism looked out from Geneva and expanded internationally at least as fast as Lutheranism.[11] Calvinism became the dominant form of Protestantism in many countries. Further, there was a "second Reformation" in Germany, characterized by Calvinist theology rather than Lutheran. Not surprisingly, friction erupted between the two confessions. This friction was lessened by the Peace of Westphalia, because it recognized Calvinism, as the Peace of Augsburg had not. However, intra-Protestant rivalry would be a normal facet of Protestantism throughout the latter half of the sixteenth century and well into the modern age.

Protestant Scholasticism

Once the different confessions settled into recognizable patterns and formed the kinds of institutional structures that supported their ongoing survival, Protestant churches looked to expansion and defense. One of the necessary steps toward either was education. Protestant churches could not thrive without a trained ministerial corps. Further, Protestant cities and states wanted their sons to be trained for governmental service in academies and universities that were attached to a peculiarly Protestant vision of the role of the magistrate. Part of the story of the Reformation is a story of the foundation of schools.

Once the schools were in place, identifiable curriculums came into existence. As humanistically influenced movements, one might assume that the scholastic models of Aristotelian logic would have no place in Protestant schools. However, the opposite was the case. This is true for several reasons.[12] First, scholastic models of theological argumentation did not wholly die out among Protestant theologians. While Calvin and Luther vociferously argued that these were flawed systems, they did not wholly abandon scholastic thought in their own work. Further, other Protestant theologians enthusiastically churned out theological tomes that were methodologically as Aristotelian as anything the sixteenth-century Catholics were writing.

In the late sixteenth century, this trend became more popular in Protestant thought. At least one reason for this was the polemic of the age. One of the chief theological tasks that Protestants had in the early history of their confessions was to answer theological attacks from either Catholics or other

Protestants. Scholastic patterns of thought were enormously helpful in answering polemics. As a method that was based in argumentation, scholastic models of thought helped to set the tone of theology so as to give final answers that were logically defensible.

However, while argumentation was served, questions were raised about the character of lived religion. Since scholastic patterns of thought demonstrated eternal truths, the importance of historical context was downplayed. Further, some pastors trained in this type of thought gave their congregations the impression that Christianity was about the correct belief, without a distinctly joyful participation in the lived faith of the community. This "colder" character aroused a backlash called "Pietism" across the lands of Europe, but that is a story for another volume.

Catholic Restoration

Humans desire stability. Students especially desire stability—to learn a fact so that it can be repeated at the appropriate moment. However, the period of the Reformation offered few such historical facts. Catholic reforming efforts did not simply accept the map of Europe as having been irrevocably changed. Far from it. Catholics were active in attempting to retake areas for the true church in England, in France, in the Low Countries, and even in Geneva. At times, such movements were extraordinarily successful. By the late seventeenth century, the city-state of Geneva was majority Catholic in its population. Catholic and Protestant contesting over territory would not cease for centuries, and the solutions to the religious questions offered by the Peace of Westphalia suggested continual change rather than settlement.

The Question of Toleration

Finally, the Reformation was clearly not an age of tolerance. However, the religious contests and conquests supplied the fuel for consideration of questions about the rights of religious minorities. At least some thinkers suggested that religious belief simply could not be compelled under any circumstance. So, though the Reformation era itself was not an age of tolerance, one of its enduring impacts was the beginning of the conversation about the need for religious tolerance, both for the stability of societies and for living in multi-religious cultures.

As we have tried to show in this chapter, at the end of this book, we are at the beginning of a quest for knowledge and wisdom. Many topics have received precious little space within these pages. But if the reader will grant that learning never ends, then we might accept this volume as one beginning, and an invitation to further explorations. Having done that, we may turn to our concluding thoughts.

QUESTIONS FOR DISCUSSION

1. Why did most early Protestant denominations not engage in foreign mission efforts to spread the gospel? What does this suggest about the necessities for evangelism in the early modern age?
2. Why did Protestant scholasticism arise? How might that have changed the character of the religious communities?
3. Why did religious communities in the late sixteenth and early seventeenth centuries develop patterns of tolerance? What does that fact suggest about the age?
4. What do the Catholic restorations suggest about the "settled" character of the religious questions after the sixteenth century?

SUGGESTED FURTHER READING

Armstrong, Brian G. *Calvinism and the Amyraut Heresy: Protestant Scholasticism and Humanism in Seventeenth-Century France*. Madison: University of Wisconsin Press, 1969.

Asselt, William J., van, and Eef Dekker, eds. *Reformation and Scholasticism: An Ecumenical Enterprise*. Grand Rapids: Baker Book House, 2001.

Butler, Jon, Grant Wacker, and Randall Balmer. *Religion in American Life: A Short History*. Oxford: Oxford University Press, 2002.

McKee, Elsie Anne. *Katharina Schutz Zell*. Leiden: Brill Academic Publishers, 1998.

Muller, Richard A. *After Calvin: Studies in the Development of a Theological Tradition*. Oxford: Oxford University Press, 2003.

Pettegree, Andrew, ed. *The Reformation World*. New York: Routledge, 2000.

Prestwich, Menna, ed. *International Calvinism, 1541–1715*. Oxford: Oxford University Press, 1987.

Wiesner-Hanks, Merry E. *Gender in History*. Malden, MA: Blackwell Publishing, 2001.

12

Conclusion

Ecclesia Reformata, Semper Reformanda

Ecclesia reformata, semper reformanda. This is not a sixteenth-century slogan; it was actually coined in the Netherlands in the seventeenth century.[1] But like so many other phrases that may not have been original, it caught on. Literally translated, the phrase means, "the church reformed, always having to be reformed." It was a characterization of the Reformation as a permanent mode of being for the church—that yesterday's reform could become today's abuse and would need to be reevaluated in the light of biblical witness. This meant that reforming the church would continue, that for Protestants who recognized their roots in the reforms of the early modern period, reform would not cease at some final destination but would, in some fashion, persist.

Therefore, when Protestants exclaimed, "*Semper reformanda*," they saw that the Reformation would not end. This might be true in a spiritual sense, but for a historian, the Reformation did end. For our purposes, the Reformation encompassed the entire sixteenth century and half of the seventeenth century. But the spiritual question, "Can the Reformation ever be over?" sparks our final examination.

What was the outcome of the Reformation? Did the Reformation accomplish its goals? Did the Reformation succeed? Is the Reformation over? None of these questions can easily be answered unless we disregard their fuller sense. The outcomes of the Reformation were legion—from a changed map of Europe, to a concentration of spiritual power in the hands of some princes, to a different set of possibilities for the monastic lives of women, to a new set of theological questions to ponder. That the Reformation changed Europe is beyond question. But what did those changes mean?

In this chapter, we will consider three different questions: What were some of the outcomes of the Reformation? Is the Reformation over? Did the

241

Reformation fail or succeed? We will see that after the first question, the answers to the second and third questions depend on the spiritual stance of the respondent—that is, they are not technically "historical" questions. But they are appropriate questions, fitting for the Reformation. They fit because though the Reformation was absolutely a historical event, it is unthinkable without the spiritual component. Yes, some people in the sixteenth century did some things for base motives of greed, lust, and desire for power. But just as frequently their motives were mixed: their desire to protect the true religion coincided with their desire to stamp out their (heretical) enemies.

REFORMATION OUTCOMES

One of the clearest outcomes of the Reformation era was a changed map of Europe. Instead of a Europe that was united by a single religion, countries, principalities, city-states, duchies, and kingdoms were now linked to particular confessions. It did not matter that the synthesis of a single society with a single religion had only been a mental construct, seen far more often in its failure than its success. Sweden was Lutheran, England was Anglican, Italy was Catholic. These allegiances affected politics, commerce, and military strategy. The pope no longer had even the nominal spiritual authority in many lands to persuade or threaten a ruler who transgressed.

Another important change that frequently escapes casual notice is the changed situation for clergy.[2] This change affected both Protestant and Catholic clergy. For Catholic clergy, the Council of Trent greatly clarified the path to ordination as well as regulating some of the abuses that had afflicted the practice of parish and diocesan ministry prior to the council. For Protestant clergy, the reforms of the sixteenth and seventeenth centuries raised even more new possibilities. With clerical marriage came the opportunity for clergy to have legitimate children. This phenomenon had several consequences. First, the minister's family now had a role in the ministry. Ministers were judged by how well their own children kept the written and unwritten codes of the community. Minister's wives soon had defined roles within parishes. Second, the fact that the ministry in many churches required special training separated the minister or priest from the people of the parish in ways both subtle and profound. This separation led to a kind of social classification of "clerical families," in which sons followed in their fathers' footsteps, taking the necessary steps to be educated and ordained to the ministry. An example of this phenomenon is John Wesley (1703–1791), the theologian credited with the formation of Methodism. Wesley's father, grandfather, and great-grandfather were also ministers, as was his younger brother Charles. The ministerial vocation in this family began in the Reformation and extended well into the eighteenth century. What it meant to be the clergy was irrevocably altered in the Reformation.

Another outcome that is too frequently simply assumed without being analyzed is the basic stance of opposition between Protestantism and Catholicism. This opposition was so complete that Friedrich Schleiermacher, the great German theologian of the late eighteenth and early nineteenth centuries, simply assumed that it was part of the definition of Protestant theology to oppose Roman Catholic theology. At least in part, the intensification of scholasticism in Protestant thought in the seventeenth century came about as an answer to the attacks of Roman opponents. Scholastic models of theology were seen as better fit for argumentation, and Protestantism was frequently defined not only positively as what it was, but also negatively as what it was not.

Paradoxically, new traditions marked the Protestant confessions. The same communities of belief that had attacked the ways that traditions had enshrined nonbiblical beliefs as sacred began to put their own extrabiblical convictions in privileged settings. Nowhere was this clearer than in the Lutheran communion, where allegiance to the truth of Scripture became an issue that divided Lutherans from each other. Arguments over the meaning of Scripture could finally only be judged by some standard outside of the Bible. The same kind of privileging occurred in Reformed regions, seen in the heresy trials over the issue of predestination in the early seventeenth century. Certainly Calvin had taught predestination, but in his own life he had been open to friendship and conversation with theologians such as Philip Melanchthon who had been far more leary of openly teaching predestination. The patterns of consolidation within the newer confessions demonstrate clearly that religious humans desire certainty. A variety of orthodoxies sprang up in the wake of the Reformation.

One of the greatest impacts of the Reformation was the transformation of biblical religion. This occurred in three ways that were clear to the reforming theologians as well as to the laity of the time. The first way was how the use of the Bible structured worship. The second way was the effect of the spread of the Bible into the hands of more people. The third way was the manner in which disputes were settled by recourse to Scripture. The people of Zurich, Wittenberg, and Geneva believed that the pattern of their worship life and the structure of Christian authority had been changed by attending to the Word of God. Catholic polemicists argued that this difference was overstated. But some of the differences were real.

Worship was radically transformed, especially in Calvinist and Zwinglian regions. This might be one of the more amazing facts of the Reformation. In a single generation, the central event of Christian worship changed. In the Catholic service, the eucharistic ritual was the most important event. But that

Catholic Mass was something one *watched* because it was a dramatic presentation of the mystery of the faith, full of pageantry and symbolism. In Reformed worship, the central act became the sermon. The sermon was closely modeled on a lecture and was a means of explaining Scripture to the congregation. One did not watch a sermon, but rather listened.

Second, most reformers believed that it was crucial to put the Bible into the hands of the common people. Luther and Tyndale, among others, translated the Bible into the languages of the people. Countless pastors and theologians commented on the Bible, and these commentaries were quickly made available to laypeople in their own languages. In catechisms, in classrooms, in special open courses such as the *Prophezei* in Zurich or the *Congrégations* in Geneva, reformers sought to teach the Bible to as many as would receive it. Sometimes the reforming theologians were not happy with what people did with this new biblical knowledge, but they never backed away from putting Scripture into the hands of the people.

Finally, the idea of laypeople judging the meaning of the Bible, and judging their spiritual leaders by their adherence to the gospel message, became common. Further, at least some of the people of that time themselves believed that this attendance upon the Scriptures had changed the nature of Christian religion. Robert Estienne (1503–1559) was one such figure. He was a businessman, who despite being the king's royal printer, ran afoul of the theologians at the University of Paris for some of his publishing projects. He had long printed Bibles on behalf of the university but now wanted to print a version of the Bible with commentary surrounding the text. This was a traditional project, such Bibles were common, and the commentary was called the *Glossa ordinaria*. However, Estienne wished to use a new translation of the Bible and new voices in the commentary. This so aroused the Paris theologians that Estienne felt it wise to leave, and he emigrated to Geneva. Estienne expected a country roughness in Geneva, but he found something much different:

> Here among the beasts I encountered men who proclaim God's goodness as worthy of love and celebration and preach both his grace and his mercy in their fullness, serving as Christ's ambassadors in his name. They so present him to their brethren and set forth his portrait, as it were, before their eyes that the image and face of the Son of God, previously unknown to me but now so splendidly depicted, and the new lineaments and teaching of the gospel instilled in me the greatest amazement and astonishment. For I reckoned that I had hitherto made such progress in the knowledge of Jesus Christ that I judged myself capable of being their teacher, whereas the outcome was quite different—the opposite of what I supposed. . . .
>
> Once I had removed myself far enough from those lowland wolves which pollute the minds of everyone with their flatulence, and began

to experience among these mountains instruction in Christian piety and religion which comprises God's Word and his sacraments, I consulted the Scriptures to ascertain whether the teaching I was hearing agreed with them. Since our mind is wicked and perverse, I expected to find some divergence and some noticeable omissions.

But—God be praised!—I found the greatest possible consistency, agreement and concord.[3]

Estienne was unfamiliar with this kind of preaching. He checked the teaching of the Genevan ministers against the testimony of the Scriptures. In that very practice, Estienne demonstrated that the Christian religion had been changed. It would have been almost unthinkable a century earlier for a layman to "fact check" his minister by reading the Scriptures. Granted, Estienne was a learned man. But his report leaves little doubt that the reform of biblical religion had changed the very spiritual landscape of Europe. The Bible was central to a minister's authority; his claim to authority rested upon his ability to understand and proclaim the Scriptures.

The various theologians and religious communities reworked the understanding of the nature of the church during the Reformation era. "Church" could now refer to a variety of different conceptions, as well as a variety of different institutions. For some, the church was the gathered group of true believers, easily distinguished by their rejection of the world. For others, the church was often too nebulous to define completely, but observers could discern the true church by looking for its marks, or notes. However, the lists of the marks of the church differed from community to community. For Calvin and the Genevans, two marks sufficed. These were the preaching and hearing of the Word of God, and the right administration of the sacraments. The Scots believed those two marks needed a third—the administration of right discipline. Catholicism also more clearly defined the church. For the next four hundred years, the church was formally defined by the hierarchy. To be in communion with the true church, according to Rome, was to to comply with the doctrinal and disciplinary directives of the bishops, especially when they were in general agreement.

This is not to say that many of these theories had not existed in some form prior to the reforms of the sixteenth and seventeenth centuries. However, now many of these ideas were explicitly being taught, either by an authoritative church leader, or by a group or council that had authority within a particular confession. The effect of this was enormous. As the various confessions became more set in their own new traditions, their adherents were formed ever more deeply in different ideas of the function and definition of the church—making theological conversations across the confessions ever more difficult.

Finally, the Reformation changed the way men and women thought about the path of salvation. For some, the church ceased to have the central role it had previously held. Salvation was not about what one actively did, but what grace one passively received. For others, grace was only the beginning of the process. After the reception of grace, believers had to obey God's holy law, or suffer consequences. For still others, the role of the church and its sacramental system intensified. The possibility of salvation outside the church for such Christians was severely discounted.

This new set of possibilities necessarily contributed to a new set of crises. Obviously, preachers and theologians argued about the truth of their doctrinal formulations. But perhaps less obviously, the lives and consciences of hundreds of thousands of men and women were affected. Under the doctrine of *cuius regio, eius religio*, what would happen when a ruler changed the faith of the kingdom? Further, what effect came from confessional preaching? Did people automatically accept whatever the local religious figure handed out? We know that this was not the case. The shifting ground of the Reformation contributed as much to religious and spiritual anxiety as it did to religious and spiritual confidence.

IS THE REFORMATION OVER?

When we consider the slogan *ecclesia reformata, semper reformanda*, a question arises. If the church is "always" to be reformed, can the Reformation be over? This question is less a historical question than it is a theological and ecumenical question about the relationship between Protestantism and modern Roman Catholicism. Have things changed so much between Protestants and Roman Catholics that it is possible to end this great schism, to heal the breach that divides Christians into different camps? Some have argued that the great majority of differences between the confessions have been worn away by time, or that they can be set aside by more helpful confessional language. These figures point to the joint Lutheran and Roman Catholic declaration on justification and optimistically suggest that some kind of universal union might be possible. Even if such a union is not possible because of long-standing institutional differences, some argue that the differences between Rome and Wittenberg or Rome and Geneva are a thing of the past.

The concentration upon commonalities of belief among Christians in the twenty-first century represents a worthwhile goal. One of the great Christian movements of the twentieth century was the ecumenical movement, which sought to explore how Christian denominations could repair the historical breaches that divided them. In a world that recognizes a huge diversity of religions, Protestants and Roman Catholics share far more than that on which they disagree. However, while the ecumenical goal is worthy, it should not blind analysts to the truths of either historical fact or present belief. The Protestant Reformation generated systems of belief that honestly and genuinely differed from the stances that defined Catholicism, especially after the Council of Trent. Further, in 2000 the Vatican promulgated a decree stating that most Protestant churches were not technically churches. In 2007, Pope Benedict XVI restated those convictions. The realities that came from the Reformation still animate present conversation, and to assume otherwise is theologically and historically unsound. The Reformation ended, but its impact is present throughout the Christian world.

DID THE REFORMATION FAIL OR SUCCEED?

It is occasionally proclaimed either that the Reformation failed or that it succeeded. These are extraordinary claims, as historians are generally loathe to state that huge intellectual and/or spiritual movements can be reduced to such a simple dichotomy. However, once the question is raised, it is worth considering. Obviously, if the Reformation can be said to have failed, then there is the possibility that it succeeded.

There are several manners in which one could say that the Reformation failed. First, it did not reform all of Europe. Vast numbers of people did not convert, and vast territories were rather unruffled by the reforms that unsettled other lands. Second, the reforms were frequently co-opted by secular lords whose motives were mixed with political purposes. Third, even among those who did convert confessionally, their lives did not always resemble a true picture of the gospel. But none of these charges can bear much weight with the historically trained arbitrator. Christianity had never been wholly judged by its ability to become the majority religion; if it had, it would have always been considered a failure. Even today, Christianity is not the "majority religion" in the world. The charge about politics is rather anachronistic: Catholicism had been knee-deep in politics for centuries, and the need to be "pure" of entanglements with politics represents a perspective that was foreign to the minds of many people of the sixteenth century. The lack of changes in the lives of the converted was a frequent lament of Protestant reformers themselves. Luther, Calvin, Zwingli, and Bucer all saw that the Christian life in this world was far more marked by failure than success. The Protestant reformers did not generally see themselves attempting to set up perfect human societies.

Then did the Reformation succeed? One could argue that it did. Today there are hundreds of millions of people who trace their spiritual heritage to confessions begun in the Reformation. Modern ideas of politics and economics were inestimably changed by the doctrines and consequences of the

Reformation. The methods of biblical and historical scholarship were incalculably changed by Protestant scholars for both polemical and academic reasons. But again, these statements, while all true, do not prove success for the Reformation. To judge it so is to use a set of criteria that the reforming theologians and laypeople alike would have found utterly foreign. They were not interested in making history; their ideal was to live in the now and to do so as faithfully to the Christian ideal as humanly possible.

The question then comes down to an evaluation of whether the Protestant movement was attempting something that was not humanly possible. It can be said that Protestantism attempted the impossible, that its concentration upon the mental and ethereal realm without the greater help of materiality and superstition was doomed to fail, because humans simply need those things. To that, the only possible retort is that biblical Christianity cannot finally accept human limitations. The Reformers did not set out to make utopias—far from it! They believed in the radical power of sin in a way that terrorized even their own consciences. But they accepted the radical biblical notion that Jesus the Christ calls all people to do the impossible—to be born again, as it is put in the Gospel of John, or to be baptized into death and live again, as Paul puts it.

In the end, that is the standard by which we should measure the people of the Reformation, rather than the Reformation itself. It is impossible to evaluate an impersonal historical event, except as a reflection of its founders or the figures who represented its genius. But in evaluating the Reformers and the people who acted upon the religious currents of that day, the men and women who sought to be faithful to the Lord, we should find them successful. They were not successful because they were Protestant, nor were they successful because they were Catholic. They were not successful because they introduced the world to Lutheranism or Calvinism or Mennonitism or Tridentine Catholicism.

The true success of the people of the Reformation era was that they found paths to maintain continuity with the historic Christian faith while responding to what they discerned as a divine call to reform it. Faced with enormous changes in their world, they persevered. These changes included changes in the economy, changes in the idea of the role of the state, changes even in the the idea of the extent of the physical world. As for the spiritual world, challenges were posed to the role of the church, the manner of salvation, the efficacy of the sacraments, and the nature of following Christ. Faced with a world that was transforming around them, these believers carved out answers to their questions that took seriously the historic aspect of their faith while making accommodations to their own new realities. In doing so, they lived out their faith, even when it meant changing their patterns of life. In doing so, they changed their world.

QUESTIONS FOR DISCUSSION

1. What was the significance of the "confessionalized map of Europe" after the Reformation?
2. Laypeople gained in religious importance in the Reformation era. Was that a positive or negative development, or perhaps both?
3. What was the effect of competing ideas about the path of salvation?
4. Must every age find its own way to maintain continuity with the traditions of Christianity, while reinventing the faith to speak to its own time?

SUGGESTED FURTHER READING

Hillerbrand, Hans. *The Division of Christendom: Christianity in the Sixteenth Century.* Louisville, KY: Westminster John Knox Press, 2007.

Noll, Mark A., and Carolyn Nystrom. *Is the Reformation Over? An Evangelical Assessment of Contemporary Roman Catholicism.* Grand Rapids: Baker Academic, 2005.

Ozment, Steven. *The Age of Reform, 1250–1550: An Intellectual and Religious History of Late Medieval and Reformation Europe.* New Haven, CT: Yale University Press, 1980.

———. *Protestants: The Birth of a Revolution.* New York: Doubleday, 1992.

Strauss, Gerald. *Luther's House of Learning: Indoctrination of the Young in the German Reformation.* Baltimore: Johns Hopkins University Press, 1978.

Notes

Introduction

1. Though I argue that this was a series of separate reforming movements, I will retain the term "the Reformation," but the reader should understand that term as a period of reforming efforts and movements.
2. George Huntston Williams, *The Radical Reformation*, 3rd rev. ed. (Kirksville, MO: Sixteenth Century Journal Publishers, 1992).
3. Barbara Tuchman, *A Distant Mirror: The Calamitous Fourteenth Century* (New York: Ballantine Books, 1978), xiv.

Chapter 1. What Is the Reformation?

1. Brad S. Gregory provides this important insight in his *Salvation at Stake: Christian Martyrdom in Early Modern Europe* (Cambridge, MA: Harvard University Press, 1999), chap. 1.
2. Euan Cameron has attributed the success of the Reformation to this very phenomenon, that the "flattery of Reformed preaching" was enormously attractive to people of the time. See *The European Reformation* (Oxford: Oxford University Press, 1991), 417–22. Erasmus attacked Luther for discussing things in front of the common people.

Chapter 2. The Late Medieval Context

1. Cited in Carter Lindberg, *The European Reformations* (Malden, MA: Blackwell Publishers, 1996), 24.
2. Exodus 10 records the eighth plague that God sent upon the Egyptians as a swarm of locusts.
3. Lindberg, *European Reformations*, 26. "Black Death" is the preferred term, which covers a multitude of diseases including but probably not restricted to the bubonic plague.
4. Norman Davies, *Europe: A History* (Oxford: Oxford University Press, 1996), 512.
5. Jacques Le Goff notes that the term "purgatory" did not appear before the year 1000. See *The Birth of Purgatory*, trans. Arthur Goldhammer (Chicago: University of Chicago Press, 1984).
6. Robert Kingdon has estimated that there were 400 members of the clergy in Geneva prior to the Reformation. However, when the total number of people directly involved in religious life in Geneva is counted, that number swells to 1,000. Noting that there were only 10,000 people in Geneva, this suggests that the Genevans were supporting fully 10 percent of the population as religious.

251

See Kingdon, "Calvin and the Government of Geneva," in *Calvinus Ecclesiae Genevensis Custos*, ed. Wilhelm Neuser (New York: Peter Lang, 1984), 54.
7. Bruce Gordon, "The New Parish," in *A Companion to the Reformation World*, ed. R. Po-chia Hsia (Malden, MA: Blackwell Publishing, 2004), 421.
8. Jean Delumeau makes this argument in *Catholicism between Luther and Voltaire: A New View of the Counter-Reformation* (Philadelphia: Westminster Press, 1977).
9. Although there were new religious orders at this time, we shall save our consideration of most of them for a later chapter.
10. Cardinal Jacopo Sadoleto wrote this in a letter to the people of Geneva in 1539 while he was attempting to have them return to the Church of Rome.
11. For more information, see Miri Rubin, *Corpus Christi: The Eucharist in Late Medieval Culture* (Cambridge: Cambridge University Press, 1991), 164–287.
12. See Lisa Jardine, *Worldly Goods: A New History of the Renaissance* (New York: Doubleday, 1996).

Chapter 3. The Humanistic Call for Return

1. Some scholars think of humanism as a movement with clearly definable doctrines. Others deny that this was the case, arguing instead that humanism represented a method, rather than a clearly staked-out position.
2. For an interesting consideration of Pseudo-Dionysius in the Reformation, see Karlfried Froehlich, "Pseudo-Dionysius and the Reformation of the Sixteenth Century," in *Pseudo-Dionysius: The Complete Works*, Classics of Western Spirituality (New York: Paulist Press, 1987), 33–46.
3. Basil Hall notes the sense of biblical humanism as separable from humanism in general. See Hall, "Calvin and Biblical Humanism," *Proceedings of the Huguenot Society of London* 20 (1960): 195–209. See also William Bouwsma, "The Two Faces of Humanism: Stoicism and Augustinianism in Renaissance Thought," in *Itinerarium Italicum: The Profile of the Italian Renaissance in the Mirror of Its European Transformations*, ed. Heiko Oberman and Thomas A. Brady Jr. (Leiden: E. J. Brill, 1975), 3–60.
4. The most helpful consideration of this practice is Henri de Lubac, *Medieval Exegesis: The Four Senses of Scripture*, 2 vols. (Grand Rapids: Wm. B. Eerdmans Publishing Co., 1998–2000). See also Beryl Smalley, *The Study of the Bible in the Middle Ages* (South Bend, IN: University of Notre Dame Press, 1964).
5. Erika Rummel, *The Humanist-Scholastic Debate in the Renaissance and Reformation* (Cambridge, MA: Harvard University Press, 1995), 19.
6. Guy Bedouelle, "Jacques Lefèvre d'Étaples," in *The Reformation Theologians*, ed. Carter Lindberg (Malden, MA: Blackwell Publishers, 2002), 20.
7. I follow Guy Bedouelle's consideration of Stapulensis's life as a series of stages. See ibid., 19–33.
8. Ibid., 21.
9. Ibid., 23.
10. Roland Bainton, *Erasmus of Christendom* (New York: Crossroad, 1969), 8.
11. Ibid., 12.
12. J. Laurel Carrington, "Desiderius Erasmus," in Lindberg, *Reformation Theologians*, 35.
13. John P. Dolan, introductory essay to *The Handbook of the Militant Christian*, in *The Essential Erasmus*, ed. John P. Dolan (New York: Penguin, 1964), 24.
14. Desiderius Erasmus, *Ten Colloquies of Erasmus*, trans. and ed. Craig R. Thompson (New York: Liberal Arts Press, 1957), 128.
15. "An Inquiry concerning Faith," in Dolan, *Essential Erasmus*, 220.

16. I depend here on Laurel Carrington's characterization in "Desiderius Erasmus," 37–38.

Chapter 4. The Lutheran Reform

1. Robert Kolb, *Martin Luther as Prophet, Teacher, and Hero: Images of the Reformer, 1520–1620* (Grand Rapids: Baker Books, 1999), 9.
2. Heiko Oberman, *Luther: Man between God and the Devil*, trans. Eileen Walliser-Schwarzbart (New Haven, CT: Yale University Press, 1989), 3.
3. Martin Brecht, *Martin Luther: His Road to Reformation, 1483–1521*, trans. James L. Schaaf (Philadelphia: Fortress Press, 1985), 68.
4. Helmar Junghans, "Luther's Wittenberg," trans. Katharina Gustavs, in *The Cambridge Companion to Luther*, ed. Donald K. McKim (Cambridge: Cambridge University Press, 2003), 23.
5. Ibid., 23.
6. Brecht, *Martin Luther*, 151.
7. Figuring out the value of sixteenth-century money is difficult. If one tries to use purchasing power, the value is frequently skewed by modern manufacturing or agricultural methods, which have cheapened many products. Another method is using the value of the underlying precious metal; early modern coins were valuable because of the metal they represented. In any case, rough estimates place the value somewhere between $1,000,000 and $4,400,000. However, it is somewhat more difficult than that. Many people in the United States would claim to know someone with assets of a million dollars or more, or whose salary was a million dollars or more. But how many people have a million dollars in cash, to hand over at any given time? Further, Albrecht owed interest to the Fuggers, so he had to raise a lot more.
8. Brecht, *Martin Luther*, 179.
9. Carter Lindberg, *The European Reformations* (Malden, MA: Blackwell Publishers, 1996), 76.
10. Albrecht Beutel, "Luther's Life," trans. Katharina Gustavs, in McKim, *Cambridge Companion to Luther*, 10.
11. See T. H. L. Parker's *Commentaries on the Epistle to the Romans, 1532–1542* (Edinburgh: T&T Clark, 1986), 1–4.
12. Lindberg, *European Reformations*, 94.
13. Carlos M. N. Eire, *War against the Idols: The Reformation of Worship from Erasmus to Calvin* (Cambridge: Cambridge University Press, 1986), 63.
14. For a brief overview and helpful geographical division, see Euan Cameron, *The European Reformation* (Oxford: Oxford University Press, 1991), 202–9.
15. Thomas Müntzer, "Sermon before Princes," in *Spiritual and Anabaptist Writers*, ed. George H. Williams and Angel M. Mergal (Philadelphia: Westminster Press, 1957), 66.
16. Both Erasmus's work and Luther's response are frequently unhelpfully translated as having to do with the will. The Latin is rather clear, however, that the issue at stake is the choice the will is able to make.
17. Martin Brecht, *Martin Luther: Shaping and Defining the Reformation, 1521–1532*, trans. James L. Schaaf (Philadelphia: Fortress Press, 1990), 213.
18. For a good overview of this movement, see Cameron, *European Reformation*, especially 265–80.
19. As the Augsburg Confession is still at the heart of modern Lutheran belief, it is widely available in translation. Excellent translations of both the Augsburg Confession and the Apology of the Augsburg Confession are available in

Robert Kolb, Timothy Wengert, and James Schaffer, eds., *The Book of Concord: The Confessions of the Evangelical Lutheran Church* (Minneapolis: Augsburg Fortress Press, 2001).

20. "In our quest for a systematic key to Luther's theology, these [Luther's] self-designations may serve as guides. Luther saw himself as a preacher, as a Scripture interpreter. All that can be summarized in one single term, which he helped shape and which in our modern language is referred to as a pastor. Here we see the first problem surface awaiting those trying to systematize Luther's theology: Martin Luther was not a systematic theologian. He did not develop and present his 'teachings' in concise treatises, logically arranged and secured to all sides. Luther's theology rather grew out of a concrete situation. As much as he favored reliable and clear statements on the one hand, so little would he have himself tied down to specific doctrinal formulations on the other." Markus Wriedt, "Luther's Theology," trans. Katharina Gustavs, in McKim, *Cambridge Companion to Martin Luther*, 86–87.

Chapter 5. Zwingli and Zurich

1. Gregory J. Miller, "Huldrych Zwingli (1484–1531)," in *The Reformation Theologians: An Introduction to the Theology of the Early Modern Period*, ed. Carter Lindberg (Malden, MA: Blackwell Publishers, 2002), 157.
2. Bruce Gordon, *The Swiss Reformation* (Manchester: Manchester University Press, 2002), 9. For an overview of the political foundations of the Swiss confederation, see 6–24.
3. Ibid., 49.
4. Steven Ozment, *The Age of Reform, 1250–1550: An Intellectual and Religious History of Late Medieval and Reformation Europe* (New Haven, CT: Yale University Press, 1981), 318. Ozment lists Heinrich Wölfflin, Conrad Celtis, Thomas Wyttenbach, Beatus Rhenanus, Glarean, Conrad Pellican, Conrad Zwick, and Caspar Hedio.
5. G. R. Potter, *Zwingli* (Cambridge: Cambridge University Press, 1976), 22.
6. Ibid., 39.
7. For more on Zurich, see Gordon, *Swiss Reformation*, 46ff.
8. Ibid., 51.
9. Ibid., 53.
10. Ibid., 58.
11. Scholars generally agree that Zwingli won, but they disagree on the significance of that victory. For instance, Bruce Gordon stresses the partial nature of the decision, while Steven Ozment sees the triumph as so decisive that he dates Zurich's becoming Protestant from this date.
12. See Carlos Eire, *War against the Idols: The Reformation of Worship from Erasmus to Calvin* (Cambridge: Cambridge University Press, 1986), 1–27 and 73–104.
13. Potter, *Zwingli*, 129–31.
14. In choosing the terminology of Radical Reformers for those who parted with Zwingli, I am clearly in the debt of George Huntston Williams. The terminology of Magisterial and Radical reform has become part of the language of sixteenth-century historiography. Having said that, I do not wish to give the sense that these questions are ultimately settled.
15. In Greek, the prefix *ana* means "again." Thus, the Anabaptists were those who had been baptized again. Those who received adult baptism believed that

they were the only people who had truly received baptism at all, so they rejected the term.

16. Ozment, *Age of Reform*, 332.
17. Gordon, *Swiss Reformation*, 343.
18. Ibid., 86–87.
19. Philip Benedict, *Christ's Churches Purely Reformed: A Social History of Calvinism* (New Haven, CT: Yale University Press, 2002), 39.
20. Ibid., 39.
21. Ibid., 41.
22. Karin Maag, *Seminary or University? The Genevan Academy and Reformed Higher Education, 1560–1620* (Brookfield, VT: Ashgate, 1995), 130.
23. Miller, "Huldrych Zwingli," 160.
24. Ibid., 163.
25. Ibid., 162.
26. Bruce Gordon warns against this tendency in his introduction to the collection he coedited with Emidio Campi, *Architect of Reformation: An Introduction to Heinrich Bullinger, 1504–1575* (Grand Rapids: Baker Academic, 2004).
27. Gordon, *Swiss Reformation*, 343.

Chapter 6. Radical Reform

1. Werner Packull, "An Introduction to Anabaptist Theology," in *The Cambridge Companion to Reformation Theology*, ed. David Bagchi and David C. Steinmetz (Cambridge: Cambridge University Press, 2004), 194.
2. George H. Williams, *The Radical Reformation* (Philadelphia: Westminster Press, 1962).
3. In this volume, I use "Radical" and "Anabaptist" almost interchangeably. This is not the most nuanced presentation, but it does give the beginning student a place to start.
4. Steven Ozment, *The Age of Reform, 1250–1550: An Intellectual and Religious History of Late Medieval and Reformation Europe* (New Haven, CT: Yale University Press, 1980), 277.
5. Sigrun Haude, "Anabaptism," in *The Reformation World*, ed. Andrew Pettegree (London: Routledge, 2000), 237.
6. George Huntston Williams, *The Radical Reformation*, 3rd rev. ed. (Kirksville, MO: Sixteenth Century Journal Publishers, 1992), 117.
7. The apocryphal books were those that generally were written later. While they had traditionally been part of Old Testament, they had not always been viewed as having the same authority as the other books in the Old and New Testaments. In the sixteenth century, most Protestants denied these books a place in the Bible, while the Council of Trent included them in the Bible for Catholics.
8. Williams, *Radical Reformation*, 3rd ed., 122.
9. Ibid., 123.
10. The seven gifts are wisdom, understanding, counsel, fortitude, knowledge, piety, and fear of the Lord.
11. Williams, *Radical Reformation*, 3rd ed., 134.
12. Thomas Müntzer, "Sermon before Princes," *Spiritual and Anabaptists Writers*, ed. George W. Williams and Angel Mergal, Library of Christian Classics, (Philadelphia: Westminster Press, 1957), 58.
13. Carter Lindberg, *The European Reformations* (Malden, MA: Blackwell Publishers, 1996), 158.

14. Peter Blickle, *The Revolution of 1525: The German Peasants' War from a New Perspective*, trans. Thomas A. Brady Jr. and H. C. Erik Midelfort (Baltimore, John Hopkins University Press, 1981), 195. See this for an excellent translation of the Articles.
15. Williams, *Radical Reformation*, 3rd ed., 148.
16. Ibid., 165. For a consideration of the very complicated wider political and military ramifications of the Peasants' War, see 137–74.
17. Ibid., 164.
18. Ibid., 290.
19. The text is available in translation in Michael G. Baylor, ed. and trans., *The Radical Reformation* (Cambridge: Cambridge University Press, 1991), 172–80; and in John H. Yoder, *The Legacy of Michael Sattler* (Scottdale, PA: Herald Press, 1973), 27–43.
20. Baylor, *Radical Reformation*, 173.
21. Ibid., 177.
22. Williams, *Radical Reformation*, 3rd ed., 295.
23. Ibid., 566–67.
24. Ibid., 568–69.
25. Sigrun Haude, "Anabaptism," in *The Reformation World*, ed. Andrew Pettegree (London: Routledge, 2000), 245.
26. Menno Simons, *The Complete Writings*, trans. Leonard Verduin, ed. J. C. Wenger (Scottdale, PA: Herald Press, 1956), 668.
27. Sjouke Voolstra, "Menno Simons (1496–1561)," in *The Reformation Theologians*, ed. Carter Lindberg (Malden, MA: Blackwell, 2002), 364.
28. Ibid., 363.
29. Ibid., 369.
30. Ibid., 371.
31. See "On the Ban: Questions and Answers by Menno Simons," in Williams and Mergal, *Spiritual and Anabaptist Writers*, 263–71.
32. Quoted in Voolstra, "Menno Simons," 363–64.
33. This section depends broadly upon the longer summary in Packull, "Introduction to Anabaptist Theology," 198–217.

Chapter 7. Calvin and Geneva

1. For an interesting discussion of Calvin's reputation and legacy, see Karin Y. Maag, "Hero or Villain? Interpretations of John Calvin and His Legacy," in *Calvin Theological Journal* 41 (2006): 222–37. Though Calvin's first name was clearly Jean, throughout this chapter we will follow the more normal English usage and call him John.
2. Quirinus Breen, *John Calvin: A Study in French Humanism*, with a foreword by John T. McNeill (Hamden, CT: Archon Books, 1968), 11.
3. I have covered much of this material in an earlier essay I coauthored with John Kuykendal, "The Reformed Understanding of Vocation in History," in *Called to Teach: The Vocation of the Presbyterian Educator*, ed. Duncan Ferguson and William Weston (Louisville, KY: Geneva Press, 2003), 43–58.
4. Alexandre Ganoczy notes that in August 1523, the month that Calvin arrived in Paris, an Augustinian monk had been burned alive in front of the entrance of Saint-Honoré. See Ganoczy, *The Young Calvin*, trans. David Foxgrover and Wade Provo (Philadelphia: Westminster Press, 1987), 49.
5. Ibid., 57–61.

6. Breen, *John Calvin*, 6.
7. Ganoczy, *Young Calvin*, 59.
8. François Wendel, *Calvin: Origins and Development of His Religious Thought*, trans. Philip Mairet (Durham, NC: Labyrinth Press, 1987), 21.
9. Breen, *John Calvin*, 46.
10. Ganoczy, *Young Calvin*, 72.
11. For an interesting view into works of Luther that Calvin might have been reading, see Francis Higman, "Les traductions françaises de Luther, 1524–1550," in *Lire et découvrir: La circulation des idées au temp de la Réforme* (Geneva: Librairie Droz, 1998), 201–25.
12. Wendel, *Calvin*, 36.
13. Calvin quotes *City of God* fifteen times. See Luchesius Smits, *Saint Augustin dans l'oeuvre de Jean Calvin* (Assen: Van Gorcum, 1957), 1:16ff.
14. Ganoczy, *Young Calvin*, 74.
15. For a consideration of the event and Calvin's role, see Alister E. McGrath, *A Life of John Calvin* (Malden, MA: Blackwell Publishers, 1990), 64–67.
16. Ganoczy, *Young Calvin*, 91.
17. Calvin's friend, Theodore Beza, wrote in Calvin's first biography that Calvin associated with Grynaeus and Capito. For other possibilities, see Ganoczy, *Young Calvin*, 91–95.
18. Ibid., 97.
19. *The Institutes of the Christian Religion* is the common name of this text. The title continues "embracing almost the whole sum of piety and whatever is necessary to know of the doctrine of salvation: A work most worthy to be read by all persons zealous for piety, and recently published."
20. McGrath, *Life of John Calvin*, 91.
21. Ibid., 91.
22. In Geneva's case, that would have represented a huge displacement of people. Robert Kingdon has estimated that as much as 10 percent of the population, or about a thousand people, was economically tied to Catholicism. In this number, he includes about 400 clergy and another 600 employees of the clergy. See Kingdon, "Calvin and the Government of Geneva," in *Calvinus Ecclesiae Genevensis Custos*, International Congress on Calvin Research, ed. Wilhelm Neuser (New York: Peter Lang, 1984), 49–67.
23. McGrath, *Life of John Calvin*, 92.
24. Ibid., 94.
25. William Naphy, *Calvin and the Consolidation of the Genevan Reformation* (Louisville, KY: Westminster John Knox Press, 2003), 33–34.
26. In my article "Calvin's Exegetical Pastor," in *Calvin and the Company of Pastors: Calvin Studies Society Papers, 2003*, ed. David Foxgrover (Grand Rapids: CRC Publications, 2004), 179–209, I have speculated that this newfound pastoral sensibility shows up in Calvin's writing of his first set of commentaries.
27. For further information on this first series of commentaries, see my essay "Calvin as Commentator on the Pauline Letters," in *Calvin and the Bible*, ed. Donald K. McKim (Cambridge: Cambridge University Press, 2006), 224–56.
28. The most accessible summary of Calvin's work on the Bible is McKim, ed., *Calvin and the Bible*.
29. The standard translation of Sadoleto's letter and Calvin's reply is contained in John C. Olin, *A Reformation Debate* (Grand Rapids: Baker Book House, 2001).

30. For a far fuller explanation of Calvin's coming to power in Geneva, see Naphy, *Calvin and the Consolidation of the Genevan Reformation*.
31. An excellent and accessible introduction to Calvin's thought is Randall Zachman, *John Calvin as Teacher, Pastor, and Theologian: The Shape of His Writings and Thought* (Grand Rapids: Baker Academic, 2006).
32. John Calvin, *Institutes of the Christian Religion*, ed. John T. McNeill (Philadelphia: Westminster Press, 1960), I.i.1.
33. Thomas J. Davis has written one of the clearest and best treatments of Calvin's doctrine of the Lord's Supper, detailing its various forms and the development of this doctrine in his thought. See Davis, *The Clearest Promises of God: The Development of Calvin's Eucharistic Teaching* (New York: AMS Press, 1995).
34. This is an extraordinarily brief summary and simplification.
35. Knox said, "Geneva is the most perfect school of Christ that ever was in this earth since the days of the Apostles. In other places I confess Christ to be truly preached, but manners and religion to be so sincerely reformed, I have not seen in any other place." Quoted in Carter Lindberg, *The European Reformations* (Malden, MA: Blackwell, 1996), 249.
36. A good source to study the spread of Calvinism outside Geneva is Menna Prestwich, ed., *International Calvinism, 1541–1715* (Oxford: Clarendon Press, 1985).
37. McGrath, *Life of John Calvin*, 17.
38. See Maag, "Hero or Villain?" Also, a simple Web search on the name "Michael Servetus" will generate several sites that condemn Calvin for his crimes, more than four hundred years after the events in question.
39. Naphy, *Calvin and the Consolidation of the Genevan Reformation*, 183.
40. Alexandre Ganoczy, "Calvin's Life," trans. David Foxgrover and James Schmitt, in *The Cambridge Companion to John Calvin*, ed. Donald K. McKim (Cambrige: Cambridge University Press, 2004), 23.
41. Peter Matheson, *The Imaginative World of the Reformation* (Minneapolis: Fortress Press, 2001), 59.

Chapter 8. English Reform

1. Diarmaid MacCulloch, "England," in *The Early Reformation in Europe*, ed. Andrew Pettegree (Cambridge: Cambridge University Press, 1992), 168.
2. For a representative of the "calm" theory, see Christopher Haigh, "The Reformation in England to 1603," in *A Companion to the Reformation World*, ed. R. Po-chia Hsia (Malden, MA: Blackwell Publishing, 2004), 135–49. For a representative of the "turmoil" theory, see A. G. Dickens, *The English Reformation*, 2nd ed. (University Park: Pennsylvania State University Press, 1991). A book dedicated to discussing the historiographical issues of the English Reformation is Margo Todd, ed., *Reformation to Revolution: Politics and Religion in Early Modern England* (London: Routledge, 1995).
3. Heiko A. Oberman, *Forerunners of the Reformation: The Shape of Late Medieval Thought, Illustrated by Key Documents*, trans. Paul L. Nyhus (New York: Holt, Rinehart & Winston, 1966).
4. Quoted in Patrick Collinson, *The Reformation: A History* (New York: Modern Library, 2004), 35.
5. Carter Lindberg, *The European Reformations* (Malden, MA: Blackwell Publishers, 1996), 311.
6. Diarmaid MacCulloch, *The Reformation: A History* (New York: Viking Penguin, 2004), 199.

7. Ibid.
8. Henry eventually married six women. Besides Catherine of Aragon and Anne Boleyn, he married Jane Seymour in 1536, Ann of Cleves in 1540, Catherine Howard in 1540, and Katherine Parr in 1543.
9. Haigh, "Reformation in England to 1603," 138.
10. Ibid., 138–39.
11. Helen Parish, "England," in *The Reformation World*, ed. Andrew Pettegree (London: Routledge, 2000), 227.
12. Quoted in ibid., 228.
13. Ibid.
14. Haigh, "Reformation in England to 1603," 142.
15. Ibid., 143.
16. Parish, "England," 230.
17. Lacey Baldwin Smith, *Fools, Martyrs, Traitors: The Story of Martyrdom in the Western World* (Evanston, IL: Northwestern University Press, 1997), 201.
18. MacCulloch, *Reformation*, 282.
19. The best recent study of sixteenth-century martyrdom is Brad Gregory, *Salvation at Stake: Christian Martyrdom in Early Modern Europe* (Cambridge, MA: Harvard University Press, 1999).
20. Parish, "England," 231.
21. Lindberg, *European Reformations*, 326.
22. MacCulloch, *Reformation*, 289.
23. Carter Lindberg sees such remaining tradition as an olive branch toward English Catholics. Lindberg, *European Reformations*, 326. Diarmaid MacCulloch rejects this notion as absurd and understands it as an effort to mollify Lutherans, showing them that England would not be a Zwinglian stronghold. MacCulloch, *Reformation*, 289.
24. MacCulloch, *Reformation*, 290.
25. Ibid., 298.

Chapter 9. Catholic Reform

1. John O'Malley, *Trent and All That: Renaming Catholicism in the Early Modern Era* (Cambridge, MA: Harvard University Press, 2000).
2. Elizabeth Gleason, "Catholic Reformation, Counterreformation and Papal Reform in the Sixteenth Century," in *Handbook of European History, 1400–1600: Late Middle Ages, Renaissance, and Reformation*, ed. Thomas A. Brady Jr., Heiko A. Oberman and James D. Tracy, vol. 2, *Visions, Programs, and Outcomes* (Grand Rapids: Wm. B. Eerdmans Publishing Co., 1995), 318.
3. Ibid., 318.
4. Ibid., 327–29.
5. Ibid., 333.
6. Michael Mullett, *The Catholic Reformation* (New York: Routledge, 1999), 70.
7. Ibid., 71.
8. Ibid., 72.
9. Ibid., 73.
10. The most significant order for Catholic reform in the sixteenth century was the Jesuits, but we shall consider them separately.
11. Gleason, "Catholic Reformation, CounterReformation, and Papal Reforms," 295.
12. Ibid., 297.

13. Anthony Wright, *The Counter-Reformation: Catholic Europe and the Non-Christian World*, 2nd ed. (Burlington, VT: Ashgate, 2005), 233.
14. Gleason, "Catholic Reformation, CounterReformation, and Papal Reform," 323.
15. "This cultivation of one's own family's interests was in reality a structural element of Italian society and an integral, even admired part of social norms in sixteenth-century Italy. Indeed, it has been shown that nepotism had a sort of moral value, contributing as it did to the central and immensely important value of *pietas*, the ideal of proper behavior toward one's family and dependents in a society which placed the collectivity above the individual." Ibid., 325. By this, Gleason is pointing out that some of the moral values of Paul III's society required him to use his position to enrich his family, thus using the papacy for the gain of the Farnese family. To fail to do so would be to fail to be a good son and brother.
16. John Patrick Donnelly, SJ, "The New Religious Orders, 1517–1648," in Brady et al., *Handbook of European History, 1400–1600*, vol. 2, 290.
17. *Ignatius of Loyola: Spiritual Exercises and Selected Works*, ed. Parmananda Divarkar and Edward J. Malatesta, Classics of Western Spirituality (Mahweh, NJ: Paulist Press, 1991), 213.
18. Donnelly, "New Religious Orders," 292.
19. Ibid., 291.
20. John O'Malley, "The Society of Jesus," in *A Companion to the Reformation World*, ed. R. Po-chia Hsia (Malden, MA: Blackwell Publishing, 2004), 226.
21. H. O. Evennett, *The Spirit of the Counter-Reformation* (South Bend, IN: University of Notre Dame Press, 1970), 45.
22. O'Malley, "Society of Jesus," 225.
23. Donnelly, "New Religious Orders," 292.
24. Ibid.
25. O'Malley, "Society of Jesus," 230.
26. See Donnelly, "New Religious Orders," and John O'Malley, "Society of Jesus."
27. Patrick Collinson, *The Reformation: A History* (New York: Modern Library, 2004), 117.
28. See Mullett, *Catholic Reformation*, 31.
29. Within each assembly, there were numerous "sessions." The sessions were consecutively numbered and did not begin again with each new assembly.
30. For the history of the Council of Trent, it is still hard to beat Hubert Jedin's three-volume work, *A History of the Council of Trent*, trans. Ernest Graf, 3 vols. (St. Louis: Herder, 1957–1963). For the text of the proceedings of the council, I have used *The Canons and Decrees of the Council of Trent*, trans. H. J. Schroeder, OP (Rockford, IL: Tan Books, 1978).
31. *Canons and Decrees of the Council of Trent*, 18–19.
32. Ibid., 42.
33. Ibid., 175.
34. Ibid., 19.
35. See William Monter, "The Inquisition," in *A Companion to the Reformation World*, ed. R. Po-chia Hsia (Malden, MA: Blackwell Publishing, 2004), 255–71.
36. Wright, *Counter-Reformation*, 16.
37. David Coleman, "Spain," in *The Reformation World*, ed. Andrew Pettegree (London: Routledge, 2000), 298.

38. Ibid., 299.
39. Monter, "Inquisition," 266–267.
40. Ibid., 267.

Chapter 10. Religion and Violence

1. Carter Lindberg, *The European Reformations* (Malden, MA: Blackwell Publishers, 1996), 244.
2. Ibid., 247.
3. Mack P. Holt, *The French Wars of Religion, 1562–1629* (Cambridge: Cambridge University Press, 1995), 41.
4. Raymond A. Mentzer, "The French Wars of Religion," in *The Reformation World*, ed. Andrew Pettegree (London: Routledge, 2000), 323.
5. Holt, *French Wars of Religion*, 44.
6. Both Mack Holt and Raymond Mentzer agree that the conflict in the seventeenth century should be included in the discussion of the French Wars of Religion. See Holt, *French Wars of Religion*, and Mentzer, "French Wars of Religion," 323–43.
7. Holt, *French Wars of Religion*, 133.
8. Mentzer, "French Wars of Religion," 340.
9. Johannes Burkhardt, "The Thirty Years' War," in *A Companion to the Reformation World*, ed. R. Po-chia Hsia (Malden, MA: Blackwell Publishing, 2004), 276.
10. Lacey Baldwin Smith, *Fools, Martyrs, Traitors: The Story of Martyrdom in the Western World* (Evanston, IL: Northwestern University Press, 1999), lists as one of the necessities of martyrdom the existence of a society divided against itself (19).
11. See Brad S. Gregory, *Salvation at Stake: Christian Martyrdom in Early Modern Europe* (Cambridge, MA: Harvard University Press, 2001), for the best analysis of martyrdom in the sixteenth century. Briefly, Gregory finds enormous commonalities among martyrdoms of the various confessional traditions.
12. Actually, the massacre included not only Protestants but also suspected Protestants and people who were accused of being Protestant.
13. The details of the St. Bartholomew's Day Massacre remain murky to this day. Certainly someone attempted to assassinate Coligny, and someone gave the order for his execution or murder. Those responsible found that events got out of hand and chose to deny their roles. This has led to a cottage industry among historians of the period in assigning blame. Confessional differences impacted the discussion, with Protestant historians frequently blaming the king or Catherine, and Catholic historians frequently blaming the Protestants for their own demise. See Barbara Diefendorf, *Beneath the Cross: Catholics and Huguenots in Sixteenth-Century Paris* (Oxford: Oxford University Press, 1991), for a consideration of the likely scenarios.
14. Ibid., 99.
15. How many thousands has been almost impossible to determine. James Smither, "The St. Bartholomew's Day Massacre and Images of Kingship in France, 1572–1574," *Sixteenth Century Journal* 22 (1991): 27–46, notes this difficulty and lists numbers as low as 1,000 and as high as 10,000 for Paris.
16. Again, figures vary. Smither gives figures that could go as high as 90,000. Smither, "St. Bartholomew's Day Massacre," 30.
17. For these accounts, see Diefendorf, *Beneath the Cross*, 102–3.
18. Ibid., 105, 145–58.

Chapter 11. Other Movements of Reform and Later Consequences

1. Michael F. Graham, "Scotland," in *The Reformation World*, ed. Andrew Pettegree (London: Routledge, 2000), 414.
2. Quoted in ibid., 417.
3. It is best to designate this as an "area," for the modern political map of the region was not yet set. The "Low Countries," as they were frequently called, made up the region of modern Belgium, the Netherlands, and Luxembourg but also included parts of what became France and Germany.
4. Guido Marnef, "The Netherlands," in Pettegree, ed., *Reformation World*, 344.
5. Joke Spaans, "Reform in the Low Countries," in *A Companion to the Reformation World*, ed. R. Po-chia Hisa (Malden, MA: Blackwell Publishing, 2004), 119.
6. Ibid., 120–21.
7. Ibid., 123.
8. Ibid., 125.
9. The standard text in the twentieth century on the history of missions was Kenneth Scott Latourette, *A History of the Expansion of Christianity*, 7 vols. (New York: Harper & Brothers, 1937–1945). He dedicated the third volume of this seven-volume magnum opus to the time frame that includes our period, 1500–1800, and called it *Three Centuries of Advance*.
10. See Amy Leonard, "Female Religious Orders," in Hsia, *Companion to the Reformation World* 237–54.
11. St. Teresa of Avila ends one of her books with prayers for "the Lutherans." The context makes clear that this was simply a way for her to refer to all Protestants.
12. A vigorous debate exists about the reasons for and legitimacy of the turn to scholastic models of thought in the later Reformation. Some scholars have derided this tendency as a failure of the spirit of the Reformation, while others have characterized it as wholly legitimate. This chapter takes no position, offers further reading below, and notes the tendency because all historians of the period note it and because its existence was important for theological developments in later time periods.

Chapter 12. Conclusion

1. Philip Benedict, *Christ's Churches Purely Reformed: A Social History of Calvinism* (New Haven, CT: Yale University Press, 2002), xvi.
2. See Bruce Gordon, "The New Parish," in *A Companion to the Reformation World*, ed. R. Po-chia Hisa (Malden, MA: Blackwell Publishing, 2004), 411–25.
3. David F. Wright, "Robert Estienne's *Nova Glossa Ordinaria*: A Protestant Quest for a Standard Bible Commentary," in *Calvin: Erbe und Auftrag; Festschrift für Wilhelm Heinrich Neuser zum 65. Geburtstag*, ed. Willem van 't Spijker, 40–54 (Kampen: Kok Pharos Publishing House, 1991), 45–46.

Index of Names of Persons

Index of Subjects

CPSIA information can be obtained
at www.ICGtesting.com
Printed in the USA
BVOW01s2236120117
473385BV00001B/4/P